DATE DUE

UND

BALL

COMPLE

BULLET

PHILIP P. MASSARO

Published by

Gun Digest® Books, an imprint of F+W Media, Inc.
Krause Publications • 700 East State Street • Iola, WI 54990-0001
715-445-2214 • 888-457-2873
www.krausebooks.com

To order books or other products call toll-free 1-800-258-0929
or visit us online at www.gundigeststore.com

Cover photography by
Philip Massaro

ISBN-13: 978-1-4402-4336-3
ISBN-10: 1-4402-4336-0

Cover Design by Dave Hauser
Designed by Dave Hauser
Edited by Chad Love

Printed in USA

10 9 8 7 6 5 4 3 2 1

For many more great
Gun Digest titles on reloading,
ballistics, and bullet selection,
visit the Gun Digest store at
www.gundigeststore.com.

Suggested titles:

CARTRIDGES OF THE WORLD, 14TH EDITION

—— ○ ——

HANDBOOK OF RELOADING BASICS

—— ○ ——

GUN DIGEST SHOOTER'S GUIDE TO RELOADING

—— ○ ——

HOW TO RELOAD AMMO WITH PHILIP MASSARO

THIS BOOK IS
DEDICATED TO MY FRIEND,
PROFESSIONAL HUNTER
JAY T. CARLSON,
WHOSE HUNT WAS CUT
SHORT MUCH TOO EARLY.
I HOPE YOU'RE HUNTING
BONGO IN VALHALLA,
BUDDY.

CONTENTS

6 Foreword

9 Introduction

10 Chapter One: The Projectile Throughout History

14 Chapter Two: Bullet Configuration and Construction

24 Chapter Three: Rimfire Revelry

40 Chapter Four: Varmint Rifles

60 Chapter Five: Medium Game Rifles

166 Chapter Six: Dangerous Game Rifles

196 Chapter Seven: Target Rifles

214 Chapter Eight: AR-Style Rifles

226 Chapter Nine: Muzzle-loading Rifle Bullets

236 Chapter Ten: Defensive Handgun Bullets

254 Chapter Eleven: Handgun Hunting Bullets

266 Chapter Twelve: Handgun Target and Plinking Bullets

FORE

For a little over a decade, I've lived at the end of a graveled, crater infested driveway, more than a half-mile off a country road with very little traffic. There are but five or six houses on this driveway, but in one of them dwells noted gun writer and master ballistician Mr. Philip Massaro. What are the odds that someone like myself, who has been reading and digesting ballistic tables for more than 40 years, ends up with a neighbor who is someone that not only loves talking rifles and cartridges as much as I do, but is as enthusiastic about hunting (and especially hunting the Dark Continent) as I am?

So when Phil asked me to write the foreword to his second book, I was at once flattered and nervous as hell. He set my mind at ease when he said, "It's what you and I talk about every day." After reading the final draft, I had to laugh, because he's right, the book indeed sounds like a collection of our conversations ov er these past 10 years.

As I write this, I'm planning my first African safari with Phil for the spring of 2015. I'll be hunting plains game in South Africa alongside Phil, and I will be accompanying him on an elephant hunt in Zimbabwe immediately after. I was planning to hunt with my 1959 Colt Coltsman in .300H&H. A truly classic caliber and a

classic rifle, right? Phil and I worked the handloaded ammunition up together, and it's a tack-driver. But, since he's hunting elephant in Zim, why not bring my .416 Rigby across the pond for plains game, and as backup for him? When I told Phil of my plans, his response was "I love it!! Stop up to the lab tonight, let's pick out some bullets, and start working up some loads". My point here is that Phil lives and breathes cartridges and ballistics, with plenty of real world experiences to back it up.

Neighbor Dave

That fact is exactly why his book is such a valuable tool to the weekend plinker, hunter, and bench-jockey alike. When you have the likes of renowned big game hunter and author Colonel Craig Boddington, and well respected African PH Jay Leyendecker contacting you for custom ammunition, you have been validated! Simply put, ammunition and ballistics are what Phil does.

Phil has the unique ability to read or see something once, and then be able to regurgitate it verbatim. As you will see in this book, his knowledge and understanding of projectiles and their use in hunting and target shooting, is comprehensive to say the least! His first hand knowledge, which has been gleaned from his safaris to Africa and hunts all over the U.S., is vast. He has seen the terminal ballistics in the form of downed game and recovered projectiles. He knows what works, and what doesn't. Phil uses this data to extrapolate the end result when selecting the bullet for its intended use.

An excellent example of this is a trip this past fall I took to Maine for deer. Now the deer of the Maine North Woods run large, they have to in order to survive those brutal winters. They tend to average 200 pounds and up on the hoof. These are big, tough deer. The way we hunt them is to find a fresh track and hopefully stalk one up to get an opportunity for a shot. This means going through alder swamps, grown-over clear cuts, and any other thick, miserable vegetation which typically limits your shots to 75 yards and under. This isn't sitting on a Sendero in south Texas, or in a box blind 50

David C. deMoulpied (left) with author Philip Massaro (J.P. Fielding photo) yards from a feeder waiting for your buck to turn broadside so you can pop him with a tiny .243. The type of hunting we do in Maine lends itself more jumping a deer out of his bed where you have a few seconds to take your shot. As anyone who's hunted enough will tell you, the shot opportunity will be brief, and the angle less than desirable.

That's where a well-built premium bullet comes in. I shoot a Remington Model 700 Classic in .350 Remington Magnum. When discussing what bullets I should use on this trip, Phil kept coming back to the 200-grain North Fork semi-spitzer. The twist rate in my barrel doesn't lend to stabilizing the larger 250-grain bullets. A short magazine length also nixed some of the other 225-grain offerings. So we were down to 200-grain projectiles. I typically shoot Hornady soft points, but wanted something more robust for these bruisers. The 180-grain Barnes X bullets were an option too, but the lower sectional density took them off my list. So we decided on the 200-grain North Forks. Phil came up with a load that was sub-MOA in my rifle, and I was ready to go! To make a very long story short, my only opportunity came on the last day of my hunt. I was walking a logging road trying to pick up a fresh track when turning a corner had a nice six-point buck walking away from me at roughly 175 yards. I grunted to stop him, and as he looked over his shoulder, I sent that North Fork into his hip and into his vitals, anchoring him on the spot. I never found the bullet, but it had broken the hip and continued until exiting by the off front shoulder. Bullet performance made my hunt successful. I doubt many cup-and-core configurations would take such a beating and remain intact. Massaro had the right of things.

This is the kind of information you will find in this book; well thought out and germane to the topic at hand. If you like talking ballistics, are going on your first safari to Africa, want to start varmint hunting, or looking to get an AR or other "Black Gun", then this tome will have something for all of you. There is a reason we as hunters or target shooters have gun vaults, because we are never satisfied with one gun or one caliber. If you are looking to expand your collection, read this book, it will point you in the right direction and answer a lot of questions you may have along the way.

It's an art to be able to write about topics like ballistics, reloading and projectiles. As I call it, "subject matter which can be as dry as a popcorn fart!" Phil is very adept at this; he writes technically when he needs to, and then throws in real world anecdotes to drive his point home. He has the gift of being able to describe why he thinks this caliber or projectile will work without boring the seasoned hunter or target shooter; yet not talking above the head of the neophyte who's just getting into the shooting sports. What you are going to get out of this book is knowledge that is tangible. If you've never hunted dangerous game in Africa or Alaska, and your PH suggests a bullet/cartridge combination, you can read Phil's section on dangerous game to understand your PH's reasoning.

When a new client gets me on the phone, and we start to discuss rifles and ammunition, I invariably send them to Phil. Most importantly, as a good friend and hunting partner of Phil's, I couldn't be happier for his well deserved success! He is the new blood in the world of outdoor writing, this is his second of many books to come, and the sky is the limit for him. Congratulations, my friend!

David C. deMoulpied
President, deMoulpied and Son
Outdoor Adventures

INTRODUCTION

If you've picked up this book, you already have an interest in ballistics. Bullets themselves, to me, are highly interesting. There is a part of me that is constantly amazed that a shooter that is worth his or her salt can place that shiny little blob of metal into a target the size of a golf ball at the length of a football field. So many people take those shiny blobs for granted, not giving a second thought as to what makes them tick, or if one design will perform better than another, that I felt a book giving a better explanation was warranted.

Perusing your local gun shop, you can find shelves filled with different types of ammunition, or component bullets (at least you could before the ammo crunch of '13-'14), and hear a vast array of opinions as to what works best. Some of those opinions are well founded, while others can be complete bunk. For the average hunter or shooter, it can be difficult to form an experience-based opinion, as there just aren't enough opportunities to evaluate the terminal performance of many different types of projectiles. My grandfather always told me "You won't live long enough to make all the mistakes on your own, so learn from those who've made them before you." I am certainly not the final voice on ballistics, but I'd like to think I've been around the block once or twice. My own love of handloading ammunition, combined with a near obsession with hunting and shooting, have given me many opportunities to see, first-hand, how many types of ammunition will perform. But, there are so many products out there that I can't test them all. What you'll find in this book are some discussions and recommendations based on my own experiences, as well as those of my friends and fellow shooters.

I truly hope you enjoy it, and that it leads you to find a bullet that makes you happy.

CHAPTER 1

Sling Stones, slayer of the mighty Goliath.

It can easily be agreed upon that our previous millennium saw the development of the firearm; from the crude matchlocks and early cannons, to the electric machine guns with computer-guided aiming systems. It is quite the story, and numerous volumes of great material have been published on the topic. That is not the focus of this book, although many great firearms will be mentioned and highlighted, as they pertain to the projectile. It is the projectiles themselves, those often overlooked and unsung he-roes of the shooting world that we all love so much, which will have their mo-ment in the sun, at the least between the covers of this volume.

Most importantly, let me make the following statement: Whether it is a ri-fle or handgun, it is the bullet, and only the bullet, which makes contact with the target. The target may be made of paper, cardboard, clay, or flesh and bone, but the target has no idea what you're holding in your hands; it only knows the bullet.

While we all love beautifully check-

THE PROJECTILE THROUGHOUT HISTORY

ered, oil-rubbed walnut stocks, high-gloss bluing, ergonomically designed grips and classy optics, the bullet is what does the work for us. Everything else is simply a guidance system for placing that bullet where we want it to go. Let's give these little shiny guys their due respect!

I'm not sure where or when in human history that Mr. Paleolithic, Esq., deduced that by throwing his rock he could dispatch that nasty animal intending to eat him without needing to be so close as to feel that animal's breath

in his face, but I am certainly glad he did. That rock, hurled through the air, striking the intended target, was probably the first example of the projectile. Man's love affair with launching things has never subsided.

Next, the spear, that simple sharpened stick, cut to a length so as to stay safe from harm, flew through the air. This worked even better, and the development of airborne weapons was underway. The atlatl, which launched the spear faster by giving a great mechanical advantage, was followed by the bow and arrow. I find it interesting that the bow and arrow seems to have made a presence in almost all primitive cultures, regardless of the distance that separated them. The mighty Goliath, who according to Scripture stood defiant at the front of the Philistine ranks towering over all others, fell not to the brute strength of David, but was smacked in the noodle by a sling stone, in perhaps the oldest tale of superior ballistics.

Projectiles gave Homo Sapien a large advantage over the creatures that threatened his existence, and that development really hasn't stopped, nor do I believe it will. The crude bullets that were launched by the first derivations of gunpowder started a branch of science called "ballistics." There are some ingenious designs that have come to light in the last 70 years, and some of our old standbys are still with us and thriving well. Let's look at the earliest designs.

During the late medieval period, at a time when mankind had developed numerous variations of leather and metal armor, and nearly perfected the castle as a means of defense, the firearm began to show its face on the battlefield. The simple lead balls could be launched so fast that they had the ability to penetrate plate armor, and with cannon the castle's walls and gates could be blown to bits and thereby breached. The cumbersome metal armor, which slowed the soldier's movement, began to be pared down as the firearms negated their effective level of protection. The firearm was here to stay.

Firearms became a more dependable source of protection and aggression in the 17th and 18th centuries. Those firearms, on both the European and North American continents, began to evolve into a tool that could be (relatively) quickly reloaded, and armies began

Round balls, the most primitive of firearm projectiles.

to shift the focus of their arsenals away from the medieval hand-held weapons and toward the firearm. However, the projectiles remained very much the same. The lead balls of specific caliber were the bullet du jour.

Something changed the game, but that something took centuries to catch on. That something was rifling. Simple grooves cut or forged into the barrel of the firearm would send the projectile spinning, and stabilize its flight. This dramatically improved accuracy, but the process was difficult and expensive to undertake. Rifling actually came to light in western Europe before the 1500s, but it wasn't until the mid-1800s that it became a given for most firearms launching a single projectile. During the American Revolution, in which British soldiers were armed with the "Brown Bess" musket (a smooth-bore firearm) and the Colonials were often armed with long rifles, the advantage of the rifled guns was very evident. The lead knuckleballs that the musket fired paled in comparison to the accuracy of the rifle, and the shift was on.

The next major development was by a Frenchman in the late 1840's; Claude-Etienne Minié produced an elongated bullet that had a slightly less-than-caliber shank and a conical shaped nose. Upon firing, the hollow base of the "Minié Ball" would expand to take to the rifling and seal the gases, and this design gave much better-long range ballistics, both in speed and accuracy. Modern bullet technology was underway, and both the Crimean and American Civil War showed the advantages. However, the material had not changed; they were still comprised of pure lead.

In 1882, Major Eduard Rubin of Switzerland changed all that when he had the bright idea to put a harder gilding metal (copper) on the outside of the bullet. This design, which generally coincided with development of early smokeless powders, produced some unprecedented velocities. Our modern cup-and-core bullet was born! The concept of a copper jacket filled with a lead core still is the most popular today. It is the common softpoint bullet so many of us use today, and can also be made in a hollowpoint or full metal jacket form.

In the 1940s, a gentleman by the name of John Nosler had a horrible experience with cup-and-core bullets while trying to kill a Canadian moose with his .300 H&H Magnum. The bullets, which would have been perfect for deer-sized game, were coming apart on the moose's shoulder. The velocities were too high, and the hide, muscle and bone of the moose too tough. This perplexed Mr. Nosler to the point that he completely redesigned the bullets. He took a copper rod, drilled out a cavity on either end (leaving a partition of copper) and after squeezing the nose portion into a spitzer shape, filled the cavities with lead. These new-fangled bullets simply couldn't come apart, because the copper partition would protect the rear core. The Nosler Partition and the premium bullet industry were born.

Fast forward 40 or so years, and you'll see Mr. Randy Brooks sitting on a piece of high ground glassing for brown bears, contemplating the finer points of bullet technology. Mr. Brooks had come to be the owner of the Barnes Bullet Company, and had a brilliant idea. His idea was to create a hollowpoint bullet comprised of pure copper. His theory was that if there was no lead core to separate from the jacket, the bullet couldn't come apart. The hollowpoint would provide good expansion, while the rear portion would retain enough energy and weight to give excellent penetration. The Barnes X, named for the shape of the expanded bullet, changed the game and ushered in an era of radical bullet ideas.

Somewhere along the line, someone (legends vary) had the brilliant idea of chemically bonding the jacket to the core, creating the bonded-core bullets we hunters love so much today.

These are but a few of the wonderful developments that have made our job as shooters much more pleasurable. In this book many different types of projectiles, made of many different materials, in many different configurations, will be discussed. Whether you are a rimfire plinker, competition handgunner, avid hunter or long range target shooter, there will be something here for you. Let's go!

The Nosler Partition, the first premium projectile.

Different rifle bullet shapes. (J.P. Fielding photo)

The bullets available to today's shooter are more complex than ever, in both design and in the materials used to make them. Modern factory ammunition is loaded with a wide array of quality bullets, and the bullets available to the handloader can be downright dizzying. An explanation of the basics is warranted, as we will be delving deeper into the specifics later on.

This book will be divided into two basic categories: rifle bullets and handgun bullets. While there will be some overlap (some rifles shoot handgun cartridges and some handguns shoot rifle cartridges), the division is based upon the application. Generally speaking, rifle bullets are designed for longer ranges and the handgun bullets are designed for short-range work. It's important to have a good understanding of bullet shapes, so as to make a well informed, intelligent decision for what will best suit your needs. Here are some of the general shapes and nomenclature associated with the bullets of today.

BULLET CONFIGURATION AND CONSTRUCTION

BULLET CONFIGURATION

ROUND BALL

A spherical projectile, most commonly reserved for the traditional muzzle-loading rifles still in use today. They are usually seated in a greased cotton patch, so as to prevent burning gasses from escaping and for ease of loading. Some round balls are seated into metallic cartridges for the purposes of practice and plinking. The round ball was the earliest available projectile for firearms.

ROUND NOSE

A bullet with a rounded nose section, or meplat (meplat is the term for the front or nose portion of any bullet). They were the first type of elongated bullets used in cartridge rifles, and are still in good use today. These bullets can have quite a bit of exposed lead at the nose, to provide good expansion, or are covered in a solid copper jacket for thick skinned game, and are generally used at shorter distances, those within 200 yards.

(above) Round-nose bullets. (J.P. Fielding photo)

(right) Flat-nose bullets, these Hornady bullets are designed for the .30-30 Winchester. (J.P. Fielding photo)

FLAT NOSE

A blunt or flat-tipped bullet, the rifle variety being designed for safety in the tube magazine of many lever-action rifles. The flat nose concept came about to ensure that the nose of the bullet couldn't pierce the primer of the cartridge in front of it in the tubular magazine, as they are loaded bullet-to-primer. Many pistol bullets are flat-tipped to provide a better frontal diameter for energy transmission.

SPITZER

A bullet with a severely curved and pointed meplat, whose name is the anglicized derivative of the German Spitzgeschoss, which roughly translates to "pointy bullet." The pointed end of the bullet is designed to allow it to slice through the air better, better resist slowing down, and therefore have a better trajectory. These bullets, introduced in the late 19th century, made a significant difference in long-range trajectory, and are the most common rifle bullets in use today.

SEMI-SPITZER

A bullet that blends the characteristics of the round nose and the spitzer; they are more pointed than a round nose, yet not as severely pointed as the spitzer. These bullets offer a better trajectory than the round nose, yet give a similar impact to the round nose on game animals.

SPITZER BOAT-TAIL

A pointed bullet whose base has been angled and tapered, so as to even better resist air drag. Most long-range match bullets for rifle competition or long-range shooting are some form of spitzer boat-tail, be they hollowpoint or otherwise.

HOLLOWPOINT

A bullet with a hollow cavity at the nose, designed to rapidly expand upon striking the target. In a rifle, spitzer hollowpoint bullets can be wonderfully accurate (although sometimes their fragile construction often precludes them from being used

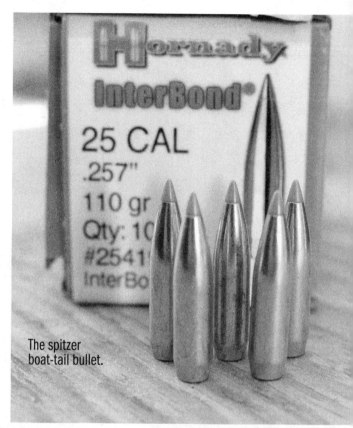

The spitzer boat-tail bullet.

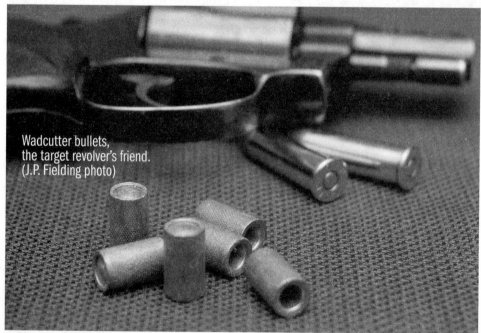

Wadcutter bullets, the target revolver's friend. (J.P. Fielding photo)

for hunting), and can provide the target shooter with some of the best results. In a pistol, the hollowpoint configuration is often used for its terminal performance in defense situations, due to its rapid expansion and impact trauma.

WADCUTTER

A pistol bullet which is a squared slug, with no taper at the nose. The name is derived from the "wad" the bullet cuts out of the paper target. These bullets may feature a hollow cavity at the base to best seal the gasses in the bore of the handgun. Having no taper at all, they may pose a problem when feeding from a spring-loaded magazine in a semi-automatic handgun. These bullets perform best in revolvers.

SEMI-WADCUTTER

A pistol bullet with the rear portion of the wadcutter design, but with a nose section tapered slightly to assist in feeding from a magazine pistol.

BULLET CONSTRUCTION

Bullet construction is a very important factor as well. It can make or break a hunting situation, or possibly save your bacon. The newer construction and makeup of today's bullets are, in my opinion, among the greatest advances in hunting technology of the last fifty years. Here are some of the basics:

PURE LEAD

The softest of bullets, used most often in round balls, and in cartridges for early-era pistol and rifles, .22 rimfire cartridges, and muzzleloading firearms. These bullets have no jacket whatsoever. In the rimfire cartridges, these pure lead bullets are often coated with wax to cut down on lead fouling within the bore.

HARD-CAST LEAD

A bullet made of lead mixed with a small amount of antimony, or other harder substance, so as to be harder than pure lead. This stiffer construction resists over-expansion upon impact and allows the bullet to penetrate into game animals better, and reduce the amount of lead fouling in the bore. They are very popular in handgun cartridges, lever-action cartridges and the blackpowder cartridges of the late 19th century.

CUP-AND-CORE

A bullet consisting of a lead core, surrounded by a gilding metal (usually copper, sometimes cupro-nickel) so as to be harder than lead and deliver good penetration, yet still malleable enough to engage the rifling in the barrel. The common softpoint bullets have varying degrees of lead exposed at the nose, as well as varying thicknesses of copper jacket. These parameters can dictate the amount of expansion on game animals. The cup-and-core bullet is the most frequently used bullet to this day. Most big game hunting bullets are of this construction, and more than likely will continue to be so. They are time-proven winners, introduced .in the 1880's and their construction allowed the great advances in velocity of the late 1800s and early 1900s.

Sierra GameKing cup-and-core bullet.

FULL METAL JACKET (FMJ)

A bullet that has no exposed lead at the nose, the copper casing completely surrounds the bullet except at the base. Military rifle and pistol bullets are mostly this type (required by the Hague Convention), and many indoor pistol ranges require a bullet to be totally encapsulated in copper so as to minimize the amount of vaporized lead in the air. In a rifle, these bullets are often used by varmint hunters who wish to preserve the pelts of coyotes, foxes, and other furbearers, as they do not expand and usually leave just a caliber-sized hole. Many military shooting competitions require the use of an FMJ, and there are many highly accurate models on the market. Some large-caliber bullets designed for penetrating the thick skin of the largest mammals are a modified version of this concept, called 'solids.' They have no exposed lead, and the jacket is of steel covered in copper.

MONOMETAL

A relatively modern design of bullet, with no lead core. These bullets are comprised of pure copper, sometimes of brass, and usually feature a hollow cavity to initiate expansion. Some feature a plastic insert at the tip to further promote expansion. This design results in a very strong bullet, which is capable of deep penetration and expansion, without the risk of premature bullet breakup. These bullets can extend the capabilities of calibers and cartridges which had previously been deemed marginal for a particular hunting scenario.

An all-copper monometal bullet, the Hornady GMX.

The Full Metal Jacket bullet

POLYMER TIP

A bullet that has a plastic or polymer tip inserted at the nose section to prevent any deformation of the meplat. The tip also acts as a method of initiating expansion and increases the ballistic coefficient of the projectile. The polymer tip is used on a wide variety of bullet types and applications, from highly frangible varmint bullets up through bullets for large game. The Hornady FTX bullet, designed to make spitzer bullets safe in a lever-action rifle's tubular magazine, uses a flexible polymer tip to avoid detonation in the magazine.

BONDED CORE

This is a bullet that has a lead core that is chemically bonded to the copper jacket, to ensure structural integrity. This process prevents the premature breakup and separation associated with standard cup-and-core bullets driven at higher than normal velocities, as frequently happens with magnum rifle and pistol cartridges. These bullets make a good choice when deep penetration is needed in addition to good expansion, or when using lighter calibers on game that traditionally requires a larger bore.

PARTITIONED

These bullets have a standard lead core and copper jacket, but feature a partition that is integral with the jacket, creating two lead cores. The concept (which is well proven) is to have the front core expand, while retaining the weight of the undisturbed rear core for penetration. This idea saw the light of day in the late 1940s, when John Nosler unveiled his Partition bullet. It remains a staple in the hunting industry, and was among the first "premium" bullets.

SOLIDS

A term used to describe the bullets designed for the heaviest of game, predominantly African dangerous game, such as the hippopotamus, Cape buf-

The modern solid, a parallel sided, homogenous metal, flat pointed demon.

falo and elephant. They can be of two designs: either a lead-core bullet with a steel jacket which is surrounded by a slight coating of copper (so as not to damage the rifling), or a monometal affair comprised of either copper (the most common design) or occasionally brass. These bullets are built for very deep, straight-line penetration, with virtually no expansion at all. Their purpose is to break heavy bone and penetrate thick hides. They are also known as "full-patch" bullets, due to the lack of exposed lead at the nose (See Full Metal Jacket).

SECTIONAL DENSITY AND BALLISTIC COEFFICIENT

There are two terms I'd like to define, and these are used to better describe the physical attributes of a particular bullet. The first is sectional density. Explained simply, sectional density, or S.D. for short, is a measurement of the ratio of the bullet's weight to its caliber, or diameter. Within any given caliber, there are bullets of varying weight, and since the diameter of the bullet cannot vary, in order to change the bullets weight it must be made either longer or shorter.

The S.D. of any bullet is represented as a decimal figure, an integer less than 1. It is derived from the following ratio: The weight of the bullet (in pounds), divided by the squared diameter of the bullet (in inches). To aid you in your calculations, and avoid the need for breaking out the abacus, there are 7,000 grains in a pound. Here's an example: we can easily figure the S.D. of a standard .30-caliber, 180-grain bullet. Divide 180 grains by 7,000 to convert to pounds and you'll get 0.025714 pounds. Square the bullet diameter of 0.308" and you'll get 0.094864. Divide the first number by the second and you will easily arrive at a S.D. of 0.271. Easy as pie!

The second term is ballistic coefficient. Ballistic coefficient, or B.C., is the term that the ballisticians use to measure a particular bullet's ability to slice through the atmosphere, or to resist air drag. This is a very complex topic, and although it is based on a scientific formula, the concept of accurately measuring B.C. is sometimes subjective and can even be the basis for argument. The ballistic coefficient of a bullet is represented by a decimal portion of a number. The higher the number is, the better the bullet will resist atmospheric drag.

So, here we sit, with all of these shapes and different constructions, in a multitude of calibers for both handguns and rifles. How can we make a decision as to what is best, or even adequate? I really wish that the great old writers like Jack O'Connor and Elmer Keith could have seen what we have available to us today; they may very well have settled, or at least eased, the debates and arguments they had. Alas, the task is left to us, so I will guide you as best I can. We will now begin to discuss proper bullet choices for each category of rifle and handgun, in detail, describing their uses and applications.

CHAPTER 3

'd be willing to bet that the majority of us who love rifles had our first experience with a rimfire rifle of some sort; more than likely with the .22 Long Rifle cartridge. It is, without a doubt, the undisputed king of the rimfire chamberings, and I'd also wager that it will wear that crown throughout my lifetime. The mild report and almost non-existent recoil make it a perfect choice for training a new shooter and establishing good fundamental shooting skills.

THE .22 LONG RIFLE

The .22LR is a great tool for hunting, plinking at cans, and target shooting, whether for fun or serious competition. For sheer fun factor, it truly is hard to

My Ruger Model 77/22, a wonderful rifle.
(J.P. Fielding photo)

RIMFIRE REVELRY

beat a .22 Long Rifle. The Long Rifle variety long ago shoved the .22 Short and .22 Long out of the spotlight (and right off the stage), but it is by no means the only rimfire cartridge popular today. The .22 Long Rifle combined the case of the .22 Long, with the 40-grain bullet of the .22 Extra Long (which has been discontinued for years), maintaining a Cartridge Overall Length of an even 1.000", and the design is classic.

The love of rimfire smallbores has prompted countless hours of research into some new offerings that are both interesting and useful. Bullet technology has followed suit. The classic setup of the .22 LR, using a 40-grain wax-coated lead bullet at 1,100 fps or so, is still offered, but even the champ has received a boost by loading some fancy

The .22 LR used a training tool, with the author's daughter Angelina. (Suzanne Massaro photo)

new bullets to better performance. Let's compare and contrast some of the offerings for the .22 Long Rifle.

As stated, the wax-coated, round-nosed lead bullet is the classic projectile for the .22 LR, and the velocities stated by the various manufacturers range between 1,050 fps and 1,250 fps. Any bullet with a muzzle velocity of less than 1,100 fps is referred to as "subsonic", as it doesn't break the speed of sound and create a sonic boom. These subsonic loads can be very effective in populated areas for pest control or plinking. Garden pests and predators that pursue livestock (my chickens are constantly harassed by raccoons and opossums) can be dealt with in a quiet manner, without alerting half the world.

The quieter ammunition is also a very valuable tool for training new shooters, as the report is so mild that the shooter develops good skills before having to deal with the sharp muzzle blast of centerfire rifles. My wife Suzie really enjoys spending time with her Savage .22 and CCI Suppresor ammuni-

tion, quietly printing tiny little groups on the target.

The traditional 40-grain roundnose bullet isn't the optimum design for long-range ballistics, but then again neither is the .22LR case. Many target-grade cartridges are made using this bullet configuration, and for good reason: they have proved over time to be very accurate.

My particular favorite rimfire rifle was a gift from my Dad, 'Ol Grumpy Pants (GP for short), for Christmas of 1985. He saw a new rimfire rifle built like a scaled-down big game rifle, the Ruger Model 77/22. It features the same integral scope mounts that the classic centerfire Model 77 has, and a good three-position safety, in addition to a stock that feels like a big game rifle. This firearm introduced me to the essence of a rifle, and it rides in the truck with me to this day. I have spent a bunch of time and money at the bench searching for the most accurate load. I have settled upon two, as they are equally accurate.

The first one I stumbled upon was

The author's wife, Suzie Q, at the bench with her favorite Savage MKII BRJ .22 LR.

the CCI MiniMag, a plated 40-grain hollowpoint, but as they are rather expensive, I also searched for a more affordable option. What I discovered was that this rifle absolutely loved Remington's Thunderbolt ammunition. The Thunderbolt runs at around 1,250 fps, which isn't the fastest around, but on the high side of the standard-velocity ammunition. There are other brands that performed well enough, but in this Ruger the Thunderbolt waxed 40-grain lead-nose would put ten shots into a dime-sized group at 35 yards.

The relatively inexpensive Thunderbolt ammo has accompanied me on

The CCI Mini-Mag rids the world of another garden pest.

many squirrel and rabbit hunts, has accounted for a couple of foxes and coyotes, numerous woodchucks, and helped me to teach my wife good rifle skills. When GP had an infestation of red squirrels (which are on license here in New York all year long) which ate holes in the soffits of his barn and proceeded to enter his domicile, Thunderbolt ammo and that Ruger sent a large number of them to meet their maker.

There are many types of ammunition that are similar to the Remington Thunderbolt: Winchester Wildcat, CCI Blazer, Federal Gold Medal Target, and the list goes on and on. If you can find it during the ammunition crunch of '13-'14, pick up as many types of ammunition as you can find and test your rifle at the range. With standard-velocity ammunition, I prefer to adjust the sights or riflescope so that the bullets are hitting dead on the bullseye at 35 yards. This gives me the ability

to make accurate hits out to 50 yards, and I test the holdover at 75 yards so I know where to hold in the event of a longer shot. Seventy-five yards is about as far as I feel comfortable with a .22LR at standard velocities.

Step things up a bit in the .22LR world and you'll find the "hyper-velocity" ammunition. Among the most popular is a brand that GP's Bicentennial Ruger 10/22 loves so much: the CCI Stinger. The light-for-caliber 32-grain hollowpoint, plated bullet is driven to over 1,600 fps, and can generate a bunch of hydraulic shock. GP can still put those Stingers into tight little groups with his Ruger, and believe me when I tell you that the rifle has seen its fair share of use over the last 38 years. Back in the late 70s, when fur prices were high, I used to accompany my father on 'coon hunts. We always kept hounds, and the fur helped the family make ends meet. That Ruger 10/22 and

The Author's Ruger Model 77/22 likes these two types of ammunition best.

a couple of magazines full of CCI Stingers would always be taken along, and the hunts were always successful. The Stinger is a bit of a unique situation, in that it uses the lighter bullet more commonly associated with the .22 Long, but maintains the C.O.L. of the .22LR by extending the case length just a wee bit. They function just fine, and have been a staple in the rimfire world for decades.

My good buddy Col. Le Frogg loves to shoot his peep-sighted target .22 rifles. He has two that he embraces: A Remington Model 513T and a sweet handling Winchester Model 75.

I've seen him put some very good groups on paper, using Remington 40-grain Golden Bullet ammunition. It's a ton of fun to plink with the peep-sighted rifles, and

Col. Le Frogg, giving the target .22 a workout.

for aging eyes they are much easier to use than traditional buckhorn iron sights. Once you get the hang of them, they are very easy to use. Le Frogg's peep sights are fully adjustable for windage and elevation, and though we tried several brands of ammo, the Golden Bullet performed best.

Speaking of the Remington Golden Bullet, my pal Marty Groppi and I had a fun day at the bench, using an old

(and sort of beat up) Mossberg .22, plinking at an empty half-keg beer barrel at 300 yards. I didn't think it could be done, but within a few minutes the faint "tink" of bullet striking metal floated back on the breeze. It required about 10 feet of holdover, but even at that distance we were hitting the target more often than not. This kind of shooting will test your marksmanship for certain! Marty would laugh that

(above) Marty Groppi, about to send another .22 downrange.

(right) Remington's Golden Bullet.

deep-throated laugh every single time we hit the keg.

I bought my younger brother Jamie an old bolt-action .22 for Christmas one year; a Mossberg with a long barrel, ten-shot magazine and iron sights only. I was amazed to watch how this rifle would group Remington's Yellow Jacket ammunition. This load features a plated lead, truncated-cone bullet of 33 grains, running at a velocity of 1,500 fps. That Mossberg simply loved sending them downrange. Jamie has used this combination with good effect for over two decades. These Yellow

Jackets utilize a lighter than usual bullet, at a higher velocity, which can help to flatten out trajectories a bit. Combine that with the longer barrel of that old Mossberg, and you can imagine how the longer shots become makeable, even with iron sights.

What ammunition you choose should be decided by what your purposes are. If you are a competition shooter, a load with a bullet that gives good long-range accuracy, such as a plated hollowpoint, might be the way to go. If you're a plinker, the lead roundnose ammunition is more than likely the way to go.

If you use your .22LR for furbearing animals, the full metal jacket ammunition will best preserve the pelts for skinning, because they do not expand at all, and simply poke a caliber-size hole through the animal. Those of you who are serious about small game, especially at the longer ranges, will want to give the plated hollowpoint bullets a whirl, to find the ammunition that gives you the best blend of velocity, trajectory and accuracy.

THE LONG AND THE SHORT OF IT

The .22 Long Rifle isn't the only variety of .22 rimfire available. Many older rifles were chambered for the .22 Short cartridge, which holds the prestigious title of being the first American-designed metallic cartridge, bursting onto the scene in 1857 in a Smith & Wesson revolver.

The .22 Short (and the .22 Long) are designed around a 29-grain bullet. Although they are slowly fading into obscurity, there are still a handful of companies that produce .22 Shorts.

CCI leads the way with three offerings: a high-velocity (1,105fps) 27-grain hollowpoint, and two varieties of the 29-grain classic: a 29-grain lead round nose at a mild 830 fps, and a stout 29-grain plated bullet at 1,080 fps.

Remington also offers their 29-grain Golden Bullet at 1,095 fps. If you have one of the petite, handy little rifles designed for the .22 Short, you can have decades of fun plinking, or chasing squirrels and rabbits during hunting season. Col Le Frogg has a neat rifle in .22 Short: the 'Winder Musket'.

Used as a training rifle for the military in the early 20th century, this well-made piece of Americana makes for a fun afternoon of shooting.

The faster loadings, with plated roundnose or plated hollowpoint can handle varmints and predators within 75 yards, although the muzzle energies drop off quickly at the longer ranges.

The .22 Long, in its original black-powder loading, offered a 25 percent powder increase over the .22 Short, while utilizing the same 29-grain lead bullet.

For the early 1870s, this was a sig-

The .22 Short.

The 'Winder Musket', a military training rifle which fires .22 Shorts.

nificant velocity gain. The case of the .22 Long is the basis for our beloved .22 Long Rifle, and for many years the Long offered a lower-cost alternative to the Long Rifle, while delivering comparable ballistics, just using the lighter bullet. Unfortunately, the .22 Long has ridden into the sunset, with very little ammunition available, as the popularity of the .22 Long Rifle has eclipsed its usefulness. The dilemma in our lifetime is that the uber-popular semi-automatic rifles that have dominated the market won't cycle with .22 Long ammunition due to a lack of energy to cycle the action.

There are ways to make some of the .22 LR rifles shoot like the lesser cartridg-

Peters .22 Long.

es. On a recent deer hunt on the Vato-ville Ranch in Texas, varmint hunting was offered as a nighttime activity, supervised by none other than Mrs. Steve Anderson, known better as Shelly. My buddy J.J. Reich from the ATK group had brought a cool Savage thumbhole stock .22 LR along, with some of the CCI "Quiet .22" ammo.

Running at 710 fps, this ammo moved so quietly and slowly that those in the group who were hard of hearing didn't know I'd shot, and those of us who watched the target for accuracy actually saw the bullet in flight. The specially-designed bullet is a copper-plated affair with a slight hollowpoint, skived to break into three longitudinal pieces upon impact.

The skunks of Texas still fear me...

Perhaps I should clarify: .22 Short, .22 Long and .22 Long Rifle all share the same rim and body diameter, they simply differ in length. Think of it along the same lines as shotshells: in 12 gauge you can fire 2 3/4" 3' and even 3 ½" shells from a 3 ½" chamber. You can safely fire .22 Short, .22 Long and .22 Long Rifle ammunition from a .22 Long Rifle chamber, but the semi-automatic rifles and pistols may not cycle with the lighter loading of the

(left) CCI sub-sonic .22 LR ammunition; Suppresor and Quiet .22.

(below) The segmented remains of CCI Quiet .22, in ballistic gelatin.

(bottom) L-R .22 Short, .22 Long, .22 Long Rifle.

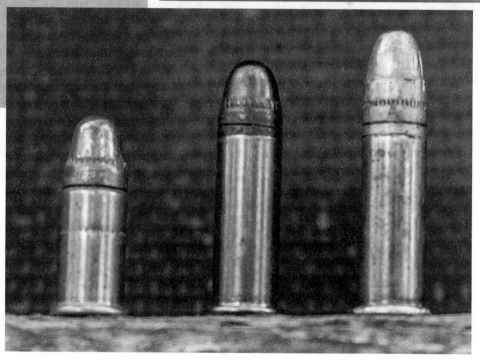

Short and the Long. It is not safe to fire .22 Long or Long Rifle in a chamber marked .22 Short, nor to fire .22 Long Rifle in a chamber marked .22 Long.

If you have a bolt-action or single-shot in .22 Long Rifle, there should be no problem firing any of the above mentioned ammunition, including the subsonic rounds that lack the energy to cycle a semi-automatic action.

THE .22 WMR

The other popular .22-caliber rimfire is the .22 Winchester Magnum Rimfire. It is a design unrelated to the rim and body specifications of the .22 Long Ri-

The .22 Winchester Magnum Rimfire, a decided improvement over the .22 Long Rifle.

fle family, being based on the obsolete .22 WRF, in a longer case.

The .22 WMR, or '.22 Mag' as it is commonly called, uses a thicker case, so as to operate at higher pressures, having a C.O.L. of 1.350", and drives the same 40-grain bullet that the .22 LR uses at a velocity of just over 2,000

fps. The velocity gain allows the newer bullet styles to really shine, in both retained energy and improved trajectory.

For the hunter who likes the idea of rimfire ammunition, and does most of their varmint hunting at ranges inside 125 yards, the .22 WMR may very well be your baby. At 100 yards, it has the same velocity the .22LR has at the muzzle, and there are a wide choice of bullets available for it. The classic round-nosed 40-grainers are certainly on the menu, but so are the spitzer point, polymer-tipped gems that have made a huge difference in the centerfire rifle.

The hollowpoint bullets offer plenty of hydraulic shock on the large varmints like coyotes and foxes, or if you're after fur there are FMJ bullets which can minimize pelt damage. Let's take a look at how the different bullets for the .22 Mag. can affect downrange performance.

We can safely assume that all the regular loadings for the .22 WMR are capable of maintaining a 100-yard zero, without a rise of more than 1.75" at the high point of trajectory. Bullets range between 30 to 50 grains, with few exceptions.

Federal's offerings illustrate the differences; we'll use a 100-yard zero for demonstrative purposes. The V-Shok ammunition, loaded with a 30-grain Speer TNT hollowpoint, leaves the muzzle at a zippy 2,200 fps, and at 150 yards - about as far as one would regularly use a .22 Mag - drops five inches.

The Federal Champion line uses a 40-grain FMJ, at a muzzle velocity of 1,880 fps, yet drops only six inches at the 150 mark. The heaviest bullet Federal offers, a 50-grain in the Game Shok line, runs at 1,530 fps, but drops eight inches at 150 yards. The holdover can be compensated for, but the striking energies are a different story. The heavy bullet, although it starts out slower, retains 131 ft.-lbs. at 150 yards, while the lightest bullet, which has a definite velocity advantage, only retains 89 ft.-lbs.

at the same distance.

For my uses, I prefer the middle-of-the-road 40-grain loading, which balances the trajectory, yet still gives 112 ft.-lbs. of energy at the distance that I draw the line for this cartridge.

OTHER RIMFIRE CARTRIDGES

In the early 1970s, Remington released the 5mm Remington Magnum Rimfire, one of the first attempts at commercial success with a rimfire round of less than .22 caliber. It offered a 30-grain bullet at 2,300 fps, in a case that was built to withstand higher pressures than the .22 WMR could handle, and the .204" diameter bullets did their job well. But, marketing being marketing, it didn't catch on, and that's a shame. I know Col. Le Frogg loved his Remington Model 591, and used it with good effect.

THE .17S

Among the rimfires, the .22 caliber still reigns supreme, but it isn't the only game in town. The 21st century has seen two rimfire greats join the throng. The .17-caliber rimfires have been with us since 2002, with the .17 HMR (Hornady Magnum Rimfire) leading the pack.

The idea was to offer a case based on the .22 WMR and maintaining the same C.O.L. as the .22 WMR, but shouldered and necked down to hold .172-diameter bullets, to offer a flatter trajectory. The good folks at Hornady came up with a sound design, utilizing a 17-grain jacketed projectile (instead of the standard plated rimfire bullet), delivered at 2,550 fps. With a 100-yard zero, this whiz-bang rimfire adds about 50 yards to the trajectory of the .22 WMR, dropping 8" at the 200-yard mark.

There are some drawbacks, such as wind. The light 17-grain bullet is very susceptible to wind drift, especially at the longer ranges. To maintain the flat trajectory a spitzer boat-tail bullet is loaded, mostly with a polymer tip, but sometimes in a hollowpoint configuration.

These bullets offer quite a bit of hydraulic shock and tend to be frangible to the point of being explosive. They have been known to make a bit of a mess on small game, especially at the shorter ranges. But the sharp pointed bullets can be very accurate, with many guns shooting less than minute-of-angle. Hornady offers three bullet weights: 15.5 grains, the standard 17-grain, and a 20-grain hollowpoint. The 'heavy' 20-grain bullet

The flat shooting .17 Hornady Magnum Rimfire.

The .17 Mach II,
based on the CCI Stinger.

leaves the muzzle at 2,350fps, and would be my choice for the small game animals on the bigger end of the scale, including fox and coyote.

Based on the success of the .17 HMR, Hornady decided that it wasn't done with rimfire research. As a companion to the HMR cartridge, in 2004 they announced the arrival of the .17 Mach 2.

This cartridge was based on the CCI Stinger case, which is just a bit longer than a standard .22LR, but again necked down to hold the .172" diameter 17-grain jacketed bullets. Muzzle velocities average 2,100 fps, much better than the .22 Long Rifle stuff, and drop only 14" at 200 yards. They offer an accurate, well-made small game and target round. The Mach 2 is as susceptible to wind drift as its big brother, but if you're a fan of the .17 bores, this can be a ton of fun. It is also possible to rebarrel your favorite .22 Long Rifle to .17 Mach 2, for a new experience. Ammunition is a tad more expensive than the .22 stuff, but in this environment of .22 scarcity, you may find the .17 stuff easier than the popular Long Rifle ammo.

If you do opt for the .17, in either configuration, I would suggest that you pick up a quality .17-caliber cleaning rod, as most of the conventional rods won't fit the tiny bore. Lyman and Tipton both make a great rod for the .17s, along with the appropriate jags and brushes.

For both the .17 rimfires, I do like the fact that the bullets are jacketed instead of plated, as this gives the very light bullet a better structural integrity when using them against bigger varmints and game animals. Hornady has done a very good job in introducing a pair of innovative and useful rimfire cartridges.

As a handloader, I am vexed by the fact that I simply can't load my own rimfire cartridges, but I'm also thankful that the ammunition companies make as many great products as they do. When (and if) the rimfire drought subsides, grab a bunch of different types of ammunition for your favorite rimfire, and have fun finding out which load or loads your rifle likes best.

CHAPTER 4

The .243 Winchester makes a great varmint round. (J.P. Fielding photo)

While in pursuit of the smaller mammals that the Creator placed on this Earth, a specialized setup is certainly warranted. It is necessary to have a rifle/optic/ammunition combination that will allow for hitting tiny distant targets in a wide variety of situations. It is one of the places where the premium riflescope will certainly show its worth, and the bull barrel will prove a worthwhile investment.

If your rifle likes factory ammunition, so be it, but the uber-accurate handloads will prove the effort well worth the time and effort. The varmint-class rifle runs the gamut of calibers rang-

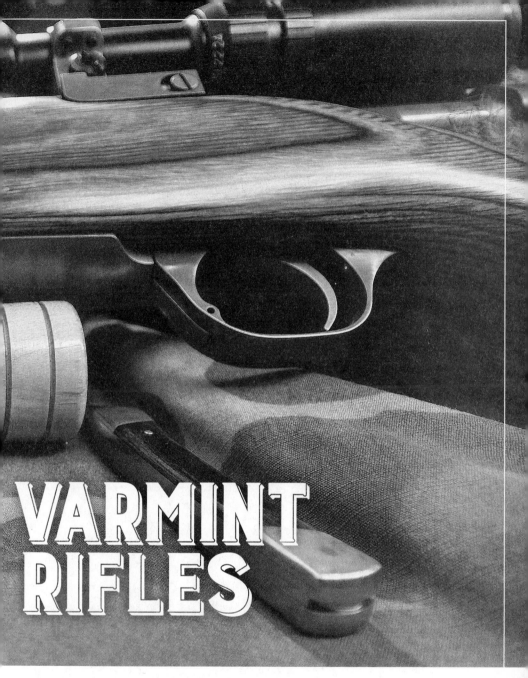

VARMINT RIFLES

ing from the diminutive .17s up to and rarely including the all-around .30s, with some exceptions on both sides of the scale. The rare rifles chambered for calibers smaller than .172" diameter, such as the .14 Flea, certainly exist, but the specialized ammunition, bullets and cases are beyond the scope of this tome. And if you're shooting varmints with an 8mm or a .338, good for you, but it certainly will be a target of opportunity, rather than a dedicated varmint rig.

For the most part, the varmint setups range from the .17s up to and including the .25s, with some rare exceptions. If you are a western hunter, where the prairie dogs and jackrabbits abound, in addition to the coyotes that prowl the prairie, you'll have ample opportunity to use your varmint rifle. If you reside in the eastern U.S., the generous seasons for furbearers, including the abundant eastern coyote, larger than his western cousin, fox, both red and grey, fisher, bobcat and their ilk gives the serious varmint hunter a reason to own two or more varmint rigs, with several different loads in each.

Depending upon your quarry, and your intent, there are many different projectiles for the varmint hunter, and they can be lumped into categories that do particular jobs. One thing is for certain; varmints can present shots at many different ranges, from up close and personal in the woods in the case of coyotes and foxes, to everything-you've-got-in-the-bag while shooting the far side of a prairie dog town or calling coyotes across a stubble field.

The projectiles designed for varmints are generally one of two types: either a highly-frangible expanding bullet, capable of delivering large amounts of hydrostatic shock (The Brotherhood of the Red Mist, I've heard it called), or a full metal jacket affair designed to penetrate without expansion, so as to best preserve the fur pelts.

The hollowpoint bullets, along with the polymer-tipped spitzers, are designed to give fantastic expansion. The jackets tend to be on the thin side, and when that is combined with the high velocities of the larger cartridges, it can generate that famous "red mist." Some are designed to break up at the slightest impact, to avoid ricochets and prevent bullets from flying all over the county.

The full metal jacketed bullets, which were initially a military design dating back to the 19th century, are the friend

Berger's fantastic .204-caliber 55-grain hollowpoint bullet delivers plenty of hydraulic shock.

of the pelt hunter. They do not expand, and if shots are placed properly, there will be one or two caliber-sized holes in the pelt, rather than the huge mess a highly-frangible expanding bullet can create.

When I'm serious about hunting coyotes, I load my .22-250 with Winchester 55-grain FMJs, and they certainly get the job done. Let's take a look at the different calibers for varmint hunters and which bullets make the most sense for them.

THE .17 CALIBERS

Starting with the smallest of the brood, the .17s, the choice of bullets is a bit more limited than some of the bigger calibers. Bullet weights range between 15.5 grains, up through the (relatively) large 37 grains.

All of them are designed for use on varmints, although I have a dear friend who actually uses a .17 Reming-

Full Metal Jacket bullets minimize pelt damage.

ton as a deer rifle, as it is legal here in New York. He is a crack shot, and extremely picky about the shots he'll take. Although I wouldn't use this caliber on anything larger than a coyote, I must admit we've sat at his table, dining upon venison he harvested with the tiny .17 Rem. That aside, the .17s, from the newest .17 Hornet, through the .17 MachIV and .17 Fireball, to the .17 Remington, make one of the best midrange varmint guns around. For the littlest guy of this bunch, the .17 Hornet, Hornady likes to use the 17-grain bullet mostly associated with the rimfire cartridges.

The most popular bullet weights for the bigger cases are the 20 and 25-grain bullets. Hornady makes their famous V-Max bullet, with its polymer tip and frangible jacket in both of those weights.

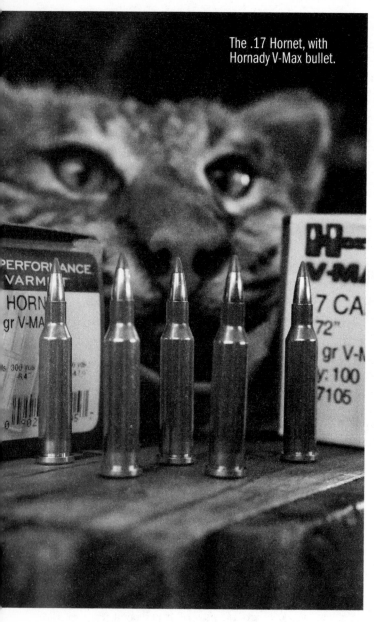

The .17 Hornet, with Hornady V-Max bullet.

includes a 20-grain bullet for the .17s in both polymer tip and hollowpoint configurations, and they both feature a very thin jacket, especially toward the bullet tip, to generate huge amounts of hydraulic shock. As a note, all of the bullets I've mentioned are of flat-base design.

The handloader can really make the various .17s shine. They can be finicky little rifles when they want to be, and if your particular barrel doesn't quite agree with the harmonics that factory ammunition produces, handloading can be good for what ails you. The bullets I've outlined are definitely available as component parts, as well as being loaded into factory ammunition. Just like the .17 rimfire cartridges, cleaning the bore of your .17-caliber rifle often will certainly help maintain the level of accuracy you're after.

One point to watch regarding the .17 caliber cartridges: they are very susceptible to the effects of wind drift. The 17 and 20-grain bullets are wonderful stuff for calm conditions, but you should really take a look at the wind drift charts and practice shooting in windy conditions to get a handle on how to dope the wind with the tiny bullets.

They are devastating on the smaller varmints, like ground hogs and prairie dogs, and can stop foxes and 'yotes in their tracks. Berger makes a fantastic 25-grain flat-base hollowpoint varmint bullet, featuring their very accurate J4 jacket. I've seen this bullet produce ¼" groups from a Remington 700 in .17 Remington. Nosler's Varmageddon line

THE .204 CALIBERS

Remington introduced the 5mm Rimfire in the year I was born, 1971, and it was immediately an oddball. The 5mm bore diameter has never been largely popular, and although the little rimfire had its few enamored followers, it was discontinued in the mid 70s, and the bore diameter lay dormant for decades. That is until, Ruger and Hornady teamed up to create the .204 Ruger in 2004.

They took the .222 Remington Magnum, shortened the neck and sharpened the shoulder, then necked it down to hold the 5mm or .204" bullets. It was an immediate hit. It offers the flat trajectory and screaming, 4,000+ fps velocities of the .17s, yet less recoil that the fast .22 centerfires for long days of shooting. Hornady, Remington, Winchester and Federal all offer good factory ammunition, loaded with a variety of projectiles.

Hornady's 32-grain and 40-grain V-Max give explosive performance and great accuracy, and Remington has a 32-grain boat-tail AccuTip as well. Invariably, the 32-grain bullet is the most popular in .20-caliber. The Winchester and Federal factory loads are designed around this bullet, and for good reason: it works.

In Wyoming, after we had all tagged out on antelope on the famous 88 Ranch, we joined Mike Henry, the ranch owner, on a mission to help curb the local jackrabbit population explosion. He was proud as a peacock to show me his new rifle, chambered in .204 Ruger. We quickly determined that using the rifle, fueled by Federal Premium 32-grain V-Shok ammunition with the Nosler Ballistic Tip against distant jacks gave us an almost unfair advantage. The cute little buggers carry rabbit fever, and 13 jacks will eat as much as one head of cattle per day on the prairie.

Given the drought situation in '06, this presented a problem for ranchers.

The Ruger .204, a continuation of the 5mm cartridges.

Bunnies at over 200 yards were not safe by any means, and the cattle on the ranch were certainly happy to recover their grazing turf. There are other bullets as well, and if you are a fan of the heavier bullets, as I am, Hornady's 45-grain hollowpoint may appeal to you. The additional weight helps defy the wishes of the crosswinds, yet still delivers plenty of energy at long ranges in spite of lower muzzle velocities. The .204 Ruger has a little brother, based on the .223 Remington cartridge, instead of the .222 Magnum. Todd Kindler's .20 Tactical is a solid design, although it remains a specialty order. It may be a touch more efficient than the .204 Ruger, but the difference between them is on par with the difference between the .308 and .30-'06. Under field conditions, there is little or no visible difference. Which is not to slight the .20 Tac., but to praise it. As a matter of fact, from a handloader's perspective, it is much easier to find .223 Remington brass to create .20 Tac than it is to find .222 Mag for the .204 Ruger.

Among the specialty bullets, Berger brings a bunch of flexibility of the .20s, producing a 35-grain flat-base varmint bullet, as well as a 40-grain boat-tail and an uber-long 55-grain boat-tail for the long-range work.

Either way, both cartridges benefit from a good selection of factory ammunition and component bullets to raise hell with the varmints. Take some time to find what works for you, and create the red mist until your heart's content with one of the .20s.

THE .22 CENTERFIRES

Now you're speaking my language. You are definitely in my wheelhouse when we're talking .22 centerfires. From the diminutive .22 Hornet and .218 Bee, up through the .22-250 Remington and .220 Swift there is a .22 centerfire that can fit everyone's needs. The bullets available for them are numerous, so please bear with me, and I'll do my best to cover the spectrum as best I can.

The .22 Hornet was the first centerfire to use the .224" bullet of the famous rimfire design, pushing the velocity envelope with heavier charges of black powder and thicker case dimensions, in a rifle capable of withstanding the greater pressures. The older .22 Hornet rifles have a bore diameter slightly

The .22 Hornet, one of the oldest of the .22 centerfires.

smaller than today's guns, requiring the use of .223" bullets rather than the standard .224" bullets, so be sure and check your bore diameter.

The traditional bullet weight for the Hornet is the 46-grain spitzer, but I've had luck with many different types. Factory stuff is available with Remington's 35-grain AccuTip, which should show a slight bump up in velocity, as well as Nosler's Ballistic Tip, which has a great reputation for both accuracy and explosive downrange performance. Both Sierra and Hornady make component bullets for the Hornet, and they're fine choices.

Available as a pointed softpoint, they work perfect at Hornet velocities, and are offered in both 40 and 45 grains. But other bullets work well in the old cartridge, including some choices you'd think would be better off in bigger cases.

My pal Ronnie Hardy, of Hardy's Custom Turkey Calls, uses his Hornet to cull whitetail deer on his ranch in West Virginia. He had called to ask me to try and replicate the factory loads when he couldn't get them during the ammo crunch of 2013, but I talked him into trying another bullet. I recommended a 53-grain flat-base Sierra hollowpoint spitzer. With a suitable load of Alliant 2400, the Hornet proved to be an accurate load and an effective killer. Mind you, Ronnie is a patient hunter, who is willing to wait for the perfect shot to present itself, and will not take a shot with a questionable angle. In my personal opinion, the venerable Hornet makes a great varmint gun when ranges are within 200 yards, but that's about it.

The Hornet's little brother, the

The .218 Bee, the Hornet's little brother.

.218 Bee, is another rimmed cartridge that has projectiles that are specifically designed for it.

Most bullets made for the Bee are flat points, because most of the rifles are tube-fed lever actions and require flat-point bullets. I've spent quite a bit of time shooting a Bee, although it wasn't a lever gun, it was Col. Le Frogg's Ruger No. 1, and it was a shooter. Even with its mild velocity and low B.C. flat points, hitting targets out to 200 yards was no problem at all.

I chose the Hornady 45-grain Bee bullet, and when loaded over IMR 4227, it worked out well for me. If you've got a single loader, have some fun toying with the match-grade bullets available in .224" diameter, you can have a blast at the bench shooting the Bee, and its lack of recoil makes it a great choice for woodchucks in the summer, and a nice handy rifle for foxes and coyotes.

The other .22 centerfires share the same types of bullets, just launched at different velocities. From the mild .22 PPC and .222 Remington, to the famous .223 Remington, up through the speedy .22-250 Remington and .220 Swift, there is a plethora (Si, El Guapo, a plethora) of great varmint bullets. The goal is pretty much the same: super accuracy and explosive terminal performance. The Speer TNT line of bullets is one of many that fit this bill.

They feature the very thin jacket that allows for rapid expansion, and a very soft, pure lead core. Most of the TNT product line features light-for-caliber bullets, but the .22-caliber TNTs are offered in 50 and 55 grains. These have worked very well in my pet .22-250 and GP's .223 Remington. My Ruger .22-250 loves the 55-grainers, and woodchucks shudder at the mere mention of it.

Sierra makes great bullets, and their varmint bullets are no exception. The

(right) Sierra BlitzKing 55-grain bullets.

(below) The explosive .22-caliber 50-grain TNT hollowpoint.

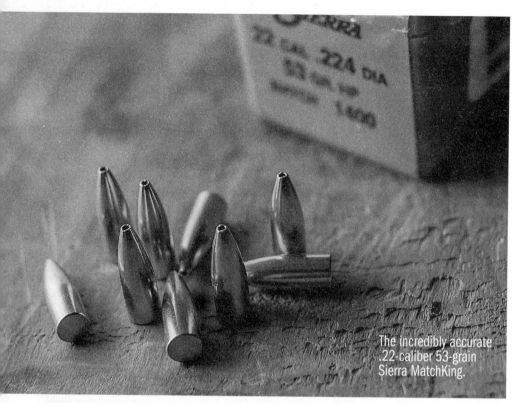

The incredibly accurate .22-caliber 53-grain Sierra MatchKing.

Hornady's Superformance .223 ammo.

BlitzKing line is a polymer-tipped bullet, and delivers the goods on varmints.

Although I'm bending the rules a bit, I like to use the Sierra MatchKing bullets on varmints, even though Sierra does not recommend them for hunting. They offer an unprecedented level of accuracy, and they hit hard. It isn't uncommon for my .22-250 to put three 53-grain MatchKings into a group of 3/8ths of an inch. I've taken many woodchucks, rogue skunks, chicken-eating foxes and other plagues on civilized society with this combination.

The factory ammunition for the .22 centerfire varmint guns is better than it has ever been. It doesn't give the varmint hunter the freedom of choice that handloading your ammo does, but when you find a load that your chosen rifle likes, you are certainly in business. Hornady's Varmint Express and Superformance lines feature the deadly V-Max bullet, and they deliver the goods.

The Black Hills ammunition that features Barnes Varmint Grenade stuff is aptly named. These bullets pretty well define frangible, yet they hold together even in the fastest twist-rate barrels, and can most certainly create the red mist! Remington's Premier Disintegrator gives hunters the option of lead-free bullet technology in common cartridges and bullet weights, while maintaining the necessary level of frangibility.

The Barnes Varminator in the 50-grain weight makes a good choice for the smaller-cased .22 centerfires.

.223 Remington, loaded with heavy-for-caliber 69-grain Sierra hollowpoint bullets.

Federal Premium Ammunition offers varmint fodder in the common calibers, utilizing both Speer's fine projectiles and the Nosler Ballistic Tip we've come to love. They are also a fine source of loaded ammunition featuring Sierra bullets.

Depending upon the chosen cartridge, you can adjust bullet weight to match the power level. For instance, if you shoot a .222 Remington, I'd look at the 40, 45, and 50-grain bullets, to maintain high velocities. In the .223 Remington, you can get away with some of the longer bullets, like the 62, 69 and 74-grain bullets, if your barrel's twist rate allows.

Twist rate is something we should

whining - my beloved .22-250 Remington usually comes with a twist rate of 1:14", or at best a 1:12", and this precludes the use of bullets over 55 grains. This is disappointing, because if any case could push those heavy bullets, it would be the .22-250. The .220 Swift, that darling of the 1930s that first broke the 4,000 fps mark, also suffers from the same slow twist rate. I can only suppose that our forefathers failed to envision the use of long-for-caliber bullets for the .22 centerfires.

The frangible bullets are only half of the equation for the varmint hunter, as there is a faction of the varmint hunting world that hunts furbearers seriously. The challenge of outsmarting the highly intelligent and cunning predators appeals to many, and each season many hunters get to extend their season throughout the winter by grabbing a set of calls and calling in the toothy furbearers.

To best preserve the pelts, a full metal jacket, military-style bullet serves best, and because the .223 Remington has been adopted by the U.S. military and the United Nations as the 5.56mm NATO, there is a wonderful supply of 55-grain bullets in this configuration. Most manufacturers offer some sort of FMJ designed bullet in their factory loaded ammunition, and as a handloader I've found some great inexpensive bullets that are a great value to the hunter in pursuit of fur. When I'm serious about collecting coyote and fox pelts in their winter prime, these are the projectiles you'll find in my kit.

My .22-250, and GP's .223 both love Winchester's 55-grain boat-tail spitzer FMJs, and both the rifles can put them into sub-MOA groups. These inexpensive projectiles have given us many seasons of good service, and do very little damage to pelts. They have dropped coyotes and foxes in their tracks, and also work well for summertime woodchucks that raid the garden annually. Most bullet companies offer a good

discuss here, as it directly affects the potential bullet choice. It takes a fast twist rate, like 1:8" or even 1:7" to stabilize the longest .22-caliber bullets. Many of today's AR platform rifles, especially those set up for long-range target work, offer this fast rate of twist, and they can certainly handle these bullets. But - and please pardon my

FMJ in their .22 bullet lineup, at the very least designed for the 5.56x45 or .223 ammunition. If you can't find the cartridge you love loaded with an FMJ, you can always contact someone to handload you some for your furbearer hunting.

So, in regard to the .22 centerfires, check the twist rate of your rifle and pick a good frangible bullet or FMJ to best enjoy your varmint and predator hunting.

THE 6MMs

The rifles chambered for 6mm, or .243" bores, have the distinction of being just about the lightest caliber capable of doing double duty on the varmint/predator sized game, yet being fully capable of taking the antelope/deer sized animals. The heavier bullets in 6mm diameter are usually reserved for big game, but there are some wonderful varmint-class bullets, in the 55 to 80-grain weights that will work perfectly. Whether the marking on your barrel says .243 Winchester, 6mm Remington, or .240 Weatherby, the twist rate of these rifles will all perfectly stabilize the varmint-weight bullets.

It's not until we get into the big game bullets that we start to see twist issues, but we'll discuss that in the Medium Game chapter. There are those who feel that for a long day of shooting, like while hunting

prairie dogs and the like, that the recoil of the 6mms as compared to the .17 or .22 centerfires can become a bit stiff, but I've never had a problem with using a standard-velocity .243 bores for extended shooting sessions. If you've chosen a 6mm as your deer/antelope rifle, one of the benefits of using it as your varmint rifle is the added trigger time with the same setup, which will allow you to become very proficient with your fetchin' iron. As the old adage goes: "Beware the man with one gun, he probably knows how to use it."

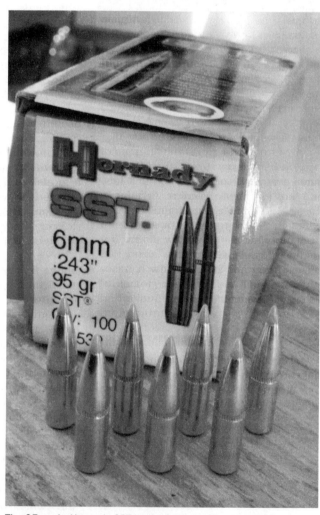

The 95-grain Hornady SST ammo will stabilize in both the .243 Winchester and 6mm Remington.

The .243 Winchester has been America's favorite son among the 6mms, and for very good reason. Like its dad, the .308 Winchester, it can be housed in a compact, short-action rifle, and has been made in bolt-action, lever-action and autoloading rifles over the years.

It shares its parental reputation for inherent accuracy, and the recoil it generates is mild enough for shooters of all statures to handle effectively. It makes for great coyote medicine, and the .243 bullets buck the wind better than the smaller-diameter bullets. Load some 70-grain Speer TNT hollowpoints at a velocity in the ballpark of 3,400 fps, and watch the magic happen. For even lighter (and faster) bullets, Nosler has a 55-grain projectile in their Varmageddon series. These are offered as a standard hollowpoint, or with a black polymer tip, and are devastating upon impact. The low sectional density and thin jacket will guarantee rapid expansion.

The .244 Remington, also known as the 6mm Remington, suffered a devastating blow to its reputation when Remington decided to produce it with a twist rate that wouldn't stabilize the long 100 and 105-grain deer bullets, but that certainly doesn't handicap its effectiveness as a varmint cartridge.

The reason for the cartridge having two names is that Remington made a valiant effort to reintroduce the case with a different rate of twist, but the .243 Winchester had gained too much ground at that point in time. The same choices for a good varmint projectile that apply to the .243 Winchester can apply to the .244/6mm Remington.

The flat-base Berger 6mm bullet, great for varmints and furbearers alike.

Using bullets lighter than 100 grains, the .244 has more case capacity than the .243 Winchester, as the .244 Remington is based on the longer 7x57 Mauser case. I like the .244 loaded with the slower-burning powders, as they can maximize the potential of the bigger case, especially with the lighter varmint-weight bullets. I've seen Col. Le Frogg's Ruger 77 in 6mm Remington push Sierra 75-grain hollowpoint bullets into tight little groups, while giving enough speed to create a very flat trajectory at the longer distances woodchucks and prairie dogs are hunted. These longer distances show the benefits of the boat-tail bullets, reducing the air drag out past 250 yards.

Weatherby's .240 Magnum certainly offers a case large enough to give a trajectory like a frozen rope, but it comes at a cost. Firstly, recoil will ramp up dramatically when compared to the mild-shooting .243 and .244, and secondly the bullet choices in factory-loaded ammunition are very limited. However, if you pick the 85-grain spitzer (the lightest factory offering) you've still got a decent choice for varmint work. Handloading the big Weatherby gives the shooter all the flexibility he or she would ever want within the 6mm realm, and were I to shoot the .240, I'd certainly take advantage of that fact.

The FMJ selection in 6mm caliber is a bit more limited than the .224" bullets, but they exist nonetheless. Sierra makes a worthy 90-grain 6mm FMJ, and I know Hornady made an 80-grain FMJ at one point in time, but I no longer see it listed as an available option. If you're a furbearer hunter, you may want to hoard whatever remaining supply of these that you can find.

THE QUARTER BORES

The .25-caliber rifles have long been an American favorite, beginning with the .25-20 Winchester, designed in 1892. Soon after, the .25-35 was introduced by Winchester in the radical new Model 1894, and it wasn't long until the wildcatters whose names would soon be revered began to modify the popular rimless cases of the late 19th and early 20th centuries to hold .257" bullets.

They are the big brother to the 6mms, but where the 6mms are often considered a varmint gun that is big game worthy, I feel that the .25s are a big-game gun that are varmint worthy. Either way you look at it, the .25s make a great varmint gun when the proper bullet is used. While the 110, 117 and 120-grain bullets really prove the worthiness of this caliber, the 100-grain and lighter bullets will be devastating on the varmints.

The smaller .25s I've mentioned, like the .25-20 and the .25-35 were 19th century developments that used the tubular magazine in lever-action repeating rifles, and necessitated the flatpoint bullets that prevented detonation with the magazine. The smaller of the two, the .25-20, was always designed as a varmint-class rifle, appearing in the classic '92 Winchester. The little case works well with 60-grain and 86-grain flatpoint bullets, but the slow velocities that the case generates limits it to an effective range of about 150 yards. The .25-35 Winchester was introduced in 1895, and was based on the .30-30 Winchester. It has the case capacity to use the full complement of .257" bullets, and makes for a cool package in the classic 1894 Winchester. Factory ammunition is very limited, but Winchester did reintroduce the cartridge in the new incarnation of the '94, and offers a 117-grain roundnose bullet. This will handle even Godzilla-sized coyotes, out to 200 yards.

The rimless .25s are an entirely different story. The forerunner, the .250/3000 Savage, earned its place in shooting history by being the first cartridge to break the 3,000 fps mark in 1915. The Savage Model 99 in which it was chambered was, and still is, a handy and great-shooting lever-action, and was probably one of the first cartridges fully capable of being a varmint/deer rig. The 87-grain bullets are a smidge light for elk-class animals, but are good for deer-sized game, and even better for woodchucks, foxes and coyotes.

Although factory ammo is also limited for this venerable case, I have handloaded 87-grain Sierra Varminter spitzers for my clients, and the reports were phenomenal. Accuracy hovered around the ½" mark for three-shot groups, and Texas 'yotes dropped dead in their tracks, from the cup-and-core bullet of lower sectional density. There are many good bullets in the 80 to 90-grain weight, like the Speer Hot-Cor (which has a reputation for being very soft) and the 85-grain Nosler Ballistic Tip Varmint. If you really want to push the velocity envelope, grab some Sierra 75-grain hollowpoints and start showing the prairie dogs exactly who is boss.

(left) The Sierra 87-grain .257" diameter varmint bullet.

(below) 100-grain Speer .25-caliber hollowpoints.

The next step up the power ladder is the .257 Roberts, based on a necked-down 7x57mm Mauser. The "Bob" is a cool cartridge, delivering better velocities than the 250/3000, yet still very mild recoil. Almost all of the factory ammunition available is designed for big game, using 110 through 120-grain bullets, but the lighter component bullets that work in the 250/3000 case can certainly be handloaded for varmint work, and at Bob velocities they certainly hit hard. That sweet polymer-tipped boat-tail Nosler Ballistic Tip at 85 grains will shoot plenty flat and generate all sorts of hydraulic shock.

The undisputed king of quarter bores is the former wildcat, the .25-'06 Remington. Although it has been around since the second decade of the 20th Century, it remained a wildcat until Remington put a ring on it in 1969. The bastard son of the .30-'06 Springfield made its own niche by launching those .257" bullets faster than any other cartridge save the behemoth .257 Weatherby Magnum. Texas hunters in particular have embraced the .25-'06 Remington, and it does great double duty on deer/hogs and varmints alike.

Federal Premium loads the 85-grain Nosler Ballistic Tip in their V-Shok line of ammunition, and they ought to be hell on varmints. Any good light weight hollowpoint bullet, like the Speer TNT, or Sierra hollowpoint, will wreak havoc on the smaller rodents, and the .25-'06 offers plenty of accuracy and wind-bucking capability to hit distant targets on windy days.

I've found the .25-'06 likes the slower-burning powders, like Alliant's Reloder 22 and Hodgdon's H4831SC, as these allow the handloader to realize the full velocity potential of the Springfield-based case. Barrel heat can pose a bit of a problem if you have a sporter-weight barrel, especially on hot days when you're sending a bunch of lead downrange at prairie dogs, but for the fur hunter the .25-06 shouldn't pose a problem.

Using the .257 Weatherby on varmints can test the mettle of the shooter, as that big case burns a lot more powder, and the recoil and muzzle blast ramp up quickly. However, if the .257 is your baby, it will certainly work. Factory ammunition is a limited prospect, and quite expensive, but if you can reload your own ammunition, costs can be cut in half and you can use a varmint-worthy bullet.

THE 6.5s THROUGH .30 CALIBERS

While intended for much larger game than small varmints, these calibers are often used when the opportunity to kill predators or varmints presents itself. I've probably shot more coyotes during our New York deer season than any other time, firstly because

I'm out afield all day, and secondly the coyotes absolutely love to dine upon the gut piles left in the deer woods.

I've used whatever big-game rifle I had in hand to dispatch the fawn-killing carnivores, but the deer bullets for the .308 Winchester and .300 Winchester Magnum that I usually hunt with will make quite a mess of the song dogs. Still, in that particular scenario, my objective is to rid the hunting area of as many coyotes as possible to ensure a healthy deer population, so I'm not too worried about it.

When a .308 Winchester was the only centerfire rifle I owned, I loaded up a bunch of 125-grain Nosler Ballistic Tip bullets at a velocity of just under 3,000fps, and I'll tell you that the low sectional density bullet, when combined with the high velocity, dropped coyotes

in their tracks. The fur was ripped to shreds, so I didn't use them for long. Instead, I found that the inexpensive military ball ammunition, which uses a 147-grain FMJ, gave the same killing power and did much less damage.

My suggestion for those who want to use their deer rifle in this fashion would be to find the lightest-weight full metal jacket available for their caliber, whether it's a .270 Winchester or 7mm Remington Magnum, and enjoy the time in the outdoors hunting coyotes with friends.

For the summertime fun of hunting woodchucks, again I prefer a highly frangible bullet in whichever caliber you use, and I like the light-for-caliber choices. Speer makes a TNT bullet for almost all calibers .308" and below, and as advertised, they are very soft.

Some of the cavernous cases, like the 7mm STW and the .300 Remington Ultra Magnum can generate force enough to separate the jacket from the copper cup, so be careful if you're trying to use the lightest bullets in a super-magnum. I've seen Col. Le Frogg tear 87-grain hollowpoints apart with a .264 Winchester Magnum. It was funny at the time, but extremely dangerous.

Nosler's famous Ballistic Tip is offered in two configurations; one for big game, and a special varmint model. You'd do well to take full advantage of these, as they shoot very accurately and generate all sorts of hydraulic shock. The same can be said of the Berger varmint series.

Do your research, and try and find some ammunition that will give you the performance you're after in your varmint rifle. If it's offered by the factory, that's wonderful, but if not, reloading may be in your future to obtain that ammunition that will do the best job.

The Speer 7mm 115-grain hollowpoint, light-for-caliber to give explosive performance.

The 8mm Remington Magnum with 220-grain Sierra Game King boatails. (J.P. Fielding photo)

CHAPTER 5

Without a doubt, in the hunting world this group of rifles is what is used most often, on practically all continents. Within this chapter, I will cover the range of animals from pronghorn antelope and javelina up through eland and moose. There is a huge amount of overlap, and many correct answers to the same question. However, by choosing the proper projectile, we hunters can neatly and humanely dispatch the game animals we are pursuing, or make a sensible middle-of-the-road choice if on a hunt that involves multiple species.

With today's advancements in bullet

MEDIUM AND LARGE GAME RIFLES

construction and technology, the list of suitable calibers and cartridges has changed from the previously accepted minimums, and absolutely warrants a revisit to the classic campfire discussions so the hunter can make a well educated decision that is both fair to the game animal and the hunter.

There are usually legal minimums set up by a particular country, province or state, so please be sure and heed the local laws while digesting this material. In my home state of New York for example, we are allowed to pursue deer and black bear with any centerfire rifle. Now it really doesn't make a whole lot of sense to head to the mountains with the intention of shooting a black bear

Author's Catskill Mountain whitetail taken with .308 Winchester and 165-grain Nosler Partition.

while toting your .17 Remington or .22-250, yet it would be perfectly legal. On the flip side of that coin, the .243 Winchester or 6.5x55 Swede would very effectively kill a 150 lb. leopard, yet the Tanzanian established minimum for dangerous game is a .375" bore or larger, so be sure and know the game laws well.

I don't think I'd be out of line by stating that the whitetail deer is the most widely hunted game animal in North America, and that the wild boar is the animal most hunted across the globe. On the average, the two are of similar weight, yet Sus Scrofa has some God-given features that can make him a tougher customer. A thick hide and a gristle

plate covering the vitals can require a stoutly-constructed bullet to put him down. Likewise, moose require a different level of killing power than does a pronghorn, and an impala will fall much easier than an eland.

The factory ammunition of the 21st Century is better than it has ever been, but even with the wide selection of choices available to the modern hunter, there are still some fantastic bullets out there that can't be purchased from a major company. Hornady offers wonderful ammunition that features their own lineup of good bullets, Federal Premium loads a good selection of different manufacturers products, and even Remington utilizes the good bullet designs of Swift and other companies. Berger bullets, which for years were only available for use as a component part, are now loaded for hunting in ABM ammunition, and Norma is using Woodleigh bullets in addition to their own designs.

Things are slowly changing, and there are avenues open now that can satisfy the desire to hunt with a particular bullet/cartridge combination you've been dreaming of. That premise is the basis of my own custom ammunition company, Massaro Ballistic Labo-

Massaro Ballistic Laboratories, a fully custom ammunition shop.

ratories, but there are others out there. Superior Ammunition from Michigan was among the first to offer this type of service, and ProGrade is another that comes to mind, but a short Internet search will reveal more like us. My own company is completely custom; with a phone call you can get any feasible centerfire cartridge with the bullet that you want to use, made just like a custom pair of shoes.

Smaller commercial operations, like Double-Tap, will listen to their customers and turn out the product if the demand is there. And, there is always the option of getting into handloading ammunition yourself. That will allow you to get the exact ballistic performance you're after, in both accuracy and velocity. Most bullet companies offer load data on their websites that will easily get you where you'd like to be. Let's get you on your way to making the proper choice.

.22 CENTERFIRES

I've put it in print before, and I'll say it here again. Many people ask me my opinion on using a .22 centerfire as a big game rifle, and my opinion is this: In the hands of a highly experienced shooter, one who is willing to take his or her time to wait for the proper shot angle, the .22s can be effective killers. Invariably, the most popular of them all, the .223 Remington, is used annually to account for many tons of meat. However, it is also responsible for much wounded game as well. I feel that for the beginner or young shooter, a .22 centerfire is not enough gun. I have seen experienced hunters, with dozens of heads of game to their credit, wound deer with a .223 and frangible bullets.

Better put, the shot that was placed on the game animal would have been lethal with a heavier bullet (in this par-

Two good choices, if you want to hunt deer with your .22 centerfire.

The all-copper Hornady GMX, shown in section.

ticular situation), and the lack of energy, penetration and bullet structure led to a lost and crippled animal. Bullet weights are light, and when the shooting angle gets funky penetration can pose a problem with cup-and-core bullets.

That said, there has been much progress made in the field of well-constructed bullets for the .22s, and if you're the shooter who feels comfortable taking one afield, I think you'd be well served by using one of them. Most of bullets that will deliver the best performance on antelope, deer and hogs are over 55 grains, so be sure and verify that the twist rate of your rifle will stabilize bullets of that length. I do feel that deer, antelope and small hogs are as large as a hunter should ethically go when using one of the .22 centerfires. When the game gets larger than that, you're really asking for trouble.

The 50-grain Barnes TSX and the 60-grain Nosler Partition are both available in factory-loaded ammunition and either would make a decent choice for using the .22 centerfire on medium game. The heavy construction of these premium bullets will help to give the necessary penetration to destroy the vital organs and kill quickly without prematurely breaking up. Swift's Scirocco II is available as a component bullet, and weighing in at 60 grains, offers bonded-core and polymer-tip boat-tail construction, which will optimize the performance of the .22 centerfires. The Hornady GMX, a bullet comprised entirely of gilding metal, is available in 50-grain weight. The GMX has worked well for me in larger calibers, and should work well in the small centerfires.

Certainly there are many fans of the cup-and-core bullets available for the .224" diameters, and they do work, but they do not provide the penetration that the premium bullets do. The Hornady InterLoks, Sierra GameKings, and Speer HotCors can be wonderfully

Federal 55-grain soft points for the .22-250. A premium bullet would better serve the hunter at .22-250 velocities.

accurate, but when using them on larger game you must be even more critical when picking your shots. Avoid bones when possible, and do your best to get the bullet into the soft heart and lung tissue, and I'd advise using the heaviest bullet that your rifle will shoot accurately.

THE SWEET SIXES

These are what I consider the best minimum for medium game up to and including deer and antelope. I don't think the sixes are a good choice for caribou, elk or bigger game, but like the .22 centerfires, there are folks who

use them. I like to use the heavy-for-caliber bullets when I head afield with a 6mm, like the 90, 100 and 105-grain offerings. On deer-sized game the traditional bullets will work just fine, providing that you do your job and put the bullet where it belongs. I've used some 100-grain Sierra GameKings and Pro-Hunters in a .243 Winchester to print very pretty groups, and those same bullets worked very well on our whitetail deer. My good pal Fred Schultz has used the .243 Winchester in a Model 70

The Fusion makes a good choice for the 6mm.

Westerner since we were kids, and he's had deer drop from that rifle as if they were pole-axed.

He has used handloaded 100-grain Hornady InterLock bullets for decades now, and will more than likely continue to effectively do so. The Remington Core-Lokt and Winchester Power Point bullets have been a factory-loaded standard for years, and they will kill very effectively as well.

The higher-end cup-and-core bullets, like a Hornady SST, Berger VLD Hunting or Combined Technologies Ballistic Silver Tip can be used to

Hornady's 100-grain boat-tail cup-and-core bullet, a decent choice for an all-around 6mm bullet.

The 6mm Remington, with its slower twist rate, can stabilize the 100-grain, whereas the .244 Remington could not.

Berger's sleek 105-grain 6mm bullet.

deliver one-shot kills, and the accuracy potential is certainly there. The sharp polymer tip and boat-tail construction retain the most energy of any bullet design, and that's important for the relatively light 6mm bore.

Be sure and use the heavier weights in this caliber, as they are designed for big game and the jackets will be thicker, in opposition to the lighter varmint style bullets previously outlined. Hornady loads the 95-grain SST for both the .243 Winchester and 6mm Remington in their Superformance ammunition line, and this would make a great long-range antelope and whitetail deer load.

If you intend to use your 6mm to hunt the larger mule deer or caribou, the premium bullets deserve an audition with your rifle. The Speer Grand Slam is available in a 100-grain weight, and with its lead core of differing hardness, it will hit hard and give good expansion without premature breakup.

Norma loads its proprietary Oryx bullet for the .243 Winchester, in a 100-grain configuration. This bullet is designed to be soft in the frontal portion, having a thin jacket and non-bonded core. However, things change halfway down the bullet, as the jacket gets thicker and the core is then bonded to the jacket. This gives all the expansion you'd want and weight retention approaching 90%, for great penetration. Norma has a winner here.

Winchester has a neat bullet for the .243 Winchester and .243 WSSM: the XP3. It's essentially a cross between the Barnes TTSX and a Nosler Partition, in that the front section of the bullet is all copper with the hollowpoint and polymer tip, but Winchester has put a lead core at the base. I haven't used them personally, but those who have tell me it's a solid performer, and at 95 grains it gives good expansion and good weight retention.

The monometals, like the Barnes TTSX and Hornady GMX, both in

80-grain weight, can make the 6mm shine. They feature a polymer tip and though apparently light for caliber, they will hold together and give you good penetration. I recently used the Federal Premium Trophy Copper 85-grain load in a Savage Compact Hunter in .243 Winchester on a deer hunt at the famous Vatoville Ranch in Eldorado, Texas.

Author's Texas whitetail taken with the Federal .243 Winchester 85-grain Trophy Copper load.

The body size of Texas deer (125 to 150 pounds) can be adequately handled by one of the 6mms, and the solid copper bullets make a sensible choice for adequate penetration. When my buddy and guide, Ben 'Brother' Lawrence, nudged me to show me the giant seven point buck that had just come into view, I settled the rifle's crosshairs on the buck's vitals, on a quartering-away shot. One tickle of the trigger at 113 yards and the tall-racked buck literally dropped where he stood. I can't quite print what Brother's actual remarks were, but suffice it to say that he was very impressed with the bullet. One lung was jellified, and the bullet coursed upward after hitting a rib, breaking the buck's spine. Lights officially out.

Federal .243 Winchester 85-grain Trophy Copper load.

The bonded-core bullets make a wise choice as well, and those that are polymer-tip boat-tails will retain more energy at longer ranges, as well as give the flat trajectories that the 6mms are famous for. Swift's Scirocco, Hornady's InterBond and Nosler's AccuBond will perform very well at even the highest velocities. They make a great choice for the fastest 6mms: the .243 WSSM (Winchester Super Short Magnum) and .240 Weatherby Magnum.

THE QUARTER BORES

America has had a long love affair with the .257" bore diameter. As we discussed in the varmint chapter, the .25-20 and .25-35 rimmed cartridges started the ball, but the release of Savage's .250/3000 saw the .25s become a serious contender for deer-size game, propelling the 87-grain bullets to that then magical velocity of 3,000 fps. The .257 Roberts is another classic, and the long-time wildcat-turned-factory darling, the .25-06 Remington hogs the majority of the stage time. The new kid at school, the .25 WSSM and the .257 Weatherby Magnum fill the magnum velocity slots.

These cartridges have a wide velocity difference, and the bullet used for each should be chosen carefully to give optimum performance. Although they offer a significant weight increase and better frontal diameter than the 6mms, the .25s are still a bit light to be considered for an 'all-around' medium to big game rifle.

The .25s are, undoubtedly, stellar performers on game from javelina and antelope up to and including wild boar,

The .25-06 works best with cup-and-core bullets in the heavier weights. (J.P. Fielding photo)

whitetail, and mule deer. You could even push the envelope as far as caribou, but that's where I'd draw the line. Elk and similar-sized animals seem to call for a bit more bullet weight and frontal diameter. The .25 bores are limited to 120 grains of bullet, but within the aforementioned applications that will work just fine.

The oldest .25s, the .25-20 and .25-35 are rarely used by serious hunters, but those who do are constantly on the hunt for ammunition. The .25-20 is available with only the 86-grain softpoint, while the .25-35 is produced with the 117-grain softpoint. These bullet weights will perform well in these mild cartridges, as their velocity does not warrant the use of the premium bullets of today. Ranges are generally close for these old timers, so if they appeal to you, try to use them within their effective ranges.

There are some great bullets on the market for the .25 calibers, and that just adds to the usefulness of this caliber. The .250/3000 Savage has few choices among factory loads, primarily the Remington 100-grain Core-Lokt, but if you are a handloader, you can put some great combinations together.

I've loaded the Sierra 87-grain flat base bullet for clients with fantastic results. The light bullets are perfect in the moderate-velocity cartridges, so long as the intended target is the smaller variety of whitetail deer. If you were grabbing your .250 for a hunting trip afar, I'd hedge my bets by using a 100, 117 or 120-grain bullet in case a weird angle shot is all that is presented. For both the .250/3000 and the .257 Roberts, I feel that standard cup-and-

The 250/3000 Savage with 87-grain Sierra and 110-grain Nosler AccuBond. (J.P. Fielding photo)

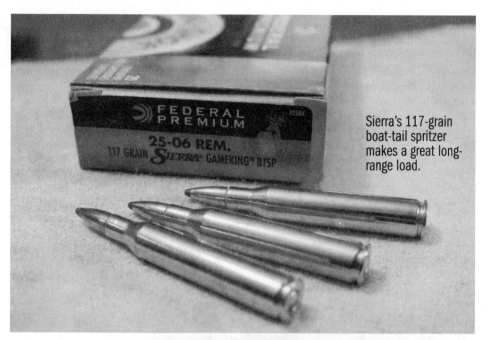

Sierra's 117-grain boat-tail spritzer makes a great long-range load.

core bullets will perform perfectly. I like the polymer-tipped cup-and-core for the milder .25s as well, and the Hornady SST and Nosler Ballistic Tip have proven to be capable of extreme accuracy. The uber-accurate Berger VLD could also fit in this category, and their 115-grain hollow-point would make a good choice for any of the middle-to-larger .25-caliber cases.

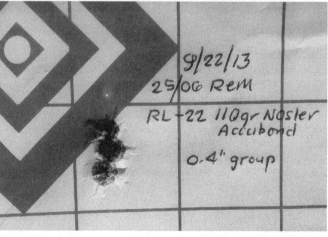

Step up to the .25-'06 Remington and you'll start to see the advantages of the boat-tail bullets, as the larger cases can push the bullet to a higher velocity and really flatten out the trajectories. Much of the factory-loaded ammunition uses this style bullet, regardless of construction. I like the way the .25-'06 performs with the premium bullets, especially if you have the chance of a close shot. The velocities are just high enough

that cup-and-core bullets can make a bit of a mess if the impact distances are within 75 yards.

I have had great success using Nosler's Ac-cuBond 110-grain bullet in the .25-'06, giving excellent accuracy and devastating performance on deer-sized game. The bonded core gives great stability upon impact, preventing premature breakup while giving deep penetra-

The accuracy potential of the .25-06 with 110-grain AccuBonds.

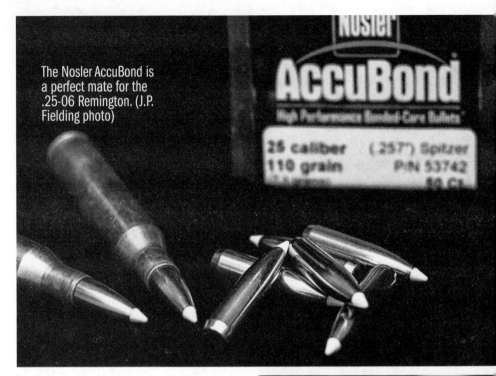

The Nosler AccuBond is a perfect mate for the .25-06 Remington. (J.P. Fielding photo)

tion. The same could be said about the Swift Scirocco II, and the Hornady Interbond. This style of bullets is, in my opinion, the optimum blend of bullet integrity and downrange performance. The sharp polymer tip and specially-designed ogive, with a boat-tail rear, give a high ballistic coefficient for a flat trajectory and wind-bucking capabilities.

The monometals are a good choice for the faster .25s as well. A Barnes TTSX, even weighing 90 grains, can give performance on par with the heavier cup-and-core bullets. Being solid copper, with a hollow cavity, there is no jacket to separate from the core. The same principal applies to the Hornady GMX and the Nosler Etip, and if these bullets shoot accurately in your rifle, you may very well fall in love with their performance in the field.

Cutting Edge Bullets makes their Match Tactical Hunting bullet, which is also a solid copper bullet with a hollow point, but the front portion of the bullet is designed break into small 'blades'

to give serious impact trauma, while the rear portion remains caliber-sized to give you all the penetration you'd want.

The classic Nosler Partition is available in .257" diameter, and that bullet has been a great choice for big game since the 1940s. It is available to the .25 fans in a 115-grain weight, and would make a sound choice for any of the larger game animals you'd pursue with this caliber. Swift's incredible A-Frame is also on the plate, in both 100 and 120-grain weights. With a bonded core, partitioned design and giving expansion of up to 2x, this bullet has become a par-

Sectional density, anyone? The 6.5x55 Swedish Mauser and a 156-grain roundnose.

ticular favorite of mine.

The fastest .25, the big .257 Weatherby Magnum, definitely performs best when loaded with premium bullets. The premiums stand up well to the high impact velocities that this cartridge can generate, and although most factory loads for it aren't loaded with premium bullets, if you can get someone to load them, you'll notice a marked improvement in performance.

The Mighty .257 Weatherby Magnum and the 100-grain Nosler.

THE 6.5MM CARTRIDGES

This caliber, while never extremely popular here in the United States, has been embraced by the rest of the shooting world. It is the lightest caliber that I feel will make a suitable choice for all non-dangerous game, including moose, elk and black bear.

The bullet weights in 6.5mm range from 100 to 160 grains, and the heavier bullets within this range have a great sectional density. This high S.D. helped to make the great reputation that the 6.5s have. They have been used in Scandinavia for over a century, and are regularly used to kill European moose and

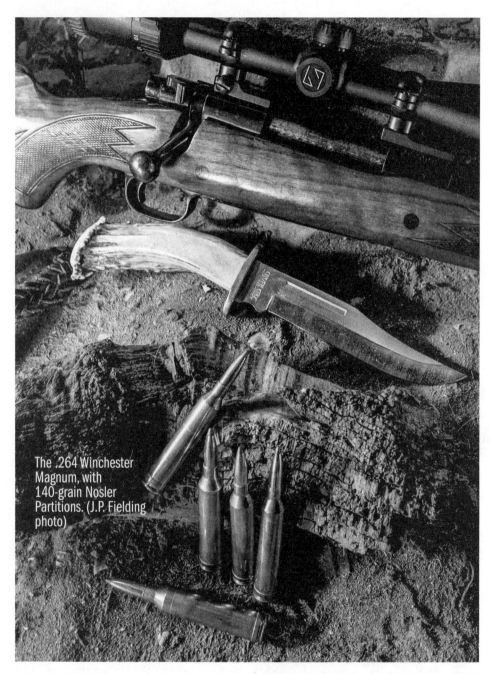

The .264 Winchester Magnum, with 140-grain Nosler Partitions. (J.P. Fielding photo)

boar.

The 6.5 bore was a favorite of Blaney Percival, head game ranger of Kenya Colony a century ago, and he used the 6.5 to regularly take lion and buffalo. Even the renowned W.D.M. "Karamo-ja" Bell used a .256" Mannlicher (read 6,5x54) to take elephant in the Lado Enclave. Now, I'm not going to even re-motely suggest that the 6.5s are an el-ephant-worthy bore diameter, but I am willing to go on record as saying that the 6.5s kill much better than their paper-ballistics would indicate.

I am a huge fan of the .264" bore, from the mild mannered 6.5x54 Mannlicher-Schoenauer and the military 6.5x55 Swedish Mauser to .260 Remington and (my personal favorite) the 6.5-284 Norma, and up to the fastest 6.5s, the .264 Winchester Magnum and the new .26 Nosler.

They can be very flat-shooting in the bigger cases, yet even the magnums have a recoil level that is tolerable to most shooters. The first magnum case that I ever fired was Col. Le Frogg's .264 Winchester, and it quickly dispelled my fear of magnum recoil, and led to a love of belted cases.

Many companies have embraced the 6.5 bore, and are producing fantastic bullets. Depending on the size of the game you are after, you can tailor the bullet choice to the job at hand. Certainly it was the long, heavy-for-caliber 160-grain roundnose, at mild speeds like 2,300 or 2,400 fps that made the reputation for the early 6.5s. I have always been a fan of heavy roundnose bullets, and this one is no exception. The Hornady InterLock 160-grain is an example, but you could certainly include the Norma Oryx 156-grain bullet as well. They have the high S.D. to give penetration that you would expect from a much larger bullet, but at the price of a lower ballistic coefficient.

Still, I wouldn't hesitate to use them within 250 yards. Just this past deer season, I took an eight-point whitetail buck with my 6.5-284 Norma with that 156-grain Oryx, and the buck flipped backward at the shot. It wasn't a long shot by any means, around 75 yards, but the bullet did its job perfectly and there was no tracking job. Those long roundnose and semi-spitzer bullets, like the 156 Oryx, make game shudder upon impact. Push them to 6.5-284 or .264 Winchester velocities, and they give you enough added energy to make you feel confident with the longer shots.

However, it is the sleek 120 to 140-grain bullets that can bring out the long-range capabilities of the 6.5s. They still offer a very good S.D., but the B.C.s of some of the spitzer boat-tail bullets are amazing. In the Mannlicher and Swede cartridges, as well as the Grendel and Creedmoor cases, you can be very well served by hunting with a well made cup-and-core bullet. The Sierra 120-grain flat-base ProHunter and the 140-grain boat-tail GameKing are both capable of hair-splitting accuracy and great terminal performance in the game fields.

Hornady's Interlock is available in

The 6.5-284 Norma with 156-grain Norma Oryx.

129 and 140-grain flat-base offerings, and both are good choices for hunting bullets. The 6.5mm Nosler Ballistic Tip, as with other calibers, has proven itself as an accurate and effective choice for medium game. The Ballistic Tip bullet and its ilk perform best at less than magnum velocities, as they are a bit on the frangible side, but for the moderate velocity cases they can be an awesome bullet.

The Nosler design is a winner, and as long as you use them sensibly, at deer-sized game, you'll have no complaints. Bump up the game size to the bigger species of deer (or African antelope) and you should be in the market for a stiffer bullet. This is the realm of the Nosler Partition, the Trophy Bonded Bear Claw, North Fork Semi-Spitzer and Swift A-Frame. All will expand reliably at the moderate velocities, but still hang tough if shoulder bones are struck. The 6.5x55 Swede and the .260 Remington, when mated with a good 140-grain bonded-core bullet, make a match that will perform surprisingly well, and kill better than its small case would suggest.

The larger 6.5mm cases are a different situation. As with any bullet, high velocity is the force that flattens out trajectories and gives better kinetic energy, but the same high velocity will produce over expansion and premature breakup upon impact. I truly believe that the three largest 6.5mm cases, the 6.5-284 Norma, the venerable .264 Winchester Magnum and the new .26 Nosler are all best served by the stronger bullets.

If you are a cup-and-core fan, be sure and find a bullet with a thick jacket to stall expansion. The bonded-core bullets, and the monometals as well, make solid choices for these big cases, especially if you anticipate an impact velocity under 100 yards. I also feel that sticking with the 140-grain and heavier bullets is a smart decision. They will retain the most energy for the longer

shots, and the higher sectional density and ballistic coefficient will deliver the finest accuracy.

For my 6.5-284 Norma, I like the North Fork 140-grain semi-spitzer. It is accurate, and the pure lead core is bonded to the pure copper jacket, for structural integrity. I feel confident and comfortable using this combination on almost all medium game up to and including elk. My custom Savage Model 116 really likes Norma's 156-grain Oryx load, driven at a velocity of 2,850 fps or so. This has shown fantastic accuracy, right out of the box, showing ½ to ¾" groups.

The .264 Winchester Magnum and the .26 Nosler can push the limits of cup-and-core bullets. I've seen Col. Le Frogg blow the core out of the lighter 85-grain cup-and-core 6.5mm bullets with his .264 Mag., and the new .26 Nosler case moves them even faster.

The high S.D. 6.5mm bullets, in 160-grain roundnose and 140-grain spitzer boat-tail.

But stick a premium bullet on the top of these cases and you've got a very potent combination in your hands. The trajectories are very flat, but the recoil level can get severe. The .26 Nosler can push 140-grain bullets over 3,300 fps, so to maximize this velocity you'll want something sleek and designed for long-range work. Nosler's AccuBond Long Range comes quickly to mind, and the Berger VLD would be a good choice for longer shots as well.

I'd also look to a Hornady GMX or Interbond for these two, and feel confident afield. Woodleigh Bullets from Australia make some great bullets for the 6.5 bores, including a 140-grain and 160-grain Protected Point. They are a semi-spitzer, with the bonded core that I like to hunt with, and although they don't have the boat-tail and sharp spitzer of some of the other bullets, I like them for the way they stay together when they hit game.

THE .270s

Since its introduction in 1925, America has had a deep affection for the

(below) A good selection of .270 Winchester ammunition. (J.P. Fielding photo)

.270 Winchester. It is the first offspring of the kingly .30-06 Springfield to be embraced by the shooting world, and it is easy to understand why. When the shooting world speaks of the ".270", more than likely they are referring to the .270 Winchester. It delivers a .277" diameter bullet at (relatively) high velocity, is easy on the shoulder, and is a very effective killer. Trajectories are flat enough to make it suitable for mountains, desert and prairie alike, and can be extremely accurate. It is just about perfect for deer, antelope, wild sheep, hogs, et al.

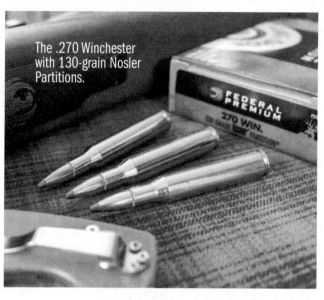

The .270 Winchester with 130-grain Nosler Partitions.

The cartridge, and the bore diameter, got a huge boost into the spotlight by being adopted by Jack O'Connor, and via his writings the cartridge gained much fame. It is one of the contestants in a major rifle debate: the great .270 v. .30-'06 rivalry.

The Nosler Ballistic Tip in .277" diameter, 130 grains.

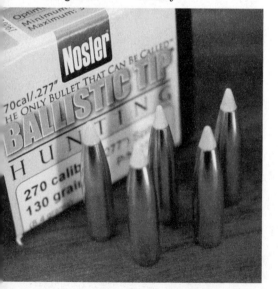

Both camps are rabid about their chosen rifle, and both have valid points. Either way, the .270 Winchester reigns supreme in this bullet diameter, even though there are other .270 bores on the market. Roy Weatherby adapted his double-radius belted magnum case to hold .277" bullets, and even Winchester tried to enhance the performance of its proven workhorse by unveiling the .270 Winchester Short Magnum. Remington joined the foray by introducing the 6.8 SPC, and although it was designed for the AR platform, it has its fans in the hunting world.

My major beef with the .270s is the choice of bullet weights. There are plenty of good bullets, but the popular weights are 130, 140 and 150 grains. I have wondered for years why a bore diameter only 0.007" smaller than the 7mm cartridges has a significantly lighter bullet choice. There are a few heavier choices, like the Nosler Partition 160-grain semi-spitzer, the Barnes Original 170-grain, and the 180-grain Woodleigh Protected Point, but these are available in component form only. The factory-loaded ammunition usually tops out at 150 grains, but then again I've never heard many complaints from

osler's 130-grain Partition in .270 Winchester.

.270 shooters. Although it isn't a bore that I hunt with often, I've shot and loaded a ton of different .270 stuff, so let's talk about some good bullet choices and the reasons for choosing them.

.270 WINCHESTER

The 130-grain bullet, which Mr. O'Connor waxed so poetic about in his .270 Winchester, is still a fantastic weight for that cartridge. Propelled at just about 3,050 fps, it provides a nice, flat trajectory, and enough striking power to kill quickly. I like the Sierra GameKing 130-grain boat-tail for deer and antelope hunting. It has been a very accurate bullet in many of the .270s I've loaded for, as many Sierra bullets have been.

The Hornady InterLock bullet is loaded in the American Whitetail line from Hornady, and I've never had a problem with any Interlock bullet at standard velocity. There are other cup-and-core 130-grain bullets for the .270 Winchester, but the Sierra and the Hornady are my favorites. Nosler's Bal-

listic Tip and Hornady's SST give the polymer-tip option for those who like the idea of a sharp point for a higher B.C., and I believe that bullet has proven itself a winner on deer-sized game.

Should you choose a premium projectile in this weight, Federal loads the excellent 130-grain Nosler Partition in their factory ammo, and that makes a good choice for larger deer, as it will retain its weight better upon impact.

Nosler themselves load the 130-grain AccuBond in their ammunition, and all of my experiences with this bullet have been positive. Another bullet that I have come to rely on personally is the Swift Scirocco II. Like the AccuBond, it has a long and tapered ogive with a polymer tip, and a boat-tail to boot, so you'll be getting the most bang for your buck (pun intended) when it comes to flat trajectory and wind-bucking capabilities.

The Swift A-Frame is available in the 130-grain configuration, and this is a very tough bullet, often retaining its weight into the high 90% range. Federal's Fusion is a relative newcomer, and its bonded core makes for a wise choice in the .270 Winchester, especially when

The Cutting Edge Bullets Raptor, in original and expanded condition.

The 150-grain Hornady roundnose, a good choice for bear hunting with your .270.

shot angles force you to break bone.

If you're into the monometal bullets (and there's good reasons to be), the 120 and 130-grainers are well represented also. Being constructed of copper, they are longer than the lead-core bullets and can deliver equal performance with less weight. Winchester loads its 130-grain Razorback XT, which is a solid copper flat-base bullet, with a deep hollowpoint for initiating expansion. The popular Barnes TTSX (Tipped Triple Shock X) is made in the 130-grain, while the all-copper Norma Kalahari, which has frangible petals that break away upon impact is loaded in the American PH lineup.

Similar to the Kalahari, The Cutting Edge MTH is another all-copper hollowpoint, lathe-turned and designed for fantastic terminal performance. The MTH is available in 120 and 130-grain weights. All of these lighter bullets will make you rethink the potential of the .270 Winchester.

The heavier 150-grain bullets are what you're going to want to reach for if you choose to take the .270 Winchester along on hunts for the larger

species. For hunting the popular black bear, a good 150-grain roundnose bullet will give you plenty of penetration to reach the vitals, even through heavy bone. Remember, even though black bears aren't the most ferocious of the Ursus clan, they still have claws and teeth and demand respect.

For elk, moose, and the African plains game, I like the heavier bullets, and especially the heavier premium bullets. Swift's 150-grain A-Frame is a wonderful choice, as is the 150-grain Nosler Partition. Hornady's all copper GMX comes in the 150-grain variety, and has worked very well in the .270 Winchester. Look long and hard at the North Fork 150-grain semi-spitzer as well. Designed to have a pure lead core, but only in the front half of the bullet, the bonded-core design will give incredible penetration.

When it comes to a big bull elk, or a big-bodied kudu bull, you want to make sure you have enough bullet to anchor your trophy, and in the .270 Winchester, I'd like to hedge my bets by using a really good 150-grain bullet that will hang together. And yes, I'll go on record as saying that with premium bullets, the .270 Winchester is a perfectly fine elk cartridge. Try a few to see how they shoot in your .270, and when you find one that shoots accurately, head afield confidently.

THE .270 WEATHERBY MAGNUM AND .270 WINCHESTER SHORT MAGNUM

These two cases have much more case capacity than does the .270 Winchester, and better the velocity by 250 to 300 fps. This velocity increase will put much more strain on the standard cup-and-core bullet. That's not to say that a traditional bullet won't work, but you'll experience more bloodshot meat, and premature bullet breakup than with a milder cartridge. The answer is a premium bullet. By either bonding the core to the jacket, or increasing the jacket thickness, or by constructing the bullet of solid copper, the premium bullets mate up perfectly with magnum cases. The premium bullets described above will work ideally in the big magnum cases.

When my buddy Craig Boddington needed a good load for his .270 WSM, we decided on the 150-grain Hornady GMX, and the end product worked out perfectly. The solid gilding metal bullets gave great penetration and quick kills, in addition to the hair-splitting accuracy that the WSM series is known for. The magnum cases will also show a strong preference for bullets on the heavier side of the spectrum.

In .277" diameter, I like the 140 and 150-grain bullets for improved stability and long-range accuracy. If you do choose a cup-and-core bullet, look to

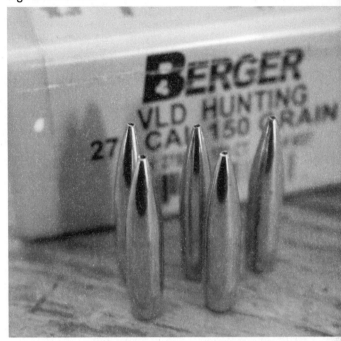

Berger's 150-grain .277" bullet is long and sleek, with high B.C. and S.D.

the heaviest weight, like the 150-grain Hornady Interlock and the 150-grain Sierra boat-tail. The Berger VLDs and Hunting bullets are another great choice for the long-range rig.

The recoil will get a bit stiffer than the sweet-shooting .270 Winchester, but if you can handle it, you'll have a hard-hitting, very flat-shooting rifle in your hands.

THE LUCKY SEVENS

This classic bore diameter is one of the two most popular in North America, and is second only to the American-as-apple-pie .30 caliber. The Seven holds the prestigious title of being the bore diameter chosen by Peter Paul Mauser for his bolt-action repeating rifle that would set the benchmark for hunting rifles for the next 130 years.

The 7x57mm Mauser, with its rimless design and accuracy potential, made the soldier that much more dead-

Federal Premium's Trophy Tipped 150-grain .270 Winchester Short Magnum load.

The original; the 7x57 Mauser.
(J.P Fielding photo)

ly, not to mention efficient. The Mauser rim dimensions are still retained by dozens of our favorite cartridges like the .30-'06 Springfield, the .280 Remington and .243 Winchester. The 7mm caliber is not exactly 7mm, the diameter of the bullets is actually 7.21mm, or 0.284"; the 7mm technically refers to the diameter of the lands within the rifle bore.

I feel that the 7mms are a good choice for the hunter who was raised like I was, in that we always chose a rifle caliber that we could use for all of our hunting, rather than having many specialized rifles (mostly because I couldn't afford them as a young man).

Like the .30s, the 7mm cartridges can be outfitted with a wide variety of bullet weights, and they will allow you to effectively hunt virtually all North American game, with the exception of the huge brown bears of Alaska (and there are those who may argue that

point with me), and for a large percentage of game across the globe. Removing the African lion, Cape Buffalo, elephant and hippo, eland and the largest water buffalo in Australia, and a good 7mm will handle the situation well. The modern bullets have made the sevens even more effective, and within the range of bullet weights, there are some that would have really opened the eyes of the hunters of yesteryear, including the revered Mr. Keith, who was (rightly so) a proponent of heavy bores and heavy bullets.

The Mauser design utilized a 173-grain bullet, at about 2,300 fps, and the combination of moderate velocity and heavy-for-caliber bullet was a perfect marriage. Perhaps the greatest champion of the 7mm Mauser was Walter Dalrymple Maitland Bell, known on the Dark Continent as "Karamoja".

The great elephant hunter used many different rifles and calibers in his pursuit of ivory across the width and breadth of Africa, but the majority of the 1,000+ elephants he killed were taken with a 7x57 Mauser, or as it was known on Great Britain, the .275 Rigby. He noted that a heavy bullet, say from a .450 Nitro Express or the like, if placed in wrong spot, did absolutely no good, but even the small cartridges, if equipped with a proper bullet, would dispatch the giant tuskers with no problem at all.

As we discussed in the 6.5mm section, I truly don't believe that any 7mm is a good match for any pachyderm, and I am convinced that Bell had a guardian angel of epic proportions, but the fact remains: he retired unscathed, and his career was a testament to proper bullet placement.

In comparison to the 7mm cartridges of today, the 7x57 falls at the bottom of the heap, with only the 7x30 Waters (the .30-30 Winchester necked down) and maybe the 7mm-08 falling below it. Modern technology has helped to develop some cartridges that can push the 7mm bullets to incredible velocities, and challenge the integrity of the classic cup-and-core bullet, but that same technology has seen newer bullets come along that can withstand those velocities, and give some new and unparalleled performance. We should look at the 7s from slowest to fastest, and pick out some good projectiles to match the cartridges' performance level.

THE 7-30 WATERS

The good Mr. Ken Waters designed his 7-30 Waters to be a high-pressure, enhanced velocity and necked-down version of the venerable 30-30 WCF, which would push the smaller diameter 7mm bullets to a very respectable velocity for a lever gun. The cartridge which bears the Waters moniker is a decided improvement over the classic 30-30 ballistics, but I think that it fell short because it was compared to the silly amount of 7mm cartridges that

the bolt guns shoot. Looking at it from a lever gun perspective, the ballistics are impressive, and offer a distinct advantage over the other lever cartridges. It requires a flat-point bullet, due to the tubular magazine, but the thicker case walls and enhanced chamber allows for higher pressures and therefore higher velocity. I like the Federal load with the 120-grain flatpoint, which totally beats the 30-30, but I would love to see what the Hornady Flex-Tip technology would do to improve upon Mr. Waters' creation.

THE 7MM-08 REMINGTON

The lower-velocity 7mm bolt-action cartridges, depending on their case capacity, can make for a good choice in an all around rifle. The 7mm-08 Remington, as much as it lacks in velocity with the heaviest of the 7mm bullets, makes a fantastic choice with the mid-weight bullets. The mild recoil and the inherent accuracy make for an impeccable combination. It's easy to teach a

Sierra's 140-grain 7mm bullet is a good choice for the smaller 7mm cases.

7-08 on larger than deer species, like elk, moose, or the African antelope, I'd choose a beefy bullet designed for large game. The Swift A-Frame, North Fork semi-spitzer, Nosler Partition, Federal Trophy Bonded and the like can give enhanced terminal performance, derived from the stout construction.

In a case as small as the 7-08, beware the monometal bullets. If you want to use them, stick with the lighter weights, as the all-copper construction will eat up a bunch of the case capacity, and thereby cut down on velocity. I like the 140 and 150-grain weights in the Hornady GMX, Barnes TTSX and Cutting Edge offerings. They make a sound choice for the larger deer species, as well as black bears.

If you're introducing a new shooter to big game hunting, and want to avoid the full-house loads (and thereby prevent a flinch early on) there are some wonderful reduced loadings on the market. Remington's Reduced Recoil line offers a 140-grain bullet at 2,360 fps, which will kill effectively out past 200 yards, without the sharp recoil associated with some of the more powerful factory ammunition. This is fantastic for building confidence early on in the hunting career.

THE 7X57MM MAUSER

The venerable 7x57mm Mauser gives a bit more flexibility to the handloader, but among the factory loadings it can seem a bit anemic. This is mostly due to the large amount of vintage rifles still on the market, which cannot handle the higher pressures of the new rifles with better metallurgy. Still, the 7x57 is a proven killer. For long-range work, the 120 to 150-grain bullets, in any configuration, should prove sufficient. The velocities are on the lower end of the spectrum, and as velocities slow down

new shooter good marksmanship skills with the 7-08, yet with the use of the 140 and 160-grain bullets, quick kills are a common occurrence.

There is something to be said for any of the .308 Winchester family of cases; they are among the most inherently accurate, easy to handload for, and will easily give good performance with factory ammunition. The diminutive case has trouble delivering the heavy 175-grain 7mm bullets at a velocity fast enough to make them expand reliably, but the premium 140, 150 and 160-grainers will give performance comparable to the cup-and-core 175-grain projectiles.

For deer and antelope-sized game, the traditional Remington Core-Lokt, Hornady InterLock, and certainly the Sierra ProHunter and GameKing bullets will perform perfectly at 7mm-08 velocities, as the bullet jackets are tough enough to penetrate deep and yet the frontal portions are soft enough to give adequate expansion for a wide wound channel.

The 7mm-08, though it lacks the look of reach, can be a good choice for a rifle to use out to 350 or 400 yards, which is about the maximum that a good shooter can ethically take game. The 7mm bullets buck the wind better than lesser calibers, and they have a frontal diameter large enough to reliably take big game. If you choose to use your

Speer's 160-grain Hot Cor bullet, good for a heavy bullet in a slower cartridge.

a whole lot of killing power without the severe recoil of the larger 7mm magnum cases. The 139, 140 and 145-grain bullets produced by Hornady, Remington, and Sellier & Bellot have produced all sorts of smiling hunters in the trophy pictures, but I feel that the 173 and 175-grain loadings will continue to perform as they have for the last century plus.

Were I to choose a classic 7x57 for my hunting rifle, I'd do my best to find two loads: one for lighter game using 120 to 150-grain bullets, and a heavy load utilizing the 160 to 175-grain bullets. I'd also want to look at the premium bullets for my heavy load.

Woodleigh Weldcores, Nosler Partitions, Barnes TSX and Swift A-Frames make a great choice for large deer species and bears; while for the lighter stuff the Hornady SST, Nosler AccuBond, Sierra ProHunter, Speer Deep Curl and Federal Fusion are excellent choice for deer, and the like. Find a pair of bullets that shoots well in your 7x57, and I'd wager you'll spend many happy days afield!

MEDIUM VELOCITY 7MMS

Bump up the case capacity to the .280 Remington, .284 Winchester, 7x61 Sharpe and Hart, and the .280 Ackley Improved, and you'll start to see velocities that can really flatten the trajecto-

the standard bullets perform very well. In my experiences, for reasons I can't exactly explain, the 7mm Mausers that I've spent any amount of time with have shown a preference for heavy bullets; they have been very accurate with the 160 and 175-grain projectiles.

That's not to say that the lighter stuff, like the 120s and 140s, weren't sufficiently accurate for hunting, but the sub-MOA accuracy came with the longer bullets. There seems to be a sort of magic with the 'heavy-and-slow' formula, as generation of hunters have brought home the bacon (or venison) with the Mauser and some good, heavy bullets. Not unlike the 7-08, the Mauser gives

The .280 Remington, loaded with 160-grain Trophy Bonded Tipped.

ries. These cartridges will also produce recoil levels that are on par with the .30-'06, and start to test the mettle of some shooters.

If used for longer shots, the cup-and-core bullets that we all love will be just fine, but if used up close, where impact velocities are high, you can start to see radical bullet breakup and jacket separation in some of the boat-tail bullets of traditional construction. I've experienced bullet failure on deer-sized game with a .280 Remington with lighter bullets and close shots. A 140-grain Remington Core-Lokt bullet at 50 yards broke up prematurely when the deer's shoulder bones were hit. This was partially my own fault, as I didn't wait for the proper shot angle, but it taught me a lesson I'd never forget. I did recover the huge-bodied eight pointer (after a bit of tracking and a follow-up shot),

but it steered me to the premium bullets to get the penetration I wanted, regardless of angle.

These snappy cases can produce some amazing results on the longer shots, as accuracy can be stellar. As a matter of fact, famed riflemaker Kenny Jarrett embraced the .280 Ackley Improved as the go-to cartridge for his "beanfield" rifle, a setup designed for the long shots across wide-open fields at deer and antelope. The higher B.C. 7mm bullets will retain their energy very well, as well as giving a flat trajectory and good wind-bucking abilities.

I've seen the .280 Remington make some excellent one-shot kills on whitetails well out past 250 yards using the polymer-tipped 154-grain Hornady SST. It is these kinds of long range shots where you'll start to see the benefits of the boat-tail bullets, in a flatter

trajectory. The Norma Kalahari, which is an all-copper bullet with a frangible front end, yet a solid rear portion, is produced in a .280 Remington 120-grain configuration in the American PH series. With a muzzle velocity of 3,100 fps, these should prove devastating on distant deer and caribou-sized animals, as well as the wild sheep of the deserts and mountains.

The Nosler Ballistic Tip, E-Tip and AccuBond all have very similar profiles, with a polymer tip and boat-tail for high B.C., yet have very

The 140-grain Partition will give good results in the 7mm cartridge.

The 7mm 150-grain Nosler Ballistic Tip is fine in lighter cartridges up close, and magnum cartridges for farther shots.

perfect for the 'lead free' areas of California, and will give performance on par with other monometal bullets.

Offered in 140 and 150-grain weights, they are a good all-around choice for big game if you've got a .280 or .284 in hand. I've had great success with the Nosler AccuBond in a number of calibers and weights, and the 7mms are no exception. They deliver all the accuracy of the Ballistic Tip, but with the bonded core they are not nearly as frangible, giving reliable expansion and flat trajectory. Give these a try in your rifle, I'd wager you'll be a happy hunter.

For a good al-around choice in the monometals, the 150-grain 7mm Nosler E-Tip works fine.

different construction. The Ballistic Tip, made in traditional cup-and-core fashion, is offered in 120, 140 and 150 grains in 7mm caliber.

I like these bullets for deer-sized game, as they are very accurate, but be careful of high velocities and close up impacts. They can be on the frangible side, which is good if they get to slow down a bit, so as to impart their energy while giving good penetration, but things can get messy if they are pushed to fast on a close shot. When I load the Ballistic Tip, I like the heavier 140 and 150-grain weights. The E-Tip is a solid copper hollowpoint,

Sierra makes a fantastic bullet for the .280-class cartridges. The Game King boat-tail hollowpoint has a very thick jacket for deep penetration, and though the core isn't bonded, these bullets can take the pounding. The bullet came to be when hunters begged Sierra for a bullet that would give the accuracy of the .30-caliber 168-grain Match King, but for hunting purposes. They listened to their customers, producing a .30-caliber 165-grain hollowpoint with four 'skives' in the hollowpoint, giving a crimped look.

While we shall discuss this further in the .30-caliber cartridge discussion, customers soon asked for the bullet in other calibers. Sierra once again responded by offering a 6.5mm in 130-grain, and two 7mm bullets: a 140-grain and a 160-grain. The 140-grain can be driven to good long-range velocity, and makes a great deer bullet. The 160-grain bullet will help you hedge your bets if black bear are also on the menu in your deer woods, or if you like a bit of a heavier bullet for mule deer or the like.

Berger makes their famous VLD hunting bullet in 7mm, and they hold some impressive tolerances with their proprietary J4 bullet jackets. Offered in 140, 168 and 180-grain weights, they have an impeccable reputation for accuracy, and their sleek ogives and boat-tails give among the highest B.C. available to a hunter. They possess all the accuracy potential of the target bullets, and are stout enough to hold up as a hunting bullet. You might lose a bit of case capacity in the .284 Winchester, but the lighter weights should be just fine.

For heavier game in the .280/.284s, look to the heavy roundnose bullets, monometals and bonded-core projectiles. The Swift A-Frame is one of my favorite bullets of all time, and in the 160 and 175-grain weights, they will allow you to use your .280 on all but the largest of game in North America.

I've loaded those bullets to take elk, moose, and African antelope and zebra.

The Nosler Partition possesses the same basic design as the A-Frame, without the bonded core. They are a great choice for large game, as they will operate perfectly at .280 velocities. The monometal bullets, including the Barnes TSX and TTSX, Hornady GMX and Cutting Edge Raptor will give you an extra confidence boost. They have very high weight retention, and will surely reach the vitals because there is no jacket to separate from the core. As with any caliber, the monometals will always be longer than the cup-and-core bullets, but you can usually get performance that you would expect from a heavy cup-and-core out of a bit lighter monometal.

If you like traditional bullets for the larger game, give some thought to heavy roundnose bullets, like the Hornady InterLock 175-grain bullet. They make a fantastic bear bullet, as you get some expansion up front, but the long shank will drive through the toughest shoulder bones.

THE 7MM MAGNUMS

The 7mm Remington Magnum has become an undeniable favorite among hunters, and it's not really hard to see why. The case capacity of the necked-down and shortened .375 H&H gives a definitive velocity advantage over the lesser cases, and that translates to higher kinetic energy values and a bit flatter trajectory. Those attractive figures come at the cost of a significant increase in recoil, but for those who can handle it, you'll find the 7mm Rem Mag to be a fantastic hunting round. Many of the basic principles I've discussed regarding the .280-class cartridges can be applied to the 7mm Magnums, including the 7mm Dakota, 7mm Weatherby Magnum and 7mm Winchester Short Magnum.

There are a few ideas I'd like to share, based on bullets I've handload-

The 150-grain 7mm Scirocco will suffice for any shot, near or far.

that can save your bacon.

If you anticipate true long-distance shots, like those past 350 or 400 yards, you'll want to shop by ballistic coefficient, as by the time your bullet hits the target it will have slowed down significantly.

For non-dangerous game, I like bullets like the Swift Scirocco II, Hornady Interbond and Nosler AccuBond for the 7 Mags, as the higher velocity is enough to get these bullets to expand sufficiently, yet they will hang together well enough to give all the penetration necessary. Some of the bullets with thinner jackets, like the Speer Hot-Cor, can make a terrible mess of edible meat when driven to magnum velocities.

The Federal Fusion should prove to be a sound choice if you'd like to use your 7mm Magnum for deer; it is just a bit tougher than the standard cup-and-cores. The Norma Oryx, with a par-

ed and factory ammunition I've spent some time with. I have found that these magnum cartridges like the longer (read heavier) bullets, as they've proved to be the most accurate. I prefer to use bullets of 150 grains or heavier. I've found that bullets that are lightly constructed can perform poorly, especially when shot distances are close.

I like premium bullets when it comes to the magnum cases, as they can stand up to the high impact velocities and yet still perform fine on the longer shots. Depending on your intended target, you can pick a few different bullets to get the exact performance you're after. A whitetail deer doesn't need either the bullet weight or construction that an elk or wildebeest or grizzly bear needs. But, if you hunt in an area inhabited by toothy mammals, be they bears or lions and leopards, you might feel a bit better knowing you've got a bullet

That speed demon, the 7mm Weatherby Magnum with 160-grain Federal Trophy Bonded Tipped projectiles.

tially bonded design, is another great bullet that is strong enough for magnum cartridges, yet soft enough to give good expansion to wreck those vitals.

In the cup-and-cores, I like the way the heavier 160 and 175-grain Sierra and Hornady bullets perform. There is plenty of sectional density there to effectively handle the magnum velocities.

Oh, by the way, if you want to get a new shooter to become comfortable with a 7mm Remington Magnum, Hornady makes a reduced-velocity load in their Custom Lite line, using a 139-grain SST, which is about 25% slower than standard loads. Remington also produces a Managed Recoil line, offering similar velocities with their 140-grain Core-Lokt softpoint.

For the bears and other toothy creatures that you might pursue with your Seven, the Nosler Partitions, Swift A-Frames, Barnes TSXs, North Fork Semi-spitzers and Woodleigh Weldcores are all smart choices. They can penetrate thick muscle and strong shoulder bones with surety, especially in the 150, 160 and 175-grain weights. The magnum cases have enough capacity to push the long and heavy bullets with plenty of oomph, and you'll be appreciative of their qualities should you stumble into an angry grizzly while stalking elk or moose!

THE 7MM SUPER MAGS

The 7mm Super-Magnums, like the 7mm STW (Shooting Times Westerner) or the 7mm Remington Ultra Magnum, push bullets to velocities that demand strong construction. While these types of cartridges are a bit too much velocity for me, there are long-range hunters that have developed an affinity for them. I'd highly recommend staying away from the lighter-for-caliber bullets with these behemoths, as they can put such strain on them that you will invariably experience jacket separation. With the high B.C bullets, the trajectory that these two can produce

is very flat, but it comes at the cost of severe recoil. Save the cup-and-core bullets for practice, I feel that you'll get the best performance from the best bullets you can get your hands on.

The premium 7mm projectiles I've outlined will stand up well to the muzzle velocities (in excess of 3,200 fps even with the 175-grain projectile) that these huge cases generate. Look at the 150 to 160-grain projectiles that combine stout construction and sleek design, they will aid in hitting the distant targets that these rifles were designed

Nosler's AccuBond, shown in section, and after impact.

for. The Hornady Interbond, Nosler AccuBond and Barnes TTSX can handle the STW and RUM, and for closer work, where the B.C. isn't as much of an issue, the A-Frames and Partitions of heavy caliber can really crush bone.

tridges, much like the 7mms, run the entire gamut of size and shape, and range from the very slow to the ultra-fast, with all stages in between well represented. There is a ton of overlap, and while each of the cartridges has its

A lineup of .30-caliber bullets, America's sweetheart.

THE ALMIGHTY .30s

If any single bore diameter had to define American ballistics, it would – far and away - be the .308. The .30-30 WCF and the .30-'06 Springfield have accomplished more than any other two cartridges of North American design. The .308 Winchester, the .30-40 Krag, .300 Holland & Holland Magnum, .300 Winchester, .300 Weatherby; they inspire and excite. Tales of the military exploits with the .30 M1 Carbine, sniper stories with the 'ought-six', adventures in the wild with a lever-action .300 Savage, all of these embody the .308-caliber bullet.

Our .30-caliber car-

fervent defenders, I will organize the cartridges (and their corresponding applicable bullets) into groups of similar performance.

Our .30-caliber bullets range from 100 grains up to the enormous 250-grainers, and they come in many different configurations. No other caliber benefits from such a diverse selection of bullets. Bullet makers usually pay homage to the .30s by offering their best bullets in a wide variety of .30-caliber weights, and usually a wider selection than most other calibers. I believe this is a direct result of the extreme differences in case size among the .30-calibers, and the huge amount of .30-caliber fans that take to the range and field.

The venerable .30-30 Winchester.

THE .30-30 WINCHESTER

The .30-30 Winchester Center Fire started the whole mess, using the .30-40 Krag's military bullet in a hunting cartridge. Introduced in 1895, in the incredible Model 1894 Winchester lever gun, it was an immediate success. The 'thutty-thutty', as Mr. O'Connor and his generation referred to it, pushed a 160-grain flatnose jacketed bullet to just shy of 1,900 fps, and this worked just fine for the hunters of the late 19th and early 20th centuries. The 170-grain load followed shortly thereafter, and I'd venture to say that this load is and was the most popular, being driven to 2,100 to 2,200 fps, depending on the company.

Within 150 yards, the factory loads with the cup-and-core 150 or 170-grain bullets work just perfectly. Expansion is good, and penetration is as well, due to the mild velocity. The major ballistic handicap of the .30-30 (beside the fact that the majority had to be fired with iron sights) is the flat or roundnose bullets they shoot. They are required to use them to prevent detonation in a tubular magazine, as the cartridges are loaded in a bullet-to-primer fashion within the tube.

Visible difference in profile of spritzer and flatnose .30-30 loads.

Hornady's LeveRevolution 160 .30-30 load.

Now, even though I have had good success with the Remington Core-Lok and Winchester Power Point loads, I truly believe that Hornady has changed the game when it comes to the old .30-30 WCF, with their LeveRevolution line of ammunition. The 160-grain spitzer boat-tail Hornady Flex-Tip bullet employs a flexible, rubbery tip on a spitzer bullet that is pliable enough to remove all possibilities of a tubular magazine detonation, and allows fans of the old lever gun to enjoy the downrange benefits of the spitzer profile bullet. With this ammunition, the .30-30, when properly zeroed, can become a 250-yard gun! This is a significant increase in ballistic performance.

In areas that prohibit lead ammunition, or if you want more velocity from a lighter bullet, Hornady also loads its 140-grain MonoFlex bullet, which combines the pliable tip with their GMX all-copper bullet. This concept is a sound one, and if you're seri-ous about using a .30-30, I'd look long and hard at this ammunition. The bullets are specifically engineered for the .30-30 case, and Hornady did a very good job. Federal is releasing a .30-30 load using their Trophy Copper bullet, and based on my past experiences with this bullet, this should also be a marked improvement on the older designs.

If you feel inclined to use your .30-30 against bears, or the larger deer species, premium bullets are available to the handloader. Nosler makes a 170-grain Partition designed for the .30-30, and Swift makes their excellent A-Frame in a 150-grain design. Both will function perfectly through the tube magazine, and give penetration that would please any hunter.

If you are a purist, and want to try your hand at hunting with hard-cast lead bullets, take a look at Falcon Bullet Company's 160-grain flatpoint. They are easy to load, and very affordable to shoot, yet are tough enough to hold together at the .30-30s mild velocity. My Winchester '94 XTR loves them, putting three into a quarter-size group at 50 yards even with my aging eyes.

AR-BASED .30s

The .30 Remington AR, the .300 Whisper and the .300 AAC Blackout are

The .300 Whisper/Blackout.

all .30-caliber cartridges designed to function through the magazine of the AR15 platform, and are catching on in the hunting fields. The Remington variety is built around the 125-grain bullets, which are very light-for-caliber. They will work, if the bullet is properly placed, but the lower sectional density doesn't give the shooter much to work with on the game animals. I'd stick to deer-sized game and smaller with this cartridge.

The .300 Whisper and .300 AAC Blackout are based on the .221 Fireball case, and are loaded with bullets between 125 grains, and the huge 220-grain. While the 125-grain load will leave the muzzle at 2,200 fps, the 220 is made to be subsonic, running at just over 1,000 fps, and generating less than 500 ft.-lbs. of energy. While the subsonic feature is very useful in certain self-defense situations, I think that sticking with the lighter bullets makes more sense in the hunting fields. We'll shed more light on these cartridges in later chapters.

THE .300 SAVAGE THROUGH THE .308 WINCHESTER

There is something to be said about the short-action .30-caliber cartridges. They offer a fantastic balance of low recoil and great terminal performance in a rifle that is lighter and handier than their long-action counterparts. I have spent much of my deer hunting career with a .308 Winchester in hand; the Ruger Model 77 was a Christmas gift from my dad, ol' Grumpy Pants. He has been a fan of the .308 Winchester since his Army training in Fort Leonard Wood, Missouri, in the summer of '68. Uncle Sam demonstrated the virtues of the short little case housed in an M14, and GP still tells stories of hitting man-sized silhouettes at 350 meters with iron sights. Shortly after returning from service, he purchased what would become his go-to rifle: a Mossberg Model 100A bolt action in .308 Winchester.

The .300 Savage with 180-grain Remington Core-Lokt bullets.

Now, ol' GP is a creature of habit, and his insistence on a good 165-grain bullet over a suitable charge of IMR4064 powder is a source of mirth around our campfire. It took many years before anyone could break him out of that mould, yet he still uses the combination with good effect, as do I. Matter of fact, when I purchased a firearm for the Mrs., I decided that the .308 Winchester was a perfect choice for an all-around rifle. I know, the .308 v. .30-'06 debate rages on, especially in the gun magazines, but it truly is a moot point, and that is due to modern bullet technology.

What the smaller .30s lack in bullet weight, they can definitely make up for in bullet construction. That goes for the .300 Savage, and I'll even include the .308 Marlin Express and the .30 T/C in that statement. The sensible bullet range for these cartridges more than likely tops out at 180 grains, but as those bullets can be driven to velocities between 2,350 and 2,650 fps, this truly isn't a handicap considering how well constructed the bullets of today are.

Modern smokeless powders have a big hand in the development of these cartridges. The .300 Savage led the pack, busting onto the shooting scene in 1920, coming just shy of the performance of the kingly .30-'06, but in the sweet-shooting Model 99 Savage lever gun. The 150-grain bullets, perfect for deer and the like, came out at 2,600 fps, and delivered fantastic terminal ballistics. The 180-grain load, while seeming anemic by today's standards, travelled at 2,350 fps, which is a perfect velocity for cup-and-core bullets. Within sane distances, these loads made history, with many satisfied customers and Savage devotees.

While there aren't many choices for factory loads in the older Savage case, I like the way some of the newer bullets work with the venerable cartridge. I've handloaded some 150-grain Nosler Ballistic Tips in the .300 Savage, and they've worked very well.

The Sierra 150 boat-tails and Hornady 150 flat-base bullets have as well. I don't know too many folks who would break out the old '99 for a brown bear hunt (although it was done, quite successfully in years past), but the idea of using the classic lever for black bear isn't absurd. I personally would look at some of good 180 roundnose bullets, like the 180 Hornady InterLock or the 180 Sierra ProHunter, if I were handloading, or the 180-grain Remington Core-Lokt factory load.

The .308 Marlin Express is a cartridge designed to approximate .308 Winchester performance in a semi-rimmed case that will function well in the lever guns. The blended powders that Hornady developed for their factory loads have given a velocity boost to the smaller cases. Using 160-grain Flex-Tip bullets and 140-grain Mono-Flex bullets specifically designed for the new case, the Marlin Express will bring the lever guns into a new light. Hornady is the foremost ammunition provider, although Remington lists a 150-grain load that should work just fine. It remains to be seen whether or not the .308ME will stick around, as it has some stiff competition from older cartridges, and the demand for attention is high among the .30s.

The .30 T/C runs a bit hotter, and with the 150 and 165-grain bullets, it can absolutely mimic the .30-'06, when loaded in the Hornady Superformance ammunition line. They use the 150-grain SST and GMX, and the 165 SST, all good bullets for anything shy of elk and moose-sized critters. Handloaders can't quite approach the velocities that Hornady obtains, but can still use the T/C cartridge with good effect. The Sierra 165-grain Game King hollowpoint boat-tail should prove to be a winner in this case, as it is plenty tough enough for the velocities of the T/C. I'd also try the Nosler 150 and 165-grain Ballistic Tips for deer and antelope, and the 150-grain Swift Scirocco II should prove to be a good all-around bullet for most big game animals. Pick a good spitzer, of decent construction, and when you put that bullet where it belongs, you'll have your game animal.

The .30-40 Krag, although developed in Sweden, was the U.S. Army's first .30-caliber cartridge. It's a rimmed cartridge, but feeds very well from the box magazine of the M1892. The Krag cartridge is, for all intents and purposes, the ballistic equivalent of the .308 Winchester. If you're in possession of a Winchester 1895 in .30-40 Krag, you have a very viable hunting rifle. The biggest issue you'll have is finding factory ammunition.

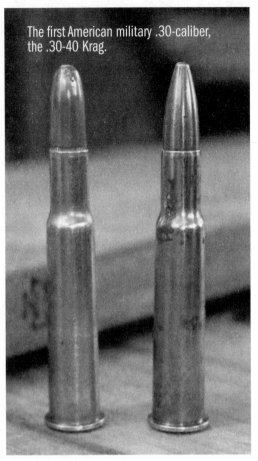

The first American military .30-caliber, the .30-40 Krag.

by the proven '06, but in a smaller case. The goal was to allow the soldier to carry more ammunition, and to consume less brass as well. At first, the ballisticians looked at the .300 Savage, but it didn't quite fit the bill. After some experimentation, the T-52, or 7.62x51mm, was unveiled. It retained the same rim specs as the '06, but in a case almost ½" shorter. Winchester beat the military to the punch, releasing the .308 Winchester in 1952.

The shooting world loved and hated it at the same time. How dare they tread upon the hallowed ground held by the .30-'06? After all, the '06 is America's favorite, and by 1952 it was completely embraced throughout the hunting world. The comparisons were immediate: The '06 has more case capacity, the .308 can't shoot the 220-grain slugs, the .308 velocities are a bit lower, and therefore it is vastly inferior, blah, blah, woof, woof. Here's the actual skinny, and although I'm absolutely certain

The classic .308 Winchester with a 165-grain Federal Fusion.

As far as I can find, Remington supplies the only loaded ammunition, a 180-grain Core-Lokt spitzer, and a good one at that. If you handload, you can greatly extend the versatility of the Krag. The bullets that I'll outline for the .308 Winchester will work perfectly for the Krag, with the addition of the great 200 and 220-grain slugs. I think a '95 with some handloaded 220 Hornady roundnose would make a classic, and very nostalgic combination.

The .308 Winchester has been a source of controversy from the time of its release. The U.S. Army was seeking a replacement for the .30-06 Springfield, believing they could profit from the advancements in smokeless powder to deliver the same ballistics provided that the debate will rage on for the rest of my days, I believe this to be true: In the game fields, no game animal will ever to be able to tell the difference between the .308 and .30-'06. There, I said it.

Now here's the why: With today's powders, and bullet technology, the velocity difference between the two is nearly pointless. While the .308 performs best with bullets in the 120 to 200-grain range, the '06 can push the heavier bullets better. Part of that problem was due to the twist rate of the early .308s (1:12"), and case capacity does come into play. But with the monometals and bonded cores and partitioned bullets of today, the playing field has been all but leveled.

There are many reasons to love the .30-'06 Springfield, and I love it as well, but we'll discuss that soon. The owner and shooter of a .308 Winchester should not feel undergunned at all. For medium and large game, this case can provide a lifetime of happy hunting. And did I mention the accuracy potential? "Inherently accurate" is a difficult term to explain, let alone embrace, but suffice it to say that it isn't hard to get a .308 to shoot well. It is chambered in almost every type of action, and the recoil level is moderate enough to allow new shooters, as well as the recoil sensitive, to master quickly.

The .308 makes what I consider to be about the perfect deer rifle. Mind you, I hunt deer in New York State primarily, and our deer can approach or top 200 pounds on the hoof. The possibility of black bears is very real, and I love the .30-caliber bullets for both of them. The bullet choices are innumerable.

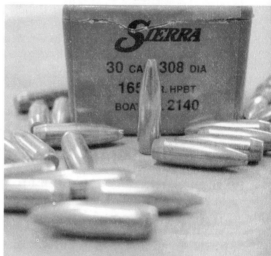

I have used many bullets between 125 and 180 grains for deer and bear, but several have jumped out at me as working very well. I absolutely love the Sierra Game King 165-grain hollowpoint boat-tail (Part No. 2140), as it is designed after the famous 168-grain Match King boat-tail target bullet, but with a very thick jacket to ensure penetration in addition to the hollowpoint expansion.

The Sierra 165-grain Game King hollowpoint boat-tail, with its skived tip and heavy jacket, has taken many whitetails.

This bullet has accounted for many whitetails, the majority of which were one-shot kills. Part of that success is due to the fact that this bullet is extremely accurate. One-half MOA is not out of the question with this load, and I wouldn't hesitate to use it for black bear. Now, for the shots here in New York, where the average is about 75 yards, that level of accuracy and a boat-tail bullet shouldn't be necessary, but we hunt thick woods, and in order to reach the target without hitting branches, one must 'thread the needle', and that accuracy comes in very handy.

I used the 125-grain Nosler Ballistic Tip for a few seasons, but I found that the lack of bullet weight and increased velocity (near 3,000 fps) didn't give the penetration I was after. I like the 165-grain Ballistic Tip much better. The .308 Winchester was designed to run best with 168-grain bullets, and the 165 and 168-grain bullets can be ridiculously accurate.

In addition to the Sierra hollowpoint, my own .308 loves the 165-grain Hornady SST, InterLock and InterBond, the 165-grain Remington Core-Lokt, and the Berger VLD Hunting. Coincidentally, all of those loads prefer IMR 4064 powder, and velocities run just around 2,600 fps. This is a recipe that will effectively kill almost all of the game animals on the North American continent, and will make a great plains game load for Africa, including the leopard. For thinner-skinned animals, the cup-and-core bullets will work perfectly, and for heavier stuff like elk, I'd go with a bonded-core bullet that shoots well. Among factory loads, the Federal Premium Vital-Shok line, featuring the 165-grain Sierra boat-tail spitzer should prove to be a good choice for a good all-around load.

The lighter 125 to 150-grain bullets can be used with good effect, with proper application. The Hornady Custom Lite series takes advantage of the 125-grain SST, at a greatly reduced velocity, for

an effective load for newer and younger hunters. The lesser velocity will prevent premature bullet breakup.

(above) Suzie Q's .308 is accurate, indeed.

(below) Suzie Q's .308 Winchester load, with 150-grain Scirocco II bullets.

My wife's .308 Winchester has a definite affinity for the 150-grain Swift Scirocco II, driven to 2,850 fps. Her Savage Lady Hunter will print three of these into a group of 0.3" at 100 yards. With the polymer tip, boat-tail and bonded core, this makes a very effective all-around load. And, mind you, this is out of a 20" barrel. That is one of the other amazing benefits of the .308: it will give great velocities out of a short barrel, and that combined with the compact receiver puts together a fantastic lightweight package that hits hard.

For the bigger stuff, I like the way the .308 delivers 180-grain bullets. Before we started handloading, ol' GP shot the 180-grain Remington round-nose Core-Lokt, and put enough whitetails in the salt to sink a battleship. At 2,600 fps, the roundnose bullets have a bit more frontal diameter, and I like the way they hit.

For my 2006 Quebec bear hunt, I chose the 180-grain Swift Scirocco II, not so much for its boat-tail and polymer tip, but for the bonded-core feature. The shot was close range, maybe 55 yards, but the bullet worked perfect on the 200+ pound boar. I also like the 180 Speer Grand Slam in the .308, as it will operate very well at this velocity. My pal Eric Post was headed to Maine, to hunt black bears over hounds, and wanted a bullet that would anchor a bear at any angle. The 180-grain Grand Slam came immediately to mind, as the

tapered jacket will give consistent expansion, yet the bullet is long enough to retain weight. Long story short, Eric's Remington Model 700 really liked this bullet, and his 175-pound sow did not. There is a bear rug that is a testament to that fact.

Take into consideration the animal you are hunting, and find the bullet that works for you. Let the bullet construction, rather than the bullet weight do its job, and the .308 will work just fine.

THE .30-'06 SPRINGFIELD

There is something about this cartridge, something that I just can't put my finger on, that makes it a contender for "Best Cartridge Ever Developed."

he .30-06 Springfield,
s American as it gets.

I mean, if you think about it, the advancements in metallurgy, smokeless powders, cartridge design and bullets should have sent the Ought-Six to its proverbial grave decades ago. Instead of fading into obscurity, as any good cartridge would do, the .30-'06 decided to inspire generation after generation, cementing its place in shooting history. I have often asked myself why, and the best answer that I can come up with is this: It works. The .30-'06 gives just about perfect velocities; not too slow so as to compromise trajectory, yet not too fast so as to have issues with premature bullet breakup, but in the fashion of Goldilocks' porridge, just right.

The original .30-'03 (predecessor to the '06) load utilized the same 220-grain roundnose bullet as the .30-40 Krag, but that didn't last very long. Three years later, the Army revised the projectile to a 150-grain spitzer, and shortened the case neck slightly, to deliver a muzzle velocity of 2,700 fps. Some famous, or soon to be famous, names embraced the .30-'06. Folks like U.S. President Theodore Roosevelt (who actually took the .30-'03 on safari), a fellow gun writer by the name of Hemingway, that Ruark guy, and even ".270 O'Connor" had a soft spot in his heart for the '06.

There are all sorts of rifles chambered for the .30-'06, from lever guns to pump actions to autoloaders to the revered bolt action and everything in between, and there are an equally overwhelming amount of bullets. The '06 can use the full gamut of .30-caliber bullets, and I've shot or loaded darn near all of them. The basic concept that we discussed for the .308 Winchester apply to the '06, except that the larger bullets are perfectly viable in the larger '06 case.

Is it sexy? No. Is it new-fangled and cutting edge? No. But it consistently delivers the goods, on any continent, season after season. The '06 will work fine with all of the 150-grain choices, from the Speer Hot-Cor bullets, to the factory-loaded Remington Core-Lokt and Winchester Power Points, and including the gamut of premiums, and they are about perfect for the deer and antelope-sized animals.

Federal's line includes the 150-grain Sierra boat-tail, the Nosler Ballistic Tip and the Fusion, among others. I think the Fusion bullet is a great deer bullet, and at '06 velocities (2,900 fps), there will be plenty of hydrostatic shock for a quick and humane kill. Were I looking for an '06 load for the open spaces of the west, I'd think long and hard about

a decent 150-grain projectile for the .30-'06. Even though they don't have the greatest S.D. values, they should prove sufficient for the task, as deer and antelope have a 'touchy' nervous system that can be easily switched off.

I really like the way the .30-'06 can handle the monometal bullets, like the Cutting Edge Raptor, Barnes TSX and Hornady GMX. The all-copper or copper alloy construction of these projectiles makes them longer than a comparable weight lead-core bullet, and the additional case capacity of the '06 will

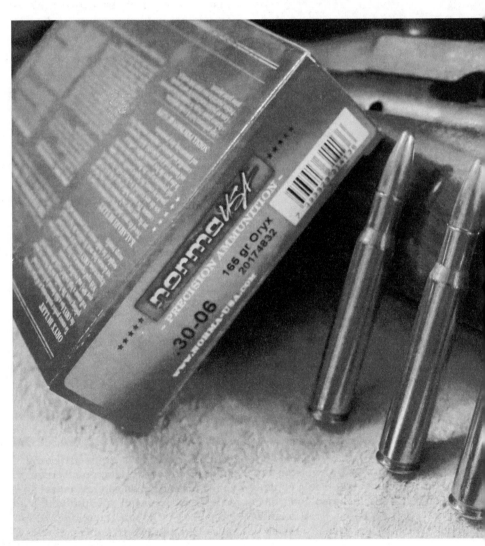

come in handy to keep velocities up. A quality monometal of 150 grains will give excellent results, creating a large wound channel yet often penetrating the entire width of the animal for quick kills.

My good pal Kevin Hicks has a WWII-era 03A3 Springfield, that has been fitted with a birdseye maple stock and a Burris Fullfield II 3-9x scope, and we handload that veteran rifle with those 165-grain Sierra Game King boat-tail hollowpoints I mentioned in the .308 Winchester section. They have resulted in some dramatic kills on some nice

bucks, including a really wide nine pointer we've dubbed 'Menorah.' We hunt the hardwoods of the Hudson Valley, and it takes some shooting skill to thread the needle and avoid the tiny branches of the young growth that populates our hunting grounds. This rifle, with these bullets (at 2,750 fps), can do just that, because the group size is well under one inch at 100 yards. Those bullets are just about perfect for whitetail deer, and I'm sure Mr. Hicks wouldn't hesitate to use them on mule deer, pronghorn or caribou.

The balanced 165-grain bullet is very popular among factory loadings, and with good reason. They have enough oomph for a decent trajectory for hunting ranges out to and beyond 350 yards, and enough sectional density to retain energy and give reliable penetration. I like the Federal 165 Fusion load; they've designed this bullet for whitetail and it's gaining a great reputation.

Hornady's Superformance '06 ammo features the 165-grain SST, GMX or InterBond bullet, and should give about 2,950 fps from your rifle. This allows you to tailor the bullet to the game at hand. The SST makes an awesome deer bullet, and the cup-and-core construction will give plenty of up-front expansion for hydrostatic shock; and the GMX and InterBond would make a good choice for elk, moose and bear, not to mention the larger African antelope that require a higher level of bullet penetration.

The Berger 168-grain VLD Hunting bullet also gives a great blend of hunting toughness and target-style accuracy. Many hunters enjoy the long-range performance of the Berger bullets. I also like the Norma 165-grain Oryx factory load for the .30-'06 Springfield, the semi-bonded core will give an excellent blend of penetration and expansion for a large wound channel.

Norma's 165-grain Oryx load, in .30-06.

The 180-grain bullets are a good all-around choice for the .30-'06 if you hunt in a place where more than one game animal may be on the menu. With a standard lead-core bullet, the 180-grainers made the great reputation that the .30-'06 has, in my opinion because these bullets operate at a velocity that will give plenty of energy, and upon impact they will retain enough weight to penetrate adequately. I've handloaded the 180-grain Sierra Pro Hunter flatbase bullet in the '06 case to obtain ½" groups at 100 yards. And, as great as the long-range benefits of the spitzer-shaped bullets are, don't overlook the classic roundnose bullet. I'm a fan of the Hornady InterLock 180-grain roundnose in the .30-'06, especially if you hunt the woods and brush lots, where shots are generally under 200 yards. It's been my experience that the roundnose bullets, with a larger frontal diameter, makes an animal shudder upon impact, and although the trajectory beyond 200 yards can't compare to the spitzers, within that distance they kill very effectively, and take up much less case capacity as they keep their weight forward.

The 180-grain premiums fit the '06 like a glove. The classic 180-grain Nosler Partition bumps up performance, and is still a very popular choice among hunters from Africa to Alaska. If you hunt moose, elk, bears and other larger game species, there are a plethora of good 180 choices.

I like the North Fork semi-spitzer, as well as the Trophy Bonded from Federal. They keep their weight forward, almost as well as the roundnose bullets, yet the bonded core prevents jacket/core separation. The Swift dynamic duo of Scirocco II and A-Frame are both fantastic 180 choices for the Springfield, with the Scirocco II giving a bit flatter trajectory (due to the polymer spitzer tip and boat tail), while partitioned A-Frame will give weight retention up into the 90% range.

A Barnes TTSX 180-grain, as loaded by Cor-Bon, will give very good results. The all-copper hollowpoint, with polymer tip, will hit hard, and is compliant with those areas that prohibit the use of bullets that contain lead. The polymer tip increases the B.C., and the increased length will help to penetrate adequately into the vitals of the larger mammals. Often when a shooter gets the Barnes bullets to shoot well from their rifle, they remain loyal to them for life. They work that well. The same can be said for the Hornady GMX and the Nosler E-Tip.

The 200 and 220-grain bullets work well in the '06 case, and although the velocities start to drop off, the heavy slugs will hit like a sledgehammer. The 220-grain Nosler Partition and Hornady InterLock are two great choices for the Ought-Six, if you want to use yours against the big brown bears of the north. They work well on smaller game as well, as the slower velocities prevent the drastic amount of bloodshot meat.

Federal is loading the 220 Speer Hot-Cor roundnose and Remington loads the 220 grain Core-Lokt, and both should prove to be very reliable. When bullets get very heavy-for-caliber, the construction is not as important as it is with the light-for-caliber projectiles, as the increased length prevents premature expansion. Plus, the long slugs look really cool too! The classic 220-grain velocity of 2,400 fps in the '06 is almost magical, as we'll see in the chapter on dangerous game cartridges.

THE .300 MAGNUMS

1925 saw the firm of Holland & Holland mate the .308" bullet with a modified .375 H&H Magnum case, to produce what we call the .300 Holland & Holland Magnum, better known in Great Britain as Holland's Super .30. It was the first commercial foray into pushing .30-caliber bullets to very fast velocities, and the case bettered the '06 velocities by 200 fps or so. Mr.

The ultra-classic .300 H&H magnum, with 180-grain Swift Sciroccos. (J.P. Fielding photo)

Roy Weatherby modified the H&H case in 1944 to unveil his curved-shoulder .300 Weatherby Magnum, pushing velocities up even further. Winchester completed its line of '06-length magnum cartridges in 1963, when they announced the .300 Winchester Magnum; and this cartridge is what I consider to be the best of the magnums in this class. Others have come and gone, with

The .300 Ruger Compact Magnum with 165-grain Hornady GMX.

.308 Cal - 150 gr - 50 ct
COPPER RAPTOR

CUTTING EDGE
BULLETS

The .300 Winchester Magnum with Cutting Edge Bullets 150-grain Raptor.

varying degrees of success.

The .300 Ruger Compact Magnum, .300 Dakota, .308 Norma Magnum, .300 Remington Short Action Ultra Magnum, and the most popular of the newbies, the .300 Winchester Short Magnum, all came upon the scene in the late 20th century and early 21st century. Generally speaking, all of them will push a 180-grain bullet from 2,900 fps to 3,200 fps, but it comes at the cost of increased powder consumption and a drastic increase in recoil. The magnum cases will make long distance shots a bit easier by flattening out the trajectories, most often hitting only six inches low at 300 yards when zeroed at 200 yards, and 18 inches low at 400 yards. The .300 magnums have velocities high enough to begin to test the structural integrity of standard cup-and-core bullets.

The father of premium projectiles, Mr. John Nosler, actually developed the Partition bullet because the bullets from his .300 H&H were blowing up on the shoulder of a big bull moose. I feel the .300 Mags perform best with premium bullets of some sort, especially in bullets lighter than 180 grains, as the velocity gains won't be offset by premature bullet breakup. I also feel that the .300s shoot best with bullets of 180 grains or longer. Or, maybe I should say that the .300s shoot best with longer bullets, with more bearing surface, as I've had some of the 150-grain monometals shoot and perform very well, the 150-grain Cutting Edge Raptor bullet in particular.

I've used my pet .300 Winchester with 180-grain Hornady and Sierra cup-and-core bullets on whitetail deer, and while the deer were most certainly dead, these bullets made a bit of a mess at 2,960 fps. The meat damage was considerably less when I switched to the Swift Scirocco II. Now, in no way am I saying that the Sierra and Hornady bullets were bad, but the high velocity of the .300 Winnie had them opening up a bit too much.

The .308" 180-grain Sierra Game King boat-tail.

When choosing a bullet for your magnum, take the game into consideration. Are you using the rifle for its flat trajectory, or for its horsepower, or both? I consider the .300 magnums to be about the perfect elk and moose rifle, as you can achieve the accuracy needed for longer shots, while the longer bullets retain energy downrange very nicely. I've used many different bullets in the .300 magnums while handloading over the years, and there are a lot of good bullets to choose from.

My own go-to load for my .300 Winchester Magnum is the 180-grain Swift Scirocco II over a suitable charge of IMR 4350 in a Norma case. It yields 2,960 fps (about equal with factory ammunition), and it extremely accurate, usually ½ to ¾ MOA. These bullets have a high B.C. (.520), a secant ogive, and 15-degree boat-tail. Combine that with a bonded core and a very thick copper jacket, and you have a recipe for success. The same bullet has worked with similar results in Neighbor Dave's 1959 Colt Coltsman, in .300 H&H Magnum. Once again we got ¾" groups and acceptable recoil, so it's a no-brainer to reach into the safe for that gun on just about any hunt. There are other bullets capable of delivering the goods in this fashion as well, like the Nosler AccuBond and E-Tip, the Hornady InterBond, Barnes TTSX, and Cutting Edge Raptor.

If it's ultra flat trajectory you're after, the 150-grain bullets are a viable option, but beware the close shots, as they are certain to make a mess unless they're well built. The 150-grain Hornady SSTs and Nosler Ballistic Tips will certainly give good accuracy, but you'll want them to slow down a bit before impact, and I'd limit the game size to large deer or maybe caribou; they aren't an elk or moose bullet at that weight. The 150s do make a great sheep bullet however, as the shots are generally well over 200 yards, and the thin skin of the wild sheep usually doesn't require a stiff bullet to penetrate.

My .300 likes that Cutting Edge Raptor I've mentioned, and we should talk about this bullet design. The Raptor is an all-copper, lathe-turned boat-tail, with a black polymer tip. The bullet weight and other tolerances are very consistent, but what happens upon impact warrants discussion. The hollowpoint nose section is designed to break apart into little blades after the initial impact, providing devastating impact trauma, and then the caliber-sized rear portion of the bullet drives deep into (and often through) the ani-

The 180-grain Swift Scirocco II in the .300 Winchester Magnum. (J.P. Fielding photo)

mal's vitals. Weight retention is often better than 70 percent, and the Raptor has proven itself on several continents. My .300 Winchester will spit them out at 3,350 fps, so it shoots very flat, and they print under one MOA.

The 165s and 168s can be a good choice for the .300s, especially in the .300 WSM, where case capacity can be compromised by the really long 180, 190 and 200-grain choices. I like the 168 Barnes TTSX in all of the cases, as the bullet is as long as some of the 180s, but the 168-grain bullet is a tried

and true .30-caliber design. For long-range deer, the 165-grain Hornady SST and 165-grain Sierra Game King hollowpoint boat-tail will prove to be winners, as the velocity can be cranked up to around 3,100 fps. I love the way the Federal Premium 165-grain Trophy Copper bullet shoots from the .300 WSM; it will expand reliably and penetrate very deep. This load showed great accuracy in my Savage rifle.

Vintage 180-grain softpoints in the .300 Weatherby Magnum. (J.P. Fielding photo)

The .300 Winchester Magnum with 180-grain Norma Oryx.

The 180-grain bullets make the .300 magnums shine, as I said earlier. These bullets have given me the best accuracy results, and they represent a good balance of high velocity and retained energy. If you like the cup-and-cores, look to the Sierra 180-grain Game King and Pro Hunter, the Speer 180-grain Grand Slam, the Berger 180-grain VLD, and Hornady's 180 SST and InterLock. They will hang together as well as any cup-and-core will.

The 180-grain bonded-core bullets are where I feel us .300 magnum shooters should be looking. The aforementioned AccuBond from Nosler (a very accurate bullet), Swift Scirocco II, Hornady InterBond and the like will give consistently good results, and a balance of weight retention and high B.C., and as most of them are boat-tailed, they will give nice long-range trajectory. Push them to .300 Weatherby velocities and you'll see them hit very hard, but even at the slightly lower H&H velocity, they perform wonderfully.

Monometal and partitioned 180-grain bullets are wonderful for the larger game. I like the way the Nosler Partition works at this weight, and I've had great results in the .300 Weatherby and .300 WSM, both cases taking Newfoundland moose very cleanly in the hands of my clients. The 180-grain Swift A-Frame, which has the partition design, but with a heavier jacket and bonded core, will make another sound choice. The A-Frame ranks among the toughest softpoints on the market. You really can't go wrong by choosing a Barnes TSX 180-grain, they have taken animals as large as coastal Alaskan brown bear, and although there may be better tools for that job, the TSX will take the largest of the deer and antelope on any continent.

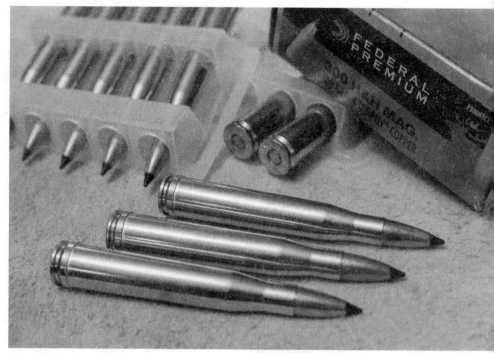

The .300 H&H Magnum with 180-grain Trophy Copper.

Bullets weighing 200 grains and over can be driven to respectable velocities, and can get the job done well. I used the 200-grain Swift A-Frame in my .300 Winchester on my first safari, and it did well on several species of plains game in South Africa. That load gave 2,700 fps, so I felt confident that I could effectively take anything from steenbok to eland, and I wouldn't hesitate to take that load for elk or moose.

The 200-grain Woodleigh Weldcore is another great bullet in this weight category, and the bonded core has earned this bullet a fine reputation. The 200 and 220 Partition, as always, make a solid choice. The Hornady 220-grain roundnose InterLock is another of my favorite bullets for these cases. I load my .300 Winchester down to a velocity of 2,425 fps with this bullet for local bear hunting here in the Catskill and Adirondack mountains, and it's worked out very well.

A 200-grain Swift A-Frame, from a .300 Winchester Magnum, recovered from an ostrich.

Look at the Woodleigh 240-grain Protected Point and the 250-grain Barnes Original if you like true heavy-weight bullets. The .300 H&H has a great track record using the 220-grain roundnose bullets in numerous factory loads, and will more than likely continue to do so. I enjoy using the round-nosed heavyweights when hunting bears over bait, as the distances will be under 100 yards and the bullets impart lots of energy to anchor the bear and avoid a follow up into the thick stuff.

New York State black bear taken with 220-grain Hornady round nose from a reduced velocity .300 Winchester Magnum. (J.P. Fielding photo)

THE .300 SUPER MAGNUMS

The cases that push .30-caliber bullets the fastest, the .300 Remington Ultra Magnum and .30-378 Weatherby, need to be mentioned in a different class. To compare them to the other .300 Magnums, these cartridges can push a 180-grain bullet to 3,350 and even 3,400 fps. This will definitely test

the strength of a bullet. I feel comfortable telling you to stay away from any cup-and-core lighter than 180 grains, and that you'd be smart to use a bonded-core or monometal that I've described in the previous section.

The .300 Remington Ultra Magnum with 180-grain Norma Oryx.

GP's favorite, the .300 Remington Ultra Magnum loaded with 180-grain flat-base Sierra Pro-Hunter bullets.

When Grumpy Pants headed to Newfoundland for moose, he (being the difficult human that he can be) insisted on a Sierra Pro Hunter 180-grain flat-base spitzer.

His Savage .300 RUM pushes them to 3,365 fps on the Oehler chronograph, and he took his moose at 250 yards, without incident, but I warned him of the results had the shot been close. He used the same load in South Africa, and on long shots at wildebeest and blesbok the amount of bloodshot meat was much larger than

it needed to be.

A client of mine used the same cartridge for a big Colorado bull elk, but with 180-grain Swift Scirocco IIs and anchored his bull without any incident. Col. Le Frogg enjoys his Weatherby Mark V in the behemoth .30-378 Weatherby, and it also shoots the 180-grain Scirocco well, in addition to

Sierra Pro-Hunter, a 180-grain flat-base spitzer.

the Nosler AccuBond. Ideally, I'd like to see them both with a Barnes TSX or Cutting Edge monometal, as I like the way these bullets perform at extreme velocities.

THE .303 BRITISH

This cartridge was the military issue of the British Empire from the late 19th century, until it was replaced by the 7.62 NATO after WWII, and as a result there were many surplus rifles on the market. In the former British colonies (U.S. aside), it remains a very popular hunting round, and that is true from Canada to South Africa, Zimbabwe and Zambia.

The ballistics of the .303, with its .311" to .312" diameter bullets (the case is named for land diameter, not groove diameter), is similar to the .308 Winchester. The case itself is rather thin-walled, and pressures need to be kept on the lower side for safety in the older rifles. Bullets for medium and large game range from 150 grains for the lighter game to the 180-grain bullets for larger stuff. The major players all make bullets for the .303, and they should keep the .303 shooters happy for some time to come.

Hornady's Custom Rifle line includes a load with the 150-grain InterLock, and the 174-grain InterLock round-nose is available as a component part. Sierra's fine Pro Hunter line offers 150 and 180 flat-base spitzers, and these will work very well at .303 velocities.

Traditionally, the .303 has been a proven game taker with the heavier bullets; the original load was a 215-grain cupro-nickel bullet with an ample charge of black powder, but time and technology has shown the lighter bullets are well constructed enough to withstand impact on game on a variety of game.

Federal makes a good 180-grain soft-point load, as does Remington. If game large than deer is on the plate, I'd look to these 180-grain bullets, but for deer, pronghorn antelope, or the lighter African game like impala, springbok, blesbok and such, a good 150-grain spitzer, like Prvi Partizan loads, or the 150 Speer Hot-Cor, will work just fine.

THE CRAZY EIGHTS

The German 8x57mm set the bar for 8mm cartridges, and it would be some years before any American cartridges were made based on this bullet diameter. Part of that issue involves the American aversion to metric bore nomenclature (no matter what, the metric system scares us) and part has to do with the similarities between the .323/8mm bore and the beloved American thirty caliber. That's a shame, because the 8mm bore is a pretty good one. It has almost the same weight range as the .30-calibers, with a bullet range of 125 grains to 220 grains, and a bit better frontal diameter.

Someone saw the light, as the late 1970s saw the release of the 8mm Remington Magnum, based on a full-length .375 H&H case, and early in the 21st century Winchester announced the .325 Winchester Short Magnum. All other 8mm offerings have come from Germany, and although they are good ones, the American market has yet to truly embrace the 8mms. The German 8x68S is a good cartridge, just 100 fps or so behind the big 8mm Remington.

For both the 8x68S and the 8mm Remington Magnum, my favorite bullet is the Sierra Game King 220-grain boat-tail spitzer. It takes full advantage of the case capacity and hard-hitting capability of the big Eights, and the design of these bullets makes for a wonderful magnum-class trajectory. With a sectional density of .301, it is plenty long enough to give deep penetration, and will deliver the results any shooter would like on elk, moose and the larger antelope of Africa. The only problem is that this bullet is only available as a component. If you handload, or if someone handloads for you, you're really going to want to give this a try.

Factory ammo for the 8mm Remington is becoming increasingly rare. Remington still offers a 200-grain Swift A-Frame, which is a great choice, but a bit stiff for the deer-sized game. It does make a great elk, moose and bear bullet though. Nosler Custom ammunition has come on the scene recently, and they are feeding some of the rare rifles, including the 8mm Remington Magnum. The 180-grain Ballistic Tip is on the menu, which will make a good long-range load for deer type game, and the 200-grain AccuBond and Partition round out the choices.

This trio of bullets will suffice for just about anything you'd want to hunt with the 8mm Magnum. That Ac-

The 8x57mm Mauser with 170-grain roundnose Remington Core-Lokt bullets.

cuBond bullet, with its boat-tail, bonded core and polymer tip, will not only buck the wind well for long-range work, but will hold up well on the close shots. If I were headed to the elk mountains or African plains with an 8 Mag in tow, I'd more than likely choose this among the factory offerings.

The 2005 SHOT show saw the introduction of the largest of the Winchester Short Magnum family, the .325 WSM. As I've stated, we Americans generally shun the 8mm bores, but Winchester rolled the dice and chambered for it anyway.

Generally speaking, it mimics the ballistics of the .300 Winchester Magnum, but with a larger bullet diameter. Winchester, in conjunction with Nosler, loads the Combined Technology 180-grain Ballistic Silver Tip and 200-grain Combined Technology AccuBond. These are essentially the same construction as the Nosler Ballistic Tip and AccuBond, but with the Winchester black Lubalox coating, designed to keep fouling to a minimum.

Double Tap Ammunition offers a good selection of the deadly Barnes TSX bullets in its product line, and these would also make a sound choice for a hunter looking to maximize the capabilities of their .325; even though the bullets will eat up a bit of case capacity, these bullets have been used for 25 years will devastating results. The 180 and 200-grain TSX will handle all the large deer species and African antelopes very well.

Winchester also offers a 220-grain Protected Hollow Point in the Power Max line, featuring a bonded core and a velocity of over 2,800 fps. This is fantastic for the bigger stuff, especially when ranges are on the close side. I imagine this would make a fantastic bear round, especially when combined with the short-action rifles that chamber for the .325 WSM. You can see why, although the bullet weights and choices in factory ammo aren't nearly as wide

as the .30s, the .325 WSM makes a lot of sense if you're a fan of the 8mm bore.

As I said, the 8x57 Mauser was the first of the 8mms on the scene, initially as a military rifle, but it didn't take long until it was used as a hunting round. It makes a great cartridge for the nostalgic, and many fantastic hunting rifles have been produced since 1905. The 150-grain bullets will give the best velocities, being the lightest, but in my own experiences the venerable cartridges shoot the most accurate with the heaviest bullets.

This is a classic example of the 'heavy and slow' mentality, but I believe this time it is with good cause. Like the 7x57mm Mauser, I think the older military-style rifles were designed to shoot the heavy bullets best, and the range tests have shown that. Hornady has embraced that wisdom, offering a 195-grain InterLock spitzer that shoots very well from the 8mm Mauser, rolling out at 2,500 fps. Prvi Partizan and Sellier & Bellot both offer 196-grain softpoints to feed the European hunting market. At this weight, there is enough bullet in a softpoint configuration to handle any hunting scenario worthy of an 8mm bullet.

For deer and black bear, the 170-grain 8mm bullets make a lot of sense. The Remington Core-Lokt 170-grain round nose will make your old 8x57 Mauser come alive in the hardwoods, because the sedate muzzle velocity of 2,300 fps will allow this bullet to mushroom well up front, but hang together for deep penetration. Mind you, this is a 200-yard load at best, but 95 percent of the shots in the woods are well under that range. Federal offers a similar load, but with a spitzer bullet which will help downrange trajectories a bit, but I still feel this is a 200-yarder at best.

One bullet I've enjoyed using in the 8x57mm is Remington's 185-grain flat-base Core-Lokt. It shot very accurately, and proved to be very effective against our New York whitetails. I handloaded

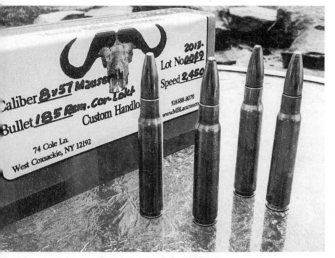

The 8mm Mauser loaded with 185-grain Remington Core-Lokts.

fashioned themselves some fantastic ammunition featuring the very same trio of bullets that I told you they load for the 8mm Remington Magnum. Tailor them to the game animal at hand, and you'll come home with your trophy if you do your part.

them to a velocity of 2,450 fps, and a sporterized WWII-era Mauser did the rest. Flat-base bullets have worked out well for me in the 8x57, as the military guns with cut-down barrels can sometimes have, well, less-than-perfect crowns.

The good folks at Nosler haven't forgotten the 8x57 fans, as they have

THE .32s

The American .32-calibers were, at one point in time, more popular than the .30s; the .32-20, .32-40 and .32 Winchester Special all have a special place in American shooting history. The first two are seldom used for game any lon-

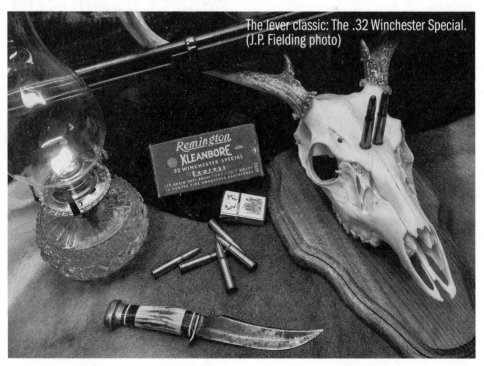

The lever classic: The .32 Winchester Special. (J.P. Fielding photo)

ger, but there are enough vintage lever guns in .32 Winchester Special to warrant a discussion.

The traditional loading, still offered by the Big Three (Winchester, Remington and Federal) consists of a 170-grain flatnose bullet (for safe loading in the tubular magazine of the Winchester Model 1894) at a muzzle velocity of 2,250; very similar to the classic .30-30 WCF load, but with the larger frontal diameter of the .321" bullet.

Now, I'm not one to argue with a classic combination, and this recipe is surely one of those, but I am old enough to recognize a brilliant idea when I see it. Hornady has nailed the lever gun upgrade in the LeveRevolution series of ammunition, and they offer the 165-grain Flex Tip bullet for the .32 Special.

That same pliable tip that increased the performance of the .30-30 WCF will give its blessing to the Special. The velocity is bumped up to 2,440 fps, and 200 to 250-yard shots are not out of the question. If you're satisfied with the traditional load, so be it, but if you're looking for an excuse to drag the Special out of the back of the safe, Hornady has the answer.

THE .338s, AMERICA'S ELK FAVORITE

In 1958, Winchester released the .338 Winchester Magnum, and American hunters were immediately intrigued. Using the bullets designed for the now-obsolete .33 Winchester (a rimmed lever gun round which was chambered in the '86 Winchester), it uses a shortened and modified .375 H&H Magnum case to drive 250-grain bullets to 2,650 fps, making it a perfect match for the big brown bears, bull elk and huge moose of North America. It also happens to work very well on the tougher antelope of Africa, such as wildebeest, kudu, sable and eland.

Mr. Elmer Keith had a lot of influence

on the design basis for this cartridge, in that he had several bad experiences with ineffective bullets in a .30-'06 used on elk, and put into print that a heavier bore and heavier bullet were needed to do the job consistently. He was part of the development of the .333 OKH, which was a wildcat that used an '06 case, necked up to hold 250-grain or larger bullets from the .333 Jeffrey.

While the .333 OKH faded into obscurity, Winchester's genius design of the .338 Winchester Magnum was received as well as the wealthy stranger at the bar that buys the next round.

To say that the .338s work anywhere on the North American continent is redundant, but what I feel is often overlooked about this particular bore diameter is its flexibility. The bullets for the .338s range from 160 grains to 300 grains, and although there may be better tools available to hunt the lighter game, any one of the .338 cases make a great choice for a wide range of larger game.

The cases for the .338 bores range from the .338 Federal, based on the .308 case, and the .338-06 A-Square, based on the '06 case, to the aforemen-

A wide selection of .338" diameter bullets.
(J.P. Fielding photo)

The .338 Federal, with 200-grain Uni-Cor bullets.

tioned .338 Win Mag, to the huge .340 Weatherby, .338-.378 Weatherby, .338 RUM, and finally to the incredible .338 Lapua. All have a place in the hunting fields (that Lapua case could be debated), and depending on your level of recoil sensitivity, there is something for you in this bore diameter.

The traditional run of cup-and-core bullets ranges between 210 and 250 grains, but it's the specialty bullets on the fringes that give the flexibility. As is true with any cartridge case, the smaller ones with limited capacity have trouble driving the largest bullets, and the cavernous cases will make a mockery of the lightest bullets, so some planning is warranted.

Should you choose to be a middle-of-the-road shooter, a good 225-grain bullet will work in any of them, but that's not the purpose of this book. Lets split the them into two groups, with the dividing line being just north of the .338 Win Mag.

Federal's decision to release the necked-up .308 makes more sense to me than does Winchester's .358, as the skinnier bullets can be driven to respectable velocities. Using this case, you're pretty much going to have to accept the fact that the heaviest bullets you can use effectively are the 225-grainers, with a few exceptions. Above that, the velocities drop off to the point where expansion is questionable.

But from 225 on down, this is a very effective case that comes in a light and handy rifle, and has many of the qualities of its parent .308 Winchester. The cup-and-core bullets in the 210 and 225-grain weights are wonderful for both the .338 Federal and the .338-'06, and the Sierra Game King in both weights are good bullets. The Speer Grand Slam comes in 250 grains, and this is a great choice for larger game, especially in the .338-06. The Grand Slam has a flat base and a flattened meplat, so even though it's a spitzer, much of the weight is kept forward and the bullet is a bit more compact, leaving room for powder in a smaller case like the .338 Federal.

Hornady and Barnes offer a good variety of differently constructed bullets, in a range of weights suitable to the lighter .338s. Look to the 185-grain GMX and TSX for your deer-sized game, as it can be driven to higher velocities, giving a decent trajectory. The 200-grain SST is another choice for deer-sized game, and would make a good bullet for mountain

goat or sheep on a combination hunt in the mountains of Alaska or western Canada. I like this bullet in the .338-'06 case as a 'lighter than elk' bullet. The classic InterLock is available in 225 and 250-grain spitzers, and a cool 250-grain roundnose. I like the roundnose in the .338 Winchester Magnum, especially for bears, where the distances are kept short.

Barnes is a bullet company making some fantastic light-for-caliber bullets, and the all-copper construction allows the bullet to hang together while creating a large wound channel. They produce the TSX and TTSX bullet in .338, from the ultralight 160 TTSX to the heavyweight 250-grain TSX. There are flat-base models, boat-tail models, and

.338 Federal with 185-grain Barnes TSX bullets.

Cutting Edge Bullets .338-caliber 176-grain Extended Range Raptor bullets.

polymer-tipped models.

Despite the lower S.D. figures, these bullets offer a longer-than-normal profile, and even the lighter 160 and 185-grain bullets will perform very well. If you're looking for a flat-shooting bullet in .338, look at the Barnes TT-SXs. Headed to Alaska? The 250-grain .338" TSX will handle any bear on the planet with authority. The 225 TSX makes a wonderful elk and moose bullet, and would be a good choice for those headed to the Dark Continent for the gamut of plains game.

Cutting Edge has the Copper Raptor available in .338, and the 176, 185 and 225-grain bullets would be perfect for the .338 Federal, .338-06 and .338 Winchester Magnum. These bullets, with their fragmenting front-end and deep hollowpoint, are lathe-turned and held to very tight tolerances. They would make a great trio for light/heavy game for the .338 enthusiast. There is a polymer tip that can be added or removed to these bullets, thereby increasing or decreasing the B.C., and I can tell you from experience that these bullets, while not cheap, are very accurate and consistent. You'll do yourself a favor by trying these out.

John Nosler's famous Partition is a staple for the .338 shooters and is available in 210, 225 and 250 grains. The 210s and 225s are a great mate for the .338 Federal, as the little case can push them to a suitable velocity for a relatively flat trajectory.

The .338-'06 case makes a very sensible choice for an all-around big game rifle when combined with the 225-grain Partition, as there really isn't too much smaller than buffalo and bison that can't be handled well by that combo, and even that is debatable.

The premium ammunition companies, like Nosler Custom and Federal Premium, offer the .338 Winchester Magnum loaded with the 250-grain Partition, to a velocity of 2,650 fps. This is a load that will get your attention! And, even though it has a flat base and relatively squat design, that bullet has developed a great reputation. It retains 80 percent-plus of its weight, and while not historically the most accurate bullet available, it makes up for that fact in being accurate enough for hunting situations and plenty hard-hitting. It's a smart choice for moose, elk, and bears, as well as hogs. I don't see this load going away anytime soon.

Nosler also loads the 250-grain AccuBond for those who love high B.C. polymer-tip bullets. It has the bonded core that I've come to love, and is one of

The .338-caliber 200-grain Nosler E-Tip, an all-copper bullet with boat-tail and polymer tip.

my favorite bullets for long range .338 Winchester loads.

Also of note is the 180-grain Ac-cuBond, in .338 caliber. This will travel at over 3,000 fps (mimicking the .300 Win Mag), and give the .338 shooter a bunch of flexibility to extend the useful-ness of his/her rifle. I've used the older 180-grain Ballistic Tip with very good results, so I would expect the bonded version to perform much the same, but with better weight retention.

Don't shy away from Nolser's 200-grain all-copper E-Tip. What a great long-range bullet that will make!

Swift makes their A-Frame and Sci-rocco II for the .338s, and they are good stuff. I've loaded the 210-grain Scirocco II in a Browning .338 Winchester Mag-num that would print them into ¾" groups all day long.

This is a great elk bullet, as the boat-tail and long ogive will help it to retain energy across the wide canyons of the

(below) The uber-accurate 210-grain .338 Swift Scirroco II, fired from the .338 Winchester magnum.

west. I believe it would perform equally well in the .338-'06 and .330 Dakota.

I also like the

A-Frames, available in 225, 250 and 275 grains. I've said it before in this book, but I'll say it again: I think the Swift A-Frame is among the best bullets available to today's hunter. It can be highly accurate, and retains weight into the 90% realm. If you want to feel confident about using a .338 on any shot angle, get your hands of some of these and watch the magic happen, so long as you put that A-Frame where it belongs.

THE BIG .338s

These cases are designed to hold a huge amount of powder, and drive the heavy bullets to velocities well over 2,900 fps. As with the biggest of the 7mm and .30-caliber cases, this kind of horsepower can prove too much for the traditional cup-and-core bullets. That's not to say that the bullets would disintegrate or anything of that sort, but

(above) The massive .338 Remington Ultra Magnum loaded with 250-grain Nosler Partitions.

(below) The 300-grain Nosler AccuBond, perfect for the .338 Lapua Magnum. (J.P. Fielding photo)

it can very easily result in superficial wounds and poor penetration. The .338 Lapua can push the 250-grainers over 3,000 fps, and while that makes a fantastic long-range target rifle, when we turn the sights onto a game animal, we have to take the bullet construction into consideration.

The .338 RUM and Weatherby's .338-.378 Magnum can hold well over 100 grains of powder. Even the .340 Weatherby will hold almost 90 grains of certain types of powder. This calls for a bullet of suitable weight to perform well once it hits fur. I think that if you've invested into a rifle chambered for one of these specialty cases, the further investment into premium projectiles is warranted.

The Barnes, Cutting Edge, Swift and others I've mentioned are almost a must for these calibers. At least a bonded-core bullet is a good minimum. Partitioned and monometal projectiles are equally wise. In .338 diameter, the lowest weight I'd generally recommend is 225 grains. Yes, you can maybe get away with some of the 210s at screaming velocity, but I think the sheer case size warrants a bit more bullet. The combination of a bullet like the 250-grain Nosler Accubond and the .338 RUM, producing a muzzle velocity of 2,850 fps will give the same trajectory as the .300 Winchester Magnum with a 180 out to 400 yards, but with 70 grains more bullet and a larger frontal diameter. If you can handle the recoil, this is winning.

The long 275-grain Swift A-Frame is also a good choice for the largest cervid, the moose, especially when they get really big in Alaska and the Yukon. It also makes for excellent insurance if you're hunting in bear turf, as this bullet will deal with the nastiest bruins on earth.

The .338 Lapua, having developed a reputation as the king of the long-range sniper rifles, is making its way into the hunting world. There is a trend, embraced by many of the hunting TV shows, of shooting game at almost unheard-of distances. This requires a very accurate rifle and ice water in your veins, yet it still comes with a risk of wounding an animal should the slightest thing go wrong.

The ethics of long-range hunting are up to you. The accuracy of the Lapua case is undeniable, and I've shot one that would print ¾" groups at 250 yards! Now that is more accuracy than is required to make a decent hunting rifle, but it sure is nice to have that kind of confidence. I like the bullets with a high B.C. for the Lapua, and again I like them 225 grains and heavier. The 300-grain Nosler Accubond, with an S.D. of .375 and a B.C. of .720 (whoa!!), this is a long-range monster. All I can say is: beware the close shots; things could get messy when hunting with a cartridge this big.

THE .348 WINCHESTER

Winchester's Model 71 came one year after the introduction of its most famous bolt-action: the Model 70. Everything that the Model 70 was to the bolt-actions, the Model 71 was supposed to be to the lever guns. Winchester superseded its famous model 1886, and the .33 Winchester, to bring the .348 Winchester to light.

Driving a 250-grain bullet to 2,350 fps (a rather magical formula), it quickly made its bones, and gained a reputation as a fantastic killer. There were 180 and 200-grain loads as well, but it was the 250-grain bullet that gained the accolades. For a couple decades it was a huge success, but the rising popularity of telescopic sights was one of the main factors in the demise of the Model 71.

In the mid fifties, Winchester discontinued the Model 71 and introduced the wicked cool Model 88, and the .358 Winchester cartridge. Quietly, fans of both the 71 and .348 grabbed up those sweet-shooting lever guns, and enjoyed shooting them. However, as with any discontinued item, availability of ammunition dwindled. The 250-grain factory load especially became a rarity. It appeared, for all intents and purposes, that the Model 71 was as dead as Sean Bean in a good movie.

Imagine my delight when I saw that Winchester had reissued the Model 71 in .348 at the 2014 SHOT show! Now the reissue itself has become a bit of a rarity, and I haven't been able to find any new Winchester ammunition, but there are some good bullets on the market. Swift offers a 200-grain A-Frame that should prove to be damned near the equal of the cup-and-core 250-grains, as far as penetration and weight retention are concerned.

Among the 250-grain bullets available, I like the cup-and-core Barnes Original, but I really like the Woodleigh Weldcore. I guess I'm a sucker for bonded-core bullets. Hawk makes a decent 250 bonded-core flatpoint as well. The tube magazine of the 71 calls for the flat and round-point bullets, as all that I've mentioned thus far are, but Hornady has once again come to the rescue by developing a 200-grain FTX bullet, and thereby giving .348 shooters a much better long-range trajectory.

As with the .30-30 WCF and .32 Special, the range and trajectory of the .348 Winchester with the Hornady spitzer load is near equal to many of the otherwise flatter-shooting cartridges. This makes the .348 Winchester fully capable of hitting targets as far out as iron sights can be practically used on game animals. The North Fork bonded-core flatpoint is offered in a 240-grain configuration and this would make a sound choice for bears and bigger cervids. The pure copper jacket is chemically bonded to the lead core, which only extends about halfway down the bullet, and the solid copper base drives deep into the biggest animals. Despite the appeal of the lighter bullets, I still like bullets in the 240-250-grain range for the big stuff; I'd set the 180s and 200-grain bullets aside for deer-size game.

THE .35s: AN AMERICAN STAPLE

There's been a soft spot in shooters' hearts for the .35-caliber cartridges for over a century, and rightfully so. The bore diameter, I believe, is derived from the simultaneous development of the American .38 Colt and associated variations and the European 9mm cartridges.

At any rate, Remington entered the rifle market in 1906 with its .35 Remington in the Model 8 autoloader. While the most anemic of the .35s, it has a very special place in cartridge history, and is the only cartridge to threaten the reign of the .30-30 WCF in the lever gun. It was picked up by Marlin in their Model 336, and still has quite a following. Col. Townsend Whelen used some bullets from the .350 Rigby Magnum to build his wildcat based on the .30-'06 case, but his namesake cartridge wouldn't be legitimized until 1987.

Winchester modified the .308 Winchester case to hold .358" bullets, and in 1955 released the .358 Winchester, and a rimmed version in 1983 as the .356 Winchester. Norma of Sweden made its foray into the .35 market in 1959 when it released the .358 Norma Magnum, based on a shortened H&H belted case. Remington hopped in the game again in 1966 with the first round of short-action belted magnums, the .350 Remington Magnum.

This is a wide variety of cases, which demand an equally wide variety of bullets. One of the cool features of the .35s is that you can shoot the light-for-caliber pistol bullets designed for the .38 Special and .357 Magnum as practice or plinking rounds. But, for hunting, you'll want to choose a .358-diameter bullet suitable for the task at hand, and that will function well in the cartridge you've chosen.

The stubby yet powerful .350 Remington magnum, shown with 250-grain Hornady roundnose and 200-grain Hornady spitzers.

REMINGTON'S .35

The .35 Remington has very little recoil, which makes it easy on the shoulder and easy for all shooters to handle. The fact that it comes (predominantly) in light, compact, and quick handling lever-action carbines is another bonus. The drawback to the .35 Remington is its throw weight. The factory ammo is generally loaded with bullets less than 220 grains, the most popular being the 200-grain roundnose bullet.

Remington makes its Core-Lokt in a 150-grain pointed softpoint load, and the 200-grain roundnose as well. Federal and Winchester also load its .35 ammo with a 200-grain roundnose soft point. These style bullets will perform perfectly at .35 Remington velocities (the 200-grain runs at a muzzle velocity of 2,080 fps); however the effective range of this cartridge is right around 150 yards. Within that range the .35 shows why it has become a woods gun classic. On deer and black bear, and game as large as elk it can kill quickly and cleanly if that bullet is put where it needs to be.

Yet again, Hornady has revamped a lever classic by offering their Flex-Tip bullet for the .35 Remington in their LeveRevolution line. The 200-grain spitzer at 2,225 fps will help to extend the range and retain more kinetic energy at the edge of the .35's range. Sighted in to be 3" high at 100 yards, the FTX bullet is only 1.8" low at 200 yards, and 18" at 300. This is a dramatic improvement for the century-plus old cartridge, and definitely worth a look if you enjoy hunting with the .35 Rem.

The .35 Remington, a long-time lever gun favorite, loaded with 200-grain roundnose bullets.

The .358 Winchester, a necked-up .308 Winchester case, loaded with the 200-grain Hornady Spitzer.

THE .356 AND .358 WINCHESTER

When the .308 Winchester gained its immediate popularity, it didn't take Winchester long to neck the case up to hold .358" bullets. Released in 1955 in the revolutionary Model 88 lever gun (a fantastic rifle!), the .358 Winchester provided a whole bunch of payload and bullet diameter in a concise and accurate package. Savage also adapted their famous Model 99 to shoot it, and it was even chambered in the epic Model 70 Winchester.

The 80's saw the rimmed version

of the .358 released in the Winchester Model 94 Big Bore, but it never really caught on. Now here's the weird thing: Winchester no longer produces ammunition for the more popular .358 Win., but it does make a 200-grain Power Point load for the .356 Winchester.

Don't ask me…

My buddy Jeff Koonz, proprietor of Coxsackie Gun & Bow, is one of the die-hard .358 Winchester fans. He hoards any and all ammunition, and his face lights up at the mention of taking his .358 afield.

My friend Mr. Jeff Koonz, proprietor of Coxsackie Gun & Bow, a firm proponent of the .358 Winchester, and .35-calibers in general.

Either one of these cartridges make a good medium-range gun, although to get the best results from these guys you're going to have to handload them. Luckily, there are boatloads of good bullets in .35 caliber that are suitable for both of these cases. As is the case with the .338 Federal, you'll have trouble pushing the big 250-grain bullets, but the 225-grain and lighter bullets can be used with great effect.

Another issue you might encounter, especially in the .358 Win., is that many of the heavier spitzer bullets will have an ogive so long that the bullet cannot be seated properly to maintain rifleman plenty of frontal diameter for a large wound channel, and although the S.D. figures aren't high, the sedate velocity will give good penetration.

Stick to roundnose bullets for the tube-magazine .356, like the Sierra I mentioned above or the Hornady 200-grain InterLock roundnose. You might want to try that same 200-grain Hornady FTX designed for the .35 Remington in your .356, as it will combat the downrange slow-down of the roundnose bullets.

Among the premiums, look to the 200 and 225-grain North Fork semi-spitzers. They will not come apart, even on the toughest shoulder bones and gristle plates. They keep enough of their weight forward that the .358 case should have no problem keeping them to the proper length. Were I heading to the pine woods for elk or cedar bogs for moose at medium ranges, I'd think long and hard about the North Fork products. Same goes for the Swift A-Frame. The 225-grain bonded-core and partitioned little gem will give fantastic performance on the biggest beasts you'd sensibly hunt with a .358 Winchester. A Barnes 200-grain TSX sitting comfortably nestled in a .358 Winchester case would also make a potent combination for a fan of the .35 bores.

THE .350 REMINGTON MAGNUM

This little fireplug of a cartridge is the personal favorite of my good pal Neighbor Dave deMoulpied. He grins ear-to-ear like a boy the day after a successful prom night, each and every time he loads up that Remington Model 700 classic for our annual jaunts into the Catskills and Adirondacks. The cartridge was one of the first attempts at making a short-action (.308 Winchester-length) magnum case based on the belted H&H design. It first saw the light of day in the Remington 600 carbine (which I think is hideous, but don't tell Dave), but the 18 ½" barrel really didn't do this cartridge justice;

the proper C.O.L. and fit the rifle's magazine. When I load for the .358, I look to bullets that tend to keep their weight forward. I prefer the flat-base bullets, like the Hornady 200-grain Interlock spitzer and the Sierra 200-grain Pro Hunter roundnose. Both of these bullets will make a great load for deer, bear and hogs. They can be driven to just over 2,400 (a wonderful velocity for cup-and-core bullets), and give the

The .358" Hornady 200-grain spitzer, perfect for the smaller .35-caliber cartridges.

it produces much better velocities and accuracy from Dave's 22" barreled 700. There are very few options available to those who shoot factory ammo; I find a 200-grain Core-Lokt from Remington and a 225-grain Partition from Nosler Custom Ammunition.

To be honest, Dave and I handloaded this cartridge from the instant he purchased the rifle, so the scarcity of the ammo was never an issue. The .350 suffers from the same length issue that the .358 Winchester does, in that the longer spitzer bullets will be seated so deep into the case (in order to maintain a C.O.L. that will feed through the magazine) that the case mouth will be on the curved ogive of the bullet rather than properly on the bullet shank. So, again we needed bullets that keep weight forward and have a short ogive. For our local whitetail deer and black bear hunting, Dave chose the 200-grain Hornady InterLock spitzer, and it worked out just fine. Velocities run around 2,650 fps, and accuracy is under one MOA. For a heavier bullet, we used the roundnose Hornady 250-grain InterLock. Not quite as fast as the 200, we still get 2,350 fps on the chrony.

Even though the cool spitzers like the Nosler AccuBonds and Sierra Game Kings are off the plate, there are great bullets out there that will work for the Three-Fitty. North Fork's 225-grain semi-spitzer is getting the nod for an African plains game safari we are planning. This weight is middle-of-the-road, within this caliber, but with the core bonded it really changes the game. Both Dave and I feel confident using this bullet on game up to and including eland, elk and moose. If you shoot Three-Fitty, give it a look.

COL. WHELEN'S .35 NAMESAKE

Developed as a wildcat in the 1920 by Col. Townsend Whelen and James Howe (later of Griffin & Howe fame), the .35 Whelen spent 67 years hiding in the cellar before Remington saw the wisdom of applying for SAAMI approval. Now, if you look at the paper ballistics, the Whelen cartridge doesn't really do much more than the .30-'06 from which it was derived. The ought-six can drive 220-grain slugs to over 2,450 fps, while the Whelen does about the same with its 250-grain slugs.

But there is something to be said for frontal diameter. The 'skinny-bullet-has-penetration vs. fat-bullet-makes-a-larger-hole' argument has been going on for decades, and will probably continue to do so. That aside, there is no denying the validity of the .35 Whelen. It could be looked on as a viable candidate for an all-around North American rifle, with an effective range of bullets from 200 to 250 grains, and relatively mild recoil, especially if your hunting regularly involves larger-than-normal creatures, or if you routinely hunt in areas haunted by bears.

Nosler's 225 AccuBond is on the menu, and as in other calibers, this bullet does its best to defy the wind and flatten out the trajectory. I'm definitely a fan of this bullet, be it for long shots on elk or mule deer in the Rockies, or gemsbok and eland in the Free State. What you have is all the benefits of the boat-tail and polymer tip, but none of the risk of jacket/core separation so often associated with cup-and-core boat-tails. Many companies load the proven Partition for the .35 Whelen, and both the 225 and 250-grain version make a great choice. I really can't think of a better bullet for bears.

Want a sweet moose bullet? Opt for the 225-grain Barnes TSX and smile in your trophy pictures. Long-range deer bullet? A Federal Trophy Bonded Tipped or Barnes 200-grain TTSX will definitely fit that bill, being driven at 2,800 fps.

Although most folks don't think of the Whelen as a deer gun, it does that job just fine. Federal's Fusion bullet is represented in the Whelen lineup, at 200 grains. This would make a great deer load. So would the Hornady Superformance 200-grain InterLock spitzer, driven to a higher velocity of 2,900 fps. That's pretty snappy!

If you feel better with a heavy bullet in your Whelen, I can't really argue with you, as I like heavy bullets myself. That safari I told you that Neighbor Dave and I were planning? I'll be bringing a .35 Whelen Ackley Improved as my heavy gun for plains game, for eland specifically, and I intend to use a 250-grain North Fork semi-spitzer in

Colonol Townsend Whelen's brainchild, the .35 Whelen.

the wildcat. I have no doubt that if I do my part, the cartridge and bullet will certainly handle an antelope approaching a ton of weight. And that wouldn't make a bad bear load either.

THE .358 NORMA MAGNUM

Norma's idea of putting a .358" bullet in a shortened .375 H&H case is a good one. This case is capable of using all of the traditional .35-caliber bullets, but with the added benefits of the heavy 275-grain bullets. Designed for Scandinavian moose, it makes a great choice for the large cervids and antelope of Africa. The downfall of the .358 Norma, if it is a downfall at all, is that it is too small to make the legal limit for dangerous game in Africa; the minimum bore being .375". I firmly believe that

with a 275-grain A-Frame, and some good solids to back it up, the .358 Norma would cleanly take a Cape buffalo.

Look to use the 225-grain bullets as minimum, as they will stay together better at Norma velocities than will the lighter bullets. I like the 250-grain Nosler Partition at 2,850 fps in this case, as loaded by Double-Tap ammunition, as well as the Norma 250-grain Oryx

at 2,750 fps. Double-Tap also loads the 225-grain Nosler AccuBond to a muzzle velocity of 3,000 fps, which would make a very impressive elk or moose load, should you be hunting in areas where long-range shots are not out of the question.

Essentially, you have a cartridge with the trajectory of the .300 Winchester using 165-grain bullets, but with the added weight and frontal diameter of a 225-grain .358. The Norma case will push all the bullets in .35 caliber at least 400 fps faster than the .35 Whelen, and although the recoil will be proportionally worse, for the shooter that can handle the heat this makes a great all-around North American heavy rifle, fully capable of handling the great bears of the northland, and at home on the African game fields on any and all plains game ever made.

THE 9.3MM CARTRIDGES: AN UNHEARD-OF WONDER

The European 9.3 mm, or .366" bore, is not very popular here in the States, but in all honesty it should be. Among the 9.3mms, there are cases that run from mild to wild. The lower-velocity cases will compare well with our .35 Whelen, while the faster cases will fall just shy of the .375 H&H Magnum. I have found this much out about the 9.3s: those who are fans of the bore diameter defend it like a rabid dog. The 9.3mm cartridges have been with us since 1900, and pre-date the venerable .375 H&H Magnum.

Being of German descent, it found great favor in its homeland as well in the German colonies that are now Tanzania and Namibia. The 9.3x74R is the oldest, and pushing the 286-grain bullets to 2,350 fps, it is a solid choice for the hunter who routinely pursues large game. It has seen a recent resurgence in the classy Ruger No. 1 single shot rifle, and the clean lines of that rifle, combined with the nostalgia factor of the long, rimmed cartridge make for a really cool package.

The 9.3x62mm, being five years the junior of its rimmed sibling, gives the same velocity from a more concise

Metric powerhouse: the 9.3x62.

case, which feeds perfectly from a bolt-action magazine. Wilhelm Brenneke's 9.3x64mm is a bit of a step up the velocity ladder, and the .370 Sako Magnum, also known as the 9.3x66mm, takes it up yet another notch. The 9.3 cartridges are on the large side for whitetail deer and pronghorn antelope, but they make a fantastic choice for hogs, bear, elk and moose.

THE 9.3X62MM

The 9.3x62mm has a pair of offerings that feature the lighter bullets. Lapua's all-copper Naturalis comes in a 220-grain configuration, and the special rubber valve at the tip is provided to initiate expansion. This would be hell on hogs, and is compliant in the lead-free zones of California. Muzzle velocity is 2,624 fps according to Lapua, and although the roundnose profile will slow things down out past 200 yards, within

that mark this will make a good medium game bullet. Norma loads their 232-grain Oryx in 9.3x62mm, at 2,630 fps, and this is a great load as well. The Oryx is skived in the nose section for good expansion, but the rear core of the bullet is bonded to the jacket. I'm thinking that if you're looking for a black bear load for the 9.3x62, this is a good choice.

I like the 250-grain Hornady GMX bullet for the 9.3x62, and I loaded this solid copper bullet for my pal Marty Longbottom for use on Texas hogs. He reports good accuracy, and I am waiting to hear if he's made bacon with it yet. The GMX is a monometal bullet with a polymer tip, and the 250-grain bullet would make a good elk and moose load, as the spitzer point will improve the B.C. and retain downrange energy. I like this bullet, along with the 250-grain Barnes TTSX, as an all-

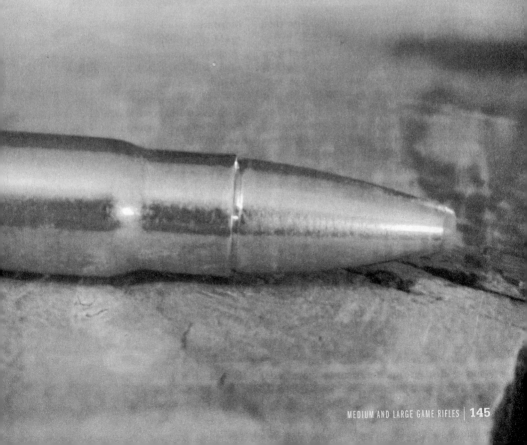

around African plains game bullet for the 9.3x62, as it will handle anything up to and including eland. Nosler loads a 250 AccuBond for the 9.3x62 in its Trophy Grade ammunition, and like other calibers, I'm a fan of that AccuBond bullet. It has a sleek profile and polymer tip, but bonding the core to the jacket removes all worries of bullet separation.

For the handloaders, the Swift A-Frame bullet is on the menu with a 250-grain bullet, and this would make a great bear load, or confidently take any moose or eland that God ever put on earth. The Cutting Edge Safari Raptor is a neat brass hollowpoint bullet, that much resembles a solid 9.3mm

bullet, but the frangible nose section breaks off into six blades that cut into the animal in a star pattern, while the rear portion of the bullet maintains caliber diameter to penetrate deep into the vitals.

For a heavy bullet in 9.3x62, there are some good 286-grain bullets, and this bullet weight seems to be ideal for the 62mm case, especially when ranges aren't much beyond 200 yards. For elk in the timber, or for the thick bushveld conditions across much of southern Africa, the 286-grain choice is a sound one.

The 62mm factory ammunition can push a 286-grain bullet at 2,360 fps, and while this weight is primar-

ily for truly large game, it could easily be used on the largest cervids and antelope. Many 9.3x62mm rifles have shown an accuracy preference for this bullet, and there are plenty of different bullets available in the 286-grain weight. The Barnes TSX, Nosler Partition, and Swift A-Frame are among the premiums, and the cup-and-core Hornady Interlock is available as well. The Lapua Mega and Woodleigh Weldcore give some different choices for those (like me) who enjoy hunting with round-nosed bullets.

All the bullets outlined here for the 9.3x62mm are also available for the 9.3x74R. Even though the case is much longer and larger, the low pressure that the 74R operates at will limit velocities to almost an exact mirror of the 9.3x62, so the applications and bullet choices are interchangeable between the two cartridges.

THE 9.3X64MM AND .370 SAKO MAGNUM (9.3X66MM)

These cases have a touch more velocity than the 62mm and 74mm cases, and work best with the premium bullets. The .370 pushes the 286-grain bullet at 2,560 fps, while the beefier 64mm has another 100 fps over that. This puts them both effectively on par with the .375 H&H Magnum. Where legal, these both make a good dangerous game cartridge, but they will also

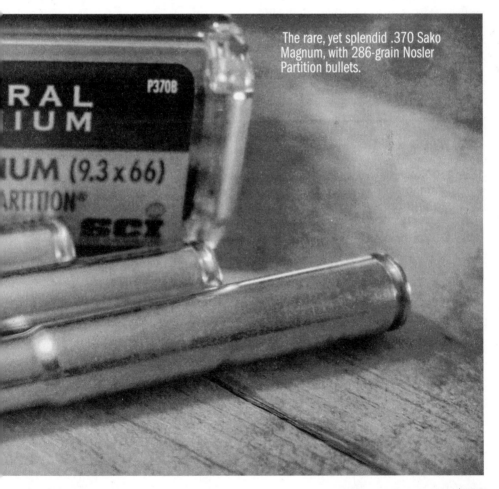

The rare, yet splendid .370 Sako Magnum, with 286-grain Nosler Partition bullets.

make for fine elk and moose rifles, as well as a fantastic black bear gun. With this kind of velocity gain, I'd like to see that 250-grain Hornady GMX used as a choice of bullet for elk, as you'd have all sorts of confidence should a longer (350 to 400 yards) shot present itself.

Federal's Cape Shok line includes the 286-grain Nosler Partition in the .370 Sako Magnum, which makes a great all-around load for game on the larger end of the scale, including any and all of the tough African game like wildebeest and eland, and would be right at home for kudu and elk. Aside from the traditional bullets, I found a bullet that should be quite interesting for any of the 9.3mms. Cutting Edge, a company becoming known for its rather radical bullet designs, offers a .366" diameter 210-grain Enhanced System Projectile (ESP) that offers all sorts of versatility. All-copper, lathe-turned, it has a deep hollowpoint and a blunt nose profile. But, you can install a polymer tip into the hollowpoint to increase the ballistic coefficient, or, and this is crazy but it works, turn the bullet around and shoot it as a solid. That's versatility!

THE .375s: CLASSICS ON BOTH SIDES OF THE POND

It seems that for almost as long as we've had metallic cartridges, there has been some sort of .375" bore available to hunters. From the venerable .38-55 Winchester and .38-56, to the workhorse .375 Holland & Holland Magnum, to the .375 and .378 Weatherbys, and even including the new kid on the block, the .375 Ruger, rifles of this bore diameter are simply fantastic.

The .38-55 Winchester was one of the first cartridges chambered in the radical new Model 1894 Winchester in 1895, but has been with us since 1876 in single-shot rifles. The .375 H&H Magnum is the African equivalent of the .30-06 Springfield, in that it will (and has) killed everything on

that continent. They are essentially on opposite ends of the power spectrum, but depending on the conditions and distance, both can be great cartridges. And, each end of the spectrum has an entirely different selection of bullets.

.375 LEVER GUNS

The .38-55 Winchester, and its cousin on steroids, the .375 Winchester, are straight-walled, rimmed cartridges, of moderate velocity. Both are designed to shoot a 200 to 255-grain flatpoint projectile, though the .375 Winchester operates at a higher pressure. It was designed for the short-lived '94 Big Bore. Winchester still makes ammunition for both cartridges. The classic .38-55 load is a 255-grain jacketed softpoint, at 1,320 fps; the low velocity is in deference to the older weapons still around.

The .375 Winchester is loaded with a 200-grain jacketed softpoint, at a much higher velocity of 2,200 fps. This illustrates the advantage of the higher pressure limits. Buffalo Bore ammunition offers a 'high-pressure' .38-55 load, with a 255-grain jacketed, bonded-core bullet moving at 1,950 fps, which should only be used in modern .38-55 rifles capable of handling the higher pressure.

Both guns are generally short-range affairs, due to low velocities and flat-nosed bullets, and many hunters leave their lever guns equipped with iron sights as a result. There are good component bullets for these guys, which will make suitable hunting cartridges. Hornady offers a 220-grain InterLock flatpoint, and Sierra makes a 200-grain flatpoint in their Pro-Hunter series. These are dependable bullets in either cartridge, as they will expand well at these velocities, yet their construction will keep them together for reliable penetration.

I would stick to deer, hog and black bear-sized game with these cartridges, though there are those who would use them for elk and moose at close rang-

The .38-55 Winchester, a cartridge that survived the transition from black powder to smokeless.

es. Both of these cartridges work very well with hard-cast lead bullets as well. You'll want to slug the rifle's bore, to be sure you get the proper diameter bullet, but if you choose a good flatpoint design of between 240 and 260 grains, with high antimony content, you'll be a happy hunter.

THE MAGNUM .375s: HOLLAND & HOLLAND, RUGER, WEATHERBY AND REMINGTON

In 1912, the chaps at Holland & Holland created what I consider to be the most useful cartridge ever designed: The .375 Holland & Holland Belted Rimless Magnum. For the period in which it was released, it was considered a medium bore, but by today's standards, and with today's bullets, it is fully capable of taking any game on Earth. Historically, both the .375 H&H Magnum, and its flanged sibling built for double rifles, were offered with three bullet weights: 235 grains for light game, and 270 and 300-grain bullets for the bigger stuff. Those weights are still with us, along with some new twists.

One of the beauties of the .375 H&H (both Belted and Flanged), and the relatively new .375 Ruger (which is essentially its ballistic twin) is that they are very shooter-friendly. The 235-grain bullets can be driven at 2,850 fps and higher, while the classic load that helped make the reputation of the .375 is a 300-grain bullet at 2,550. The range of useful bullets and velocities make the .375s in this class a truly universal choice, and here's why: although most of us here in the United States may cock an eyebrow at the idea of taking a .375 deer hunting, it is used daily across Africa to take even the smallest of the antelope, and yet with the monometal solids of today it still makes a perfectly viable elephant and buffalo rifle. It is on the heavy end for light game, but I've used it for creatures as small as steenbok, and it is on the light side as an elephant rifle, but

many thousands have fallen to this cartridge.

It is the versatility of the .375s that has earned them the title of 'universal', and if you choose your bullet wisely, you can suit the rifle to the game at hand. I'm certainly not going to say that you need a .375 to hunt smaller antelope, but if Africa taught me one lesson, it's that the 'too much gun' con-

cept doesn't hold water. Let's look at some bullet choices and their application for medium game.

The 235-grain bullets have been with us since the inception of the .375 H&H Belted magnum, and although they don't have the sectional density of the heavier bullets, they are designed to perform well on the smaller game.

There are not many 235s on the mar-

The .375 H&H with some perfectly suitable large game bullets. Left to right, the 250-grain Sierra boat-tail spitzer, 260-grain Nosler AccuBond, 250-grain Swift A-Frame, and the 300-grain Winchester Silvertip.

ket today, but one I have become enamored with is the Barnes TSX. Being an all-copper design, with a deep hollowpoint for expansion, this bullet can be pushed at velocities between 2,750 fps and almost 3,000 fps. The bullet is longer than the traditional 235-grain bullets, because copper is lighter than lead and results in a longer bullet to make up the weight difference.

These bullets are very accurate in both the .375 H&H and .375 Ruger, and at the velocities listed above will shoot very flat. Think about like this: you've got a rifle with the same trajectory as the .30-'06 with 180-grain bullets (a

The .375" diameter 235-grain Barnes TSX, a good choice for medium and large game from the .375 bore.

perfectly acceptable choice for almost all game, save the heavyweights), but with 235 grains of bullet with a much larger frontal diameter.

I've loaded this bullet for several clients who love carrying their .375 rifle and want to give it a go at elk and moose. Speer has offered their Hot-Cor semi-spitzer bullet in 235 grains, and it's an accurate bullet, but I'll have to be honest here and say that it is best reserved for target practice. I've seen it used on whitetail deer, certainly not a tough animal when compared to elk or moose or wildebeest, and the bullet seems to be very frangible. Use them to become proficient with your rifle, but keep them out of the game fields.

Kynoch loads the 235-grain Woodleigh Weldcore protected point at 2,800 fps, and while expensive, these bullets make a great choice for lighter game, especially on a mixed bag safari, or as a black bear rifle where the potential for a truly big bear exists. The Weldcore has earned a good reputation for excellent performance on game, and I don't think they'll disappoint in this configuration. The roundnose profile won't give the same flat trajectory of the Barnes TSX, but if you're hunting bushveld or bear over bait, where shots are generally less than 200 yards, this bullet will do the job very well, giving good expansion and weight retention due to the process of bonding the lead core to the copper jacket.

Cutting Edge Bullets makes a pair of .375-diameter bullets in this class, a 230-grain ESP Raptor, and a 235-grain ER (Extended Range) Raptor, that will prove to be quite impressive. As with most copper monometals, you'll get good performance out of lighter bullets, as they are longer than lead-core counterparts, and they have no jacket to separate.

The ER Raptor has a tangent ogive and a seven-degree boat-tail to maximize the downrange trajectory, and this bullet will deliver the goods upon impact. The black polymer tip initiates expansion, and the nose section breaks into a set of 'blades' that disperse to create a large impact trauma, while the remainder of the bullet stays at caliber diameter, with no expansion, to drive through flesh and bone for a quick kill.

The 230-grain ESP Raptor, as with other calibers, gives you the option of shooting the bullet as a hollowpoint, or flipped around as a solid. This is a great concept for those who wish to take smaller game on an African safari, as you can use the solid end to ensure a small-diameter entry and exit wound, without overly damaging the animal. I think it will take a bit of time for hunters to embrace the Cutting Edge idea, but I've had the opportunity to shoot their stuff and it works very well.

One newer bullet weight that has impressed me in all of the .375s of this class is the 250-grain bullet. It has a bit less recoil and a flatter trajectory than the 270-grainers, with a better S.D. than the 235s. There are a whole bunch of 250s to choose from, and I've loaded and used quite a few of them in the field. One that I really like is Sierra Game King 250-grain boat-tail. It has a decent S.D., is wonderfully accurate, and will perform wonderfully on the world's larger game.

It was this bullet that I loaded for Ol' Grumpy Pants, for his 2002 safari to South Africa, when he borrowed my Winchester Model 70 in .375 H&H. He took a 54 ½" kudu and a 39" gemsbok in the same day, and both fell like a stone to the shot. The Sierra bullet has a jacket that will allow for excellent penetration, yet frangible enough for good expansion. If you like a cup-and-core bullet for your .375, and you're after a flat trajectory, spend some time with this bullet.

The Barnes TTSX comes in 250 grains, and with the polymer tip and boat-tail you'll have a great long-range affair for any and all plains game, and a wonderful long-range setup for

America's largest deer species.

Federal's Cape Shok line has the 250 Trophy Bonded Bear Claw in its lineup, and this copper bullet with a lead core in the front half gives excellent performance. Expansion is usually over two times the original caliber and weight retention is into the 75-80 percent range. This is a great bullet in the .375s for any and all game not classified as dangerous. In my experiences, the Bear Claw has always been a reli-

The Sierra 250-grain boat-tail spitzer Game King.

able and accurate bullet, with a profile that will give good trajectories, and perform well across a wide variety of impact velocities.

The Swift A-Frame is available in the 250-grain weight, and will comfortably

handle large game. I've often described the A-Frame bullet as "meat resistant", in that it will expand very well when it meets a large animal (giving larger resistance); yet expand much less when used on the smaller animals. Let's look at it this way: if you're on safari with a .375, chances are you'll be after many different species of animals.

It's difficult to carry a suitable rifle for eland and wildebeest, and yet another that is spot on for impala, springbok and duiker. It's also difficult to find a bullet that will perform well on all those varying sizes of animals, but I feel that the A-Frame comes closest of all of them. They will whistle through a smaller antelope leaving a slightly larger than caliber-sized hole, yet expand perfectly and give that classic 'rivet' look just behind the partition. This bullet will hold up to the stresses of the larger .375 cases, and would make a good selection for the .378 Weatherby and the .375 Remington Ultra Magnum.

North Fork makes their semi-spitzer in this weight as well, and these would make a sound choice for a plains game safari, a trophy elk hunt, or a moose hunt with the possibility of a run in with bears. I've tested many North Fork bullets in different calibers, and they've proved to be winners. As with their entire line of softpoints, the pure copper jackets are bonded to the pure lead core, for a devastating wound channel. The roundish nose profile keeps some of the bullet weight forward, and the small grooves in the shank of the bullet keep the pressures lower, and actually help keep your barrel clean. This is true of all the North Fork designs, not just this 250-grain .375 bullet.

Hornady's killer GMX is made in a 250-grain configuration, and with a polymer tip and boat-tail this bullet will make a good choice for long-range work in any .375 cartridge. Being a monometal (the GMX stands for Gilding Metal eXpanding), it will be the same length as some of the cup-and-core 270-grain bullets, yet will not separate as there is no jacket or core to do so.

Nosler has embraced one of the newer bullet weights for the .375 bores: the 260-grain bullet. I like it, as it combines the high speed of the 250s while approaching the S.D. of the famous 270-grain bullets. Both the Partition and the superb AccuBond are available in this weight, and if you're a fan of either of these bullets, try the 260-grainers in your .375, regardless of the headstamp on the case. Federal Premium loads both these bullets in the Cape Shok line, and either will be a good choice for a mixed-bag safari. I like the accuracy potential of that AccuBond; it has given fantastic results in other calibers, bordering on target rifle accuracy. The 260-grain AccuBond has a B.C. of 0.473, so it will shoot flatter than some of the flat-base and round-nose bullets of this caliber and its rigid construction will make you a happy hunter.

I have found the .375s, especially the .375 Holland & Holland and .375 Ruger, to be very accurate cartridges, despite their size, with many capable of producing sub-MOA target groups. Combine that with a bullet designed for accuracy, like the AccuBond, yet fully capable of good post-impact performance and you've got a winner.

The 270-grain bullets are a classic weight in .375" bore cartridges, and they are a fine choice on the larger game. The premium 270-grain bullets have been used with good success on game as large as Cape buffalo, and they will offer deep penetration on the moose/elk/eland class of game. They are also a good choice for bear of any color. I like the Hornady 270-grain InterLock flat-base spitzer, as it shoots ¾" groups from my Winchester 70 in .375 H&H. At a velocity of 2,675 fps, this bullet will hold up well.

The premiums are the way to go if you're shooting the fast Weatherby or the .375 RUM, and I think the North Fork or the Barnes TSX would make a sensible choice for either in 270 grains. These bullets will hold up to the 3,000+ fps muzzle velocity generated by these big sticks. Look also to the 270-grain Swift A-Frame in 270 grains, should you be after the largest mammals that don't bite or gore.

The 300-grain bullets have been the bread and butter of the .375" bores for over a century, and with good cause. Factory ammunition is driven at 2,550 fps, for a good blend of velocity and low recoil. Many African Professional Hunters have discussed the best cartridges for large game, and their qualities in real-world field conditions, and nearly all of them have related that the 300-grain .375 bullet will penetrate further than any other weight in any other caliber. Often these bullets are reserved for the buffalo and elephant-sized game, but I have used quite a few of them on other game and I've been very satisfied.

The 300-grain Sierra Game King is a very good bullet, with a spitzer boat-tail design, and a very thick jacket. I've shot ½ MOA groups with this bullet over heavy charges of IMR4350, and this bullet will comfortably handle the largest of non-dangerous game.

The 300-grain Swift A-Frame shot almost as well from my .375 H&H, and it was this bullet that I took along on my first safari, taking game from the size of steenbok and springbok all the way up to eland. I was, and still am, very impressed with this bullet, and found it very effective when I took a bison in South Dakota that weighed almost a ton. It also makes a decent long-range bullet, and when we absolutely couldn't get any closer to the eland herd, I settled the rifle against the ter-

(opposite) The incredible 300-grain Swift A-Frame, a good all-around bullet for the .375 H&H.

mite mound I wanted to use for a rest, and (gulp!) had to take a 400-yard shot. Good fortune showed its face, and thanks to the drop chart I had prepared, I put the bullet where it had to go and that eland bull resides in my trophy room.

The 300-grain Woodleigh Weldcore is a favorite among many African hunters who hunt in thick bushveld conditions, where the round nose and lower B.C. figure isn't a handicap.

Are you a fan of truly heavy-for-caliber bullets? Check out the Barnes 350-grain TSX, or the Norma African PH .375 H&H load featuring the Woodleigh 350-grain softpoint at a muzzle velocity of 2,300 fps. The 'heavy-and-slow' school of thought turns your .375 into a true heavyweight. I think this wide range of bullet weights and types of construction helps to demonstrate the true versatility of this caliber, and why it's become such an irrefutable classic.

THE .44 MAGNUM: A PISTOL HERO IN A RIFLE

Dirty Harry's baby makes for a good short-range medium game rifle, as many Northeast hunters can attest. Being a re-write of the classic .44 Special, with a bit of a longer case for safety purposes, any cartridge that Elmer Keith had a hand in designing has proven to be a winner. The Ruger Model 44 carbine was centered around this cartridge, and it was also offered in my buddy Terry Marold's favorite: a Remington Model 788 bolt-action.

There are others, like the Ruger 77/44, and I think there is enough of a market to keep the lever-action and bolt-action .44 Magnum rifles in production for years to come. The round makes for a powerful, yet low-recoiling option for those of us who hunt in the woods where shots average around 75 yards. The traditional load is a 0.429" diameter, 240-grain jacketed hollow-point bullet at 1,750 fps, which Federal loads, and which will handle black bear, deer, and hogs quite well. The pistol bullets generally have a low B.C. and S.D. value, and that tends to limit both effective trajectory and penetration.

There are, however, some great newer loads that have extended the versatility of the .44, and Hornady is at the head of the pack again with their FTX bullet in the LeveRevolution line. Using a 225-grain rubber-tipped spitzer, Hornady's load gives 1,870 fps out of a 20" barreled rifle, maintaining over 1,000 ft.-lbs. of energy at the 100 yard mark.

Another company that has totally embraced the lever gun cartridges, with an unprecedented fervor, is Buffalo Bore. I first came across them when looking for a .45-70 Government load with some hair on it, so Ol' Grumpy Pants could effectively hunt bison with

his Browning Centennial Model 1886, and these folks deliver the goods.

They offer several loads for the .44 Remington Magnum, and all are worth a long look. They realize the wisdom of the lighter all-copper bullets, like the Barnes 225-grain XPB, delivered at a muzzle velocity of 1,700 fps, to the +P+ 340-grain flatpoint hard-cast lead load, designed for the strongest .44 Magnum actions. I like the 300-grain flatpoint hard-cast lead bullet at 1,770 fps, as the bullet weight will give good weight retention, and the higher velocity gives good kinetic energy. I would choose this load in a heartbeat for black bear over bait, or whitetails in the thick brush of a recently cut timber patch.

Grizzly Cartridge Company produces a great load using 270-grain Hawk bonded core, jacketed flatpoints. Bonding the core to the jacket will ensure

The .44 Remington Magnum with 240-grain hollowpoints.

the bullet will hang together upon impact, as the bonding process does not allow the jacket and core to separate. Considering that most loads for the .44 Remington Magnum are centered around pistol bullets, the fact that your projectile will hold together should engender a whole lot of confidence in your rifle.

Double Tap Ammunition offers the 300-grain Nosler jacketed hollowpoint in their lineup of semi-custom ammo, and that should prove to be a good choice for deer and black bear. Hornady loads their fabulous 240-grain XTP in their factory ammo, and I've had nothing but good results with this bullet, in any caliber. Cor-Bon uses a truncated cone hollowpoint in its 240-grain load, and Cor-Bon is another brand that has been very reliable in my experience.

The .44 Remington Magnum was never, nor ever will be, a long-range affair, but it is one of those cartridges that are so good at what they're designed to do, that it'll be around for years to come.

THE .444 MARLIN: A .44 MAGNUM ON STEROIDS

Lever gun lovers quickly took to this cartridge, and with good reason. The Marlin Model 444 lever-action rifle was introduced at a time when there was no commercially produced rifle chambered for the .45-70 Government. Marlin saw the opportunity to enter the heavy-bore lever gun market with their beefed up .44 Magnum design, and the hunting world was accepting.

Like the .35 calibers, the .444 can shoot the lighter 180 and 200-grain pistol bullets designed for the .44 Magnum, but they aren't a good choice for hunting purposes. The jacket of a pistol bullet is thinner than those of rifle bullets, so that it will expand at the lower velocities that a pistol generates.

The .444 operates best with bullets of 220 grains to 300 grains, with a thick jacket, or of hard-cast lead. Rem-

ington's Express Rifle ammunition is loaded with their 240-grain jacketed softpoint flatnose bullet, at 2,350 fps, and that combination has proved to be a very effective one for deer, hogs and black bear. For handloaders, Sierra's 240-grain jacketed hollowpoint is a good medium game bullet. But if you're after a load that might give a better trajectory, yet is tough enough to hold together on big black bears or hogs, look into Cor-Bon's 225-grain Barnes TSX load in their DPX line of ammunition. The TSX will open perfectly at .444 velocity, and this load pushes it at a muzzle velocity of 2,200 fps.

Hornady makes a beefy load for the .444, in their Superformance line. Using the InterLock 265-grain flatpoint at 2,400 fps, this is a good choice for an all-around big game load in your lever gun. The Hornady folks have also updated the performance of the .444 Marlin by making the FTX spitzer bullet, with the rubbery polymer tip designed to be safe for use in the tubular magazine of the Model 444, and giving the downrange benefits of the spitzer design.

Allow me to demonstrate the difference in trajectory and energy between similar weight bullets. Let's compare the performance, between 200 and 300 yards, of the 270-grain jacketed flatpoint load from Buffalo Bore, and the 265-grain FTX from Hornady.

Using a common muzzle velocity of 2,400 fps, and a 100-yard zero, the Buffalo Bore bullet will strike 8.2" low at 200, and 30.0" low at 300. The Hornady FTX spitzer will strike 6.9" low at 200, and 25.9" low at 300. That is an appreciable difference, should a shot at those distances present itself. The retained energy is also worth looking at. The Buffalo Bore load has 1,561 ft.-lbs of energy at 200, and 1,029 ft.-lbs at 300, while the FTX bullet has 1,729 ft.-lbs at 200 and 1,207 ft.-lbs at the 300-yard mark.

Depending on the distance, the

spitzer bullet with a higher ballistic coefficient gives a 15-20 percent advantage over the flatpoint. Now, most users of the .444 Marlin wouldn't consider it to be a 300-yard gun, but with that FTX bullet, 300 yards isn't off the menu.

If you like the heavyweight bullets for your .444, and there are lots of reasons to love them, there are plenty of good choices. Grizzly Cartridge Company offers a 320-grain flatpoint lead bullet at 2,050 fps that is heat treated for deep penetration, even if strong gristle plates or shoulder bones are hit. This load gives just shy of 3,000 ft.-lbs at the muzzle, and would be a wise choice if the shooting distances are on the short side.

Grizzly also loads its proprietary PUNCH bullet, in 300 grains at 2,000 fps, for the .444 Marlin. The PUNCH is a machined brass flatpoint bullet, with a lead insert that Grizzly designs for penetration alone. Retained weight is very close to 100 percent, and the reports indicate complete lengthwise penetration on hogs and other tough game.

.45 CALIBER CARTRIDGES

THE .45-70 GOVERNMENT: THREE CARTRIDGES IN ONE

One of the oldest metallic cartridges still in common use today, the venerable .45-70 Government has been with us since 1873. The U.S. Army adopted the Model 1873 Springfield, commonly referred to the "Trapdoor Springfield", and the initial military load used a 405-grain lead bullet over 70 grains of black powder; hence the cartridge designation of .45-70-405. It has since been shortened to .45-70, and the Government title added at the end.

The black powder loading has become a rarity in this age of smokeless powder, but some of the Trapdoor rifles, be they original or replica, are still in use today. The pressure limits of those Trapdoor ri-

The cowboy favorite: .45/70, with Remington 300-grain hollowpoint bullets. (J.P. Fielding photo)

fles are rather low, and the ammunition fired from them must be held to correspondingly low pressures. It didn't take long though, before the sporting arms began to be produced for the military cartridge. The famous Model 1886 Winchester was chambered for the .45-70, as were many Sharps rolling block single-shot rifles.

The newer lever-action rifles have been designed to withstand much higher pressures, and the Marlin 1895 and Browning 1886 are two examples. They can handle 'hotter' ammunition, and therefore generate greater energies. As I'm about to describe, there are factory loads on the market that are safe to use in these modern, stronger lever actions that are highly dangerous to use in the older style rifles.

And then, there is the Ruger No. 1 single shot, which is capable of handling all kinds of pressure. This rifle, and this rifle alone, can withstand the highest of pressures. You must be absolutely sure of the ammunition you're purchasing so as not to create a potentially fatal situation in your .45-70 rifle.

The standard factory loads are suitable for any .45-70, and are relatively anemic. They usually feature two bullets: a 300-grain jacketed hollowpoint, and a 405-grain jacketed flatpoint.

The 300-grain load operates at a muzzle velocity of just over 1,800 fps, and the Remington Express and Federal Power Shok lines adhere to this formula. For deer-sized game, the standard cup-and-core bullets will perform just fine. I've watched Ol' Grumpy Pants nearly flip deer backward with the Remington load from his '86 Browning. The 405-grain flatpoints run at a muzzle velocity of just under 1,350 fps, but if you're after boar or bear at close quarters, this is the load that made the .45-70's reputation as a heavy hitter. This load is often carried by Alaskan bear guides as backup in the alder thickets.

Hornady's LeveRevoultion line didn't neglect the .45-70 Government; as a matter of fact there are two bullets for the old thumper. The regular FTX bullet in a 325-grain weight is loaded to 2,050 fps, and will give similar benefits to trajectory as we described in the .444 Marlin section. The 250-grain Mono-Flex bullet is loaded to the same veloc-

ity, but it is an all-copper, polymer-tip spitzer. If you were looking for a long-range load for deer or hogs in your .45-70, I believe this would be a good place to start. This load should work in all the .45-70 rifles, irrespective of vintage.

When Ol' Grumpy Pants and I were heading out to South Dakota to hunt bison at the Triple U Ranch, he insisted on using his .45-70 Browning Model 1886. I told him that we should seek out a load that had a bit more kinetic energy than the standard 405-grain load. The first load we tried was Buffalo Bore's 405-grain jacketed flatpoint, at 2,000 fps, which proved to be plenty accurate. It was I who talked GP into

Federal's 300-grain hollowpoint load for the .45/70 Government.

letting me handload his cartridges for this hunt, and only because I'd discovered the Swift A-Frame, in .458" caliber, and a flatpoint 400-grainer to boot.

While with canister-grade powders I couldn't quite equal the velocity of the Buffalo Bore ammo, I did get 1,875 fps with no pressure signs at all, and the accuracy was on par with the factory stuff. I felt (and still feel) that the bonded core and partitioned bullet was a bit of a better choice for an animal the size of a bison, and when that bullet hit the tatanka's neck bone, 1,700 pounds of Americana hit the ground like a giant sack of flour.

Loads for the Ruger No. 1 can be very impressive. The 500-grain bullets can be pushed to respectable velocities, which take the .45-70 into a totally different class, truly capable of all dangerous game lighter than elephant. They can be pushed to 1,800 fps, only 300

fps behind the .458 Winchester Magnum. Load a Hornady 350-grain flatpoint to 2,200 fps, and you've got a fantastic bear load.

The premium bullets are well represented among modern .45-70 loads. The Barnes Vortex series of ammunition provides the .45-70 shooter with their 300-grain TSX flat point at 1,900 fps, while Buffalo Bore loads the Barnes 350-grain TSX at 2,150 fps. The former allows any .45/70 rifle to benefit from the performance of the famous TSX bullet, while the latter gives those with the strong actions a serious big game load to enjoy.

Federal Fusion makes a 300-grain bonded-core flatpoint, that will hold together much better than a standard cup-and-core bullet. Grizzly Cartridge loads the Hawk 405-grain bonded-core flatpoint to 2,000 fps, perfect for the biggest game this continent has to offer.

The Buffalo Bore .45/70 'Magnum' load, designed for the stronger rifle actions.

Swift's 400-grain A-Frame in .458-caliber makes a great .45/70 bullet.

The .45-70 also has the benefit of performing very well with cast lead bullets. Cor-Bon, Black Hills and UltraMax all offer mean-looking, hard-cast lead loads weighing between 350 and 450 grains, and these will perform very well on larger game, if you keep the distances sane.

THE .450 MARLIN: A LEVER GUN CARTRIDGE WITH A BELT

Hornady and Marlin teamed up to produce a cartridge that was the ballistic equivalent of the hotter .45-70 loads, without the possibility of being fired in the wrong rifle. They settled on a belted magnum design, based on the belted .458 Winchester Magnum, but with one small change: They had to make the standard .375–sized belt longer, to prevent the cartridge from chambering in any of the longer magnum chambers that use a smaller-diameter bullet, to

prevent any catastrophic results.

Released in 2000, the Marlin rifle was discontinued in 2009. Look to Buffalo Bore for a good selection of bullets, including a 405-grain jacketed flatpoint at 1,900 fps, and a big 500-grain Barnes Buster Penetrator FMJ at just over 1,600 fps. Having had a hand in its development, Hornady loads that 325-grain FTX spitzer bullet I told you of in the .45-70 section for the .450 Marlin.

I'd like to see what the .450 Marlin could do when loaded with a Cutting Edge Bullets 370-grain Lever+ Raptor. The all-copper, lathe-turned hollowpoint beast of a bullet should prove a match for any game animal on the North American continent, and damned near all that roam the African continent. I don't think that velocities for this bullet would fall very shy of 2,000 fps, if they fall shy of that number at all, and the stout construction of the Cutting Edge design would engender all sorts of confidence for the hunter who prefers the lever actions.

CHAPTER 6

DANGEROUS GAME RIFLES

When we speak of dangerous game, my ears prick up like a spaniel at the mention of a car ride. The mere fact that the entire hunt could end in loss of limb (or worse, life) is not only exciting, but defines the 'man v. nature' premise of so many adventure stories. Grizzly bears, with jowls flapping and teeth bared, lions roaring in the predawn darkness, the manner in which a leopard seemingly floats into a baited tree, the Cape buffalo, whose nickname "Black Death" is well deserved, and the mighty African elephant, weight measured in tons: these animals both frighten and excite.

It takes a hunter with great confi-

The classic .416 Rigby.
(J.P. Fielding photo)

dence in his or her field skills to pursue these creatures, and a healthy dose of respect for the possible outcome. This category of game animal certainly warrants the best hunting gear available, but no hand-rubbed walnut stock or fancy engraving has ever made the difference in life or death; it is the bullet - and only the bullet - that decides in whose favor the scales will tip.

Cartridges for this type of game extend from the 6.5mm and .270 class, for leopard alone, through the .300 and .338s for grizzly bears, and then from the 9.3mms well up into the .500s and above, for lion, buffalo and elephant. Rather than handle the idea by caliber, let's look at suitable bullets for each game animal, with some reasons for the recommendation.

LEOPARD: THE GOLDEN-SPOTTED WRAITH

The lightest of the dangerous cats, the leopard, does not require a huge bore to kill effectively. I've touched on the idea in the medium game chapter, but I believe some more light needs to be shed on the topic. A leopard is no tougher than any deer, and the same calibers and bullets that perform well on deer will effectively kill a leopard, with one little asterisk: Once a leopard is wounded, the entire game changes. They will usually seek ridiculously thick cover, and charges from wounded leopards are the stuff of nightmares.

That said, I'd pick your favorite deer bullet (and rifle), make sure you have the accuracy necessary to put that bullet exactly where your Professional Hunter tells you to, and practice, practice, practice.

The one area that I think is important is the sectional density of the bullet. Although you can kill a leopard cleanly with a light-for-caliber bullet, I like things on the heavy side of the scale, to absolutely guarantee destruction of the vitals. For example, I've cleanly killed deer with 125-grain Nosler Ballistic Tips from my little .308 Winchester, but I wouldn't venture across the pond with that load and a leopard in mind. I would however, do so with 165-grain Ballistic Tips, and quite confidently I might add.

Bullets like the Sierra Game King hollowpoint boat-tail, available in sensible weights in 6.5, .270, 7mm and .308, would make a great leopard bullet. The jacket is thickened to give good weight retention, but the hydrostatic shock from the expansion of the hollowpoint is plenty sufficient to switch the nervous system of Mr. Spots to the 'off' position. Check with the PH about

caliber minimums; Tanzania for example requires a minimum of .375" diameter to hunt any dangerous game, yet Zimbabwe allows anything above .270" diameter.

The traditional softpoints, like a Hornady InterLock or Remington Core-Lokt, if of suitable weight, can make for a good leopard bullet, but in the cartridges that deliver a higher-than-normal impact velocity, there can be excessive hide damage. Now, a taxidermist can do wonderful things, but we should avoid putting softball sized holes in the

leopard skin if we can help it.

Some of the heavier cup-and-core bullets will fit the bill perfectly, and there are no flies on a good roundnose. You want good expansion for hydraulic shock, but not so much that penetration suffers.

In a recent trip to the Federal Premium factory in Anoka, Minnesota, I had the opportunity to punch some good .30-'06 bullets into blocks of ballistic gelatin, to get a feel for the balance of expansion and penetration, and this demonstrates well what we're after in a leopard bullet. The Nosler Partition, after almost 70 years, proved to me in the lab what I'd always found in the field: that the softer nose section would open like a true softpoint and the rear core hung together for good penetration.

The Trophy Bonded Tipped gave great performance as well. It provided a huge wound channel and the bullet expanded nicely, to over two times the original diameter, while retaining weight into the 80 percent range. The Trophy Copper gave similar performance, with its copper petals well ex-

A lineup of expanded .30-'06 bullets, showing different levels of expansion and weight retention.

panded, while giving a large wound channel.

Federal's 150-grain softpoint did exactly what I thought it would: radical expansion with a much lower retained weight. Now, that bullet didn't 'fail' because it expanded so much, but it might make a bit more of a mess than would a 165 or 180-grain softpoint.

Oh, and by the way, when folks like Sierra warn us hunters not to shoot big game with match-grade bullets, they mean it. The 168 Match Kings broke to pieces in the gel, and pieces of jacket and core went all over the place, sending a shower of glass down from the ceiling. Federal, I'm sorry, and I'll replace that fluorescent light bulb.

The goal with a leopard is to have a rifle that you shoot the most accurately, as shot placement is paramount. Whether it's a 7mm Remington Magnum, .30-'06 Springfield, or some variety of .300 Magnum, putting that bullet into the vitals has never been more important.

Should you want a good leopard bullet for your 9.3mm, .375 or .416, stay away from the premium bullets altogether, and opt instead for a good cup-and-core bullet for more rapid expansion. The premiums will often punch a caliber-sized hole through the cat, which will kill him in the end, but in the meantime he may enjoy his last minutes on earth gnawing upon your person. In the 9.3mm cases, I like the Hornady 286-grain InterLock.

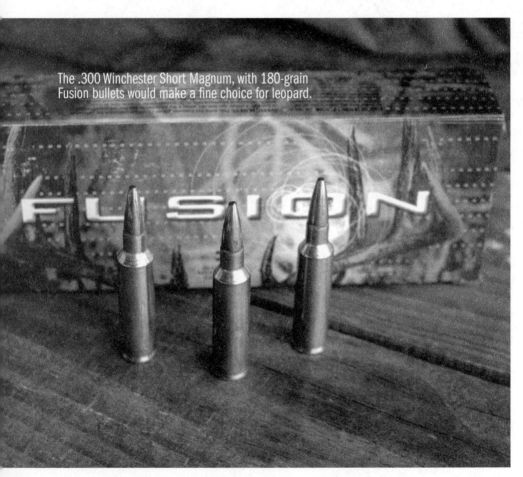

The .300 Winchester Short Magnum, with 180-grain Fusion bullets would make a fine choice for leopard.

Sierra 220-grain spitzer boat-tail, 8mm caliber, a good leopard bullet.

The Sierra 250-grain boat-tail is a good choice in .375 bore, as is the Hornady InterLock 270-grain spitzer and the 300-grain InterLock roundnose. Even a Remington Core-Lokt or Winchester Power Point will do the job well; you're after expansion here, yet you can feel confident knowing a bullet of that size and weight will clearly penetrate the entire leopard and ruin his day quickly. Same goes for the .416s and .404s: look for a classic cup-and-core roundnose or soft-point spitzer to give the hydrostatic shock that you're after, and if you put that bullet through the vitals your cat will be in the salt.

LION: TEETH AND MUSCLE COVERED IN TAWNY FUR

The largest of African cats is a totally different character than the leopard, weighing two to three times that of that spotted ninja. They also have canine teeth that can crush your skull with one bite. They are an apex preda-

tor, and have intrigued mankind from the dawn of history. Regal, brutal, terrible, magnificent, triumphant; the lion has been the stuff of wondrous tales and family crests for thousands of years.

The hunting of lion is now a political hotbed, but if you're well-heeled enough to book a safari for Simba, bullet choice is paramount. Caliber-wise, the lion demands a heavy bullet, though many have been taken (with varying degrees of success) with 6.5mm, 7mm and .30-caliber bullets. Most African countries prohibit the use of bore diameters less than .375", and that makes much sense, but some permit the use of lesser calibers. The tough, corded muscles that a lion is built of will give a bullet of lighter weight and caliber a run for its money, but there are sensible choices.

I think the 9.3mm cartridges are on par with the .375s, when it comes to good lion medicine. They can use bullets of .366" diameter from 250 to 300 grains, with the 286-grain being a good blend of speed and bullet weight. There are many 9.3s, from the 9.3x62mm and 9.3x64mm, to the .370 Sako Magnum, to the venerable and relatively sedate 9.3x74R designed for single shots and double rifles.

Were I pursuing Panthera Leo with a 9.3, I'd probably opt for the 9.3x62 in a handy rifle, or the newer .370 Sako, for its speed and hydraulic shock. Hornady's Dangerous Game series offers a 9.3x62 load featuring the 286-grain InterLock spitzer at a muzzle velocity of 2,360 fps. That bullet is heavy enough to penetrate, yet the cup-and-core design will expand very well to create a nasty wound channel.

The Federal Premium Safari line loads the .370 Sako Magnum with the 286-grain Barnes TSX and Swift A-Frame. This is one instance where I think the Swift A-Frame is a bit too good, or better put, there isn't enough lion to get that bullet to expand well. Penetration with an A-Frame is never an issue, especially at the relatively short distances at which lions are hunted. I would opt for the hollowpoint TSX in the factory load, delivered at 2,550 fps, which should open up and switch that lion to the off position.

The long, lean 9.3x74 operates at the same muzzle velocity as the 9.3x62, so the same bullets can be recommended. Were I handloading for any one of the 9.3mm for a lion hunt, I'd opt for the 250-grain NorthFork semi-spitzer, as the higher velocity would open the bullet up a bit more, creating a larger wound channel.

The .375 Holland & Holland Magnum, pushing a 300-grain bullet at 2,550 fps, is just about the perfect lion rifle. Like the leopard, you'll want a stout bullet, but not too tough. Bullet profile really doesn't matter here, as the shots on lion are generally over bait, and mostly at less than 100 paces. I like the 270 and 300-grain .375s, like the Sierra 300-grain Game King, with a tough jacket, but still a nose soft enough to give good expansion.

Norma loads the 300-grain Oryx bullet, which should prove to be a fantastic lion load. Hornady's Superformance .375 H&H load is built around the 270-grain InterLock bullet, and is just about a perfect lion bullet. A-Square made a frangible softpoint specifically for Mr. Leo: the Lion Load. It was the same size and shape as their Dead Tough, but was easily mistaken for the tougher bullet, with disastrous results. You definitely don't want to shoot a buffalo with the Lion Load. Remember, most of the premium bullets designed for dangerous game are a bit too tough to open up enough to do the kind damage you'll want to do on a lion.

I say most, because some are soft enough to do the job properly. A Nosler Partition in .375", weighing 260 grains, should give a good blend of hydrostatic shock and deep penetration, as the Partition has a reputation of being soft, up front. North Fork makes a special bullet for the cats: the 300-grain Percussion Point. Scored just behind the meplat, it will give rapid expansion in the front end, yet like the Partition, the rear portion will drive deep into the cat's vitals.

A new and different style of bullet, which should work perfect on lion, is the Cutting Edge Bullets Safari Raptor. It is an all-copper spitzer, with a black polymer tip sitting in a hollow point. The bullet's nose, once it impacts, breaks into a set of 'blades' that create severe tissue damage and trauma. The remainder of the bullet, being a solid copper slug, continues to drive through the animal, for deep penetration into the vitals. I have used them in my .300 Winchester Magnum (but not on lion), and they are very accurate. Field reports continue to roll in, with positive results. A 300-grain Safari Raptor in .375, or a .416 in 300 grains or even 325 grains, made of all copper, should handle the king of the jungle quite well.

The trio of North Fork bullets: the Flat Point Solid, the bonded core Semi-Spitzer and the Percussion Point. Shown here in .410" diameter for the .450/400 3" Nitro Express.

Cutting Edge Bullets 325-grain Safari Raptor, a lightweight choice for the .416 calibers.

A 250-grain Barnes TTSX in .375" diameter should work well, when the hollowpoint opens rapidly from the higher velocity of 2,700 fps. This would also make a good choice for a dual-purpose bullet on lion/plains game.

If you like heavy bullets, take a look at Norma's African PH load for the .375 H&H featuring a 350-grain Woodleigh Soft Point. Plenty heavy enough even for shots at the lion's rear, it should give good expansion and its weight will carry the bullet through the entire length of the cat. All that I have told you about the .375 H&H can be said for the .375 Ruger, as they are so close in performance that the lion will never know the difference.

Jumping up in caliber to the popular .416s, you'll want to be even more careful; the bullets are verily designed for thick-skinned game. Were I grabbing my beloved .416 Remington for a lion hunt, I'd load the 400-grain Hornady InterLock roundnose to an even 2,400 fps and hunt confidently. The Norma African PH load with a 450-grain Woodleigh soft point at 2,150 fps, in either .416 Remington or the epic .416 Rigby would make a close second choice. I like the thought of a heavy, slow bullet tearing large holes in the lion, so the lion doesn't tear large holes in me. I'd avoid the Hornady DGX line of ammunition, because as good as they are for buffalo and grizzly, they are probably a touch too stiff for the lion.

For those who are fans of the .458s, whether a .458 Winchester Magnum, .458 Lott or .450 Nitro Express, I'd recommend the lighter-for-caliber and inexpensive 350 and 405-grain softpoint bullets, to raise the velocity and give better expansion. They can be pushed to right around 2,400 fps from the smallest .45 safari cartridges, and will make good lion medicine. Hornady's 350-grain roundnose InterLock will fit the bill, but avoid the hollowpoint 300-grainers, as they are designed for the slower .45-70 Government, and might not give the necessary penetration for a lion.

Author's favorite dangerous game caliber, the .416 Remington Magnum, with the Norma load using 450-grain Woodleigh Weldcore bullets.

GRIZZLY: URSUS ARCTOS HORRIBILUS, THE HORRIBLE BEAR

The second largest carnivore on earth (the polar bear is bigger), these popular game animals roam the north- ern reaches of Canada and Alaska, with a presence in Montana, Wyoming and Idaho. Even the smallest of the subspecies can weigh between 400 and 800 lbs., with the coastal brown bears tipping the scales at over 1,500 lbs. That, my friend, is an animal that will get

your attention in a heartbeat. With claws that will open you like a box cutter, and teeth to match, you'll not want to save money on discount ammunition for this hunt.

They require the best expanding bullets available, and I'll recommend that you carry the biggest bore that you can shoot effectively. Please re-read the last half of that sentence; carrying an elephant rifle that you can't shoot well does you no good. You must be able to put the bullet in the bear's vitals. Ol' Grumpy Pants and I go around and around about the sensible minimum caliber for a grizzly bear. He feels that a heavy 7mm 175-grain or 220-grain .30 would work very effectively in the hands of a good shot, while I feel that heavier bullets and bigger calibers are the best tools for the job. In truth, we are both correct.

The .300 Winchester Magnum with 200-grain Swift A-Frame bullets. (J.P. Fielding photo)

The .416 Rigby with suitable premium bullets.

The bullets of today have changed the game, and a 7mm Remington Magnum loaded with 175-grain Swift A-Frames, or a .30-'06 Springfield with a 220-grain Nosler Partition will indeed kill a grizzly, even a coastal brown. They penetrate well, carry a good payload of energy and can be an effective tool. However, there are better choices, and I feel that when your life is on the line, not to mention the huge sums of money involved in hunting the great bears, it's worthwhile to pick a larger caliber.

I like what the .338 Winchester Magnum and .340 Weatherby do with 250-grain Swift A-Frames and Barnes TSX bullets, or for those who are recoil sensitive, a .35 Whelen with 250-grain Partitions or North Fork semi-spitzers would work good also. But if I were heading north to Alaska, I'd consider my .375 H&H a good choice, and my .416 Remington even better.

The 300 and 400-grain bullets will stop a charge of a wounded grizzly

bear in the thick alders or willow flats better than any lesser bullet. I like the way both these rifles shoot those Swift A-Frame bullets, and the Hornady DGX and Woodleigh Weldcore would be on the menu as well. Those DGX bullets have a copper-clad steel jacket, and a core of lead with high antimony content. These bullets will break the heavy bones and tear through the huge muscles that shroud the grizzly's vitals. Hornady's DGX load in a .416 Rigby will have a dramatic effect on even the largest coastal grizzly.

The .375 H&H, loaded with a 300-grain bullet at 2,550 fps will deliver over 4,000 ft.-lbs. of energy at the muzzle, while both the .416 Remington and its older brother the .416 Rigby give 5,000 ft.-lbs. when shooting the 400-grain bullets at 2,400 fps. You'll notice that the classic dangerous game calibers usually run at a muzzle velocity of 2,100 to 2,500 fps. This is due to the fact that most soft-point bullets perform best against large slabs of mammal at those velocities, but we'll discuss this further in the Cape buffalo section.

The larger-cased .375 bores, like the .378 Weatherby Magnum and the .375 Remington Ultra Magnum, require the best premium bullets, as their velocities are 300 or more fps faster than the .375 H&H. The recoil ramps up dramatically, but for the hunter who can handle it they are effective. Look to the mono-metals, like the 300-grain Barnes TSX or even the huge 350-grain TSX for an impressive grizzly load.

If you like sectional density, here is a winner: The Barnes TSX in .375" caliber, at a whopping 350 grains.

The .458 Winchester Magnum and .458 Lott, in the hands of the hunter who can hit his mark, will make any grizzly bear guide smile when he meets his hunter in camp. Or, maybe another way to put it is like this: you'll often see a .375 H&H or Ruger, a .416 of some noble house, or a .458 of some variety in the hands of a bear guide, and with good cause. These rifles can very effectively stop a bear in its tracks. The quick-handling lever-action rifles chambered to the .45-70 Government are a popular choice in the thickets of the Alaskan peninsula.

The 140-year-old cartridge is still viable there, especially when combined with the firepower of the lever action.

The 300-grain Fusion load in .45/70 makes a good bear load.

The newer rifles, capable of handling much higher pressures than the Springfield Trapdoor and its ilk, can shoot the revved-up loadings offered today. Buffalo Bore Ammunition makes a 400-grain softpoint load that runs at 2,000 fps, which will make a great grizzly load. I've loaded the 400-grain flatpoint Swift A-Frame in GP's 1886 Browning .45-70 for a bison hunt, the velocities were 1,850 fps, and it worked very well on a 1,700 lb. bull.

I would have no hesitation in using that same load on a grizzly or brown bear at under 100 yards, and that handicap is based on the iron sights on the rifle and my old eyes, not the load.

In the .458 Winchester and Lott, I like the 500-grain bullets, at velocities between 2,100 and 2,300 fps. Swift A-Frame, Nosler Partition, Hornady DGX,

Barnes TSX, North Fork semi-spitzer; they all will work just fine. Granted, this level of recoil is not for the faint of heart, these are true stopping rifles, capable of handling anything on earth with four feet and a heartbeat, but if you can shoot it, you'll feel a foot taller. And your guide will sleep that much better in camp.

Most grizzly bears are shot at relatively short range, that is, less than 200 yards. This makes it a pretty even playing field between the spitzer and round-nosed bullets, so don't discount the older design. The larger frontal diameter of a round nose generally causes a 'shudder' effect when it strikes a game animal, and often it is visible through the riflescope. I know for sure that if I were following a wounded grizzly into the willow thicket, I'd feel very comfortable with a large-diameter, heavy-for-caliber roundnose in the chamber.

Author with Cape buffalo bull in Zambia, taken with 400-grain Swift A-Frame bullets in .416 Remington Magnum.

CAPE BUFFALO: BLACK DEATH

There have been volumes of material written about the Cape buffalo: its tenacity, its adrenalin level, and its ability to soak up copious amounts of lead. Stories of hunters being gored, trampled, and thrown are not hard to find. One thing is for sure: you want to put that first bullet perfectly into the buffalo's vital organs, because a wounded Nyati is a very scary thing. There has been an ongoing campfire debate about the proper bullet for hunting buffalo, and it rages on today. Essentially, there are three schools of thought.

The first (and oldest) is that you use only bullets with no exposed lead. These are the full metal jacket, or full patch bullets, and the more modern style are constructed of a homogenous metal, that are commonly referred to as "solids." They offer no expansion, but

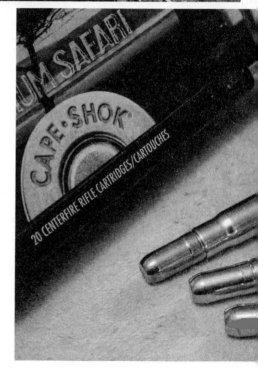

(above) 416 Remington Magnum, with 400-grain Swift A-Frame premium softpoints and 400-grain Hornady solids. (J.P. Fielding photo)

(left) The Trophy Bonded Sledgehammer solid, in .375 H&H Magnum.

give fantastic penetration. The second school of thought is to load a premium softpoint bullet for the first shot, and load the remainder of the magazine with solids for any backup shots.

This gives the advantage of an expanded bullet for the initial shot, and then the great penetration of the solids should you have to shoot the buffalo while it is running away. Shots into a running buffalo's rear are not uncommon, and the solids can penetrate the entire length of a buffalo. The third, and newest, way of thinking is that the premium softpoints of today are so well built that penetration is not an issue.

The 400-grain .416 Swift A-Frame, recovered from a Cape buffalo. Great expansion and penetration, they were resting against the off-side skin.

So which one of these ideas is right? Surely we must examine the shape and construction of the new bullets available to the buffalo hunter to make a proper, informed decision. And let me put this out there before we delve too deeply: consult your professional hunter prior to your safari and find out what he wants to see in your rifle. Ultimately, he must feel as comfortable as possible with what you're shooting, as it's his responsibility to ensure that you come home in one piece, as well as to clean up messes like wounded bovines in the thick stuff.

I think that the historical choice of 'solids only on buff' has its roots in the failure of traditional softpoint bullets.

There have been thousands of buffalo killed with the softpoints made in

the early 20th century, and the quality of those bullets has drastically improved over the last half-century. But many PHs still feel more comfortable with more penetration than expansion, and a solid bullet will "let the air out" of any buffalo. This deep penetration can pose a bit of a problem though. If there are animals behind the bull you wish to kill, the solids can (and often will) completely penetrate the entire animal, and exit with enough retained energy to kill or wound unintended targets. So a hunter must be very careful to be sure the path behind his or her buffalo is clear of other buffalo in the herd.

The traditional 'solid' is a bullet with a lead core, and a thick jacket of copper-coated steel. In an ideal world, they do not deform, expand, or bend. If recovered, they will look just as they did before being fired, but with grooves from the rifling engraved into the jacket. They are often of roundnose design; some are tapered and some have parallel sides and a hemispherical nose section. The older model Hornady solid was a fantastic bullet, as was the Kyn-

The classic "T" on the flat meplat of the Federal Trophy Bonded Sledgehammer.

och, and often both would hit to the same point of impact as softpoints in my dangerous game rifles. But, like the softpoints, the game has changed with these bullets as well.

The traditional solid still exists, but there have been major improvements made in the technology. The parallel-sided, hemispherical nose solid is still with us, but improved in the form of the monometal homogenous solid. Barnes Banded Solids and the A-Square Monolithic solid are fine examples of this style bullet. They feed without issue from the box magazine of a bolt-action rifle, and are very accurate. The flatpoint solid, with a slightly tapered nose, is a popular model as well.

The Trophy Bonded Sledgehammer was among the first to adopt this design, and it has continued today in the North Fork Flat Point Solid. Made of solid brass, these are among the toughest bullets available. For buffalo, there are some new designs that have combined several new features with the concept of a monometal solid. Firstly, the North Fork Cup Solid is very similar in design to their flatpoint solid, with the exception of a shallow cup in

400-grain North Fork Cup solids, perfect for the follow-up on buffalo.

The Woodleigh
Hydrostatically Stabilized Solids.

the nose section.

What this does is give just the slightest bit of expansion to the nose of the bullet, creating a wound channel that won't seal as easy as if it were a hemispherical-nosed solid. I really like these bullets for buffalo, and I've seen folks using them on the gamut of plains game as well, with good effect.

Woodleigh has introduced the Hydrostatically Stabilized Solid, and it is loaded by Federal Premium in their line of safari ammunition. It has a funky-looking sort of nipple on the front of the solid, and that nipple is covered with a blue polymer tip that is hemispherical in shape. This blue 'nipple hat' allows the cartridge to feed perfectly from the magazine of a bolt-action rifle, and I'm very curious to see these recovered from buffalo, and hear the results of the wound channel created.

So, with these great solids available, are they the choice for your buffalo bullet? It depends. The premium softpoints of today have progressed so far

that professional hunters are coming to depend on them exclusively. Bullets like the Barnes TSX, Federal's Trophy Bonded, North Fork semi-spitzer and Swift A-Frame have really set the standard for ideal bullet performance when it comes to Nyati.

On both of my buffalo safaris, my professional hunters were younger than I was, and both were huge fans of the Barnes and Swift softpoints. Ironically, both of them also asked me to leave the solids I had brought along in camp; they saw I had 400-grain Swift A-Frames for my .416 Remington and felt completely confident using them for any backup shots that might have been needed.

Some PHs have suggested that the Nosler Partition is a bit too soft in the nose for frontal shots, but if the weight is chosen carefully, that is, heavy-for-caliber, I believe you'll be fine. The old A-Square Dead Tough was (and still is) a favorite of mine, and one of the nice features of that bullet is that it has the same shape and profile as the Monolithic Solids that A-Square makes.

As I promised in the grizzly section, we should discuss dangerous game cartridge velocity. There seems to be a magic number for dangerous game, and for game in general, under traditional circumstances. The velocity number is 2,400 fps. It was not discovered by me, but I first read about the observation in Kevin 'Doctari' Robertson's *The Perfect Shot*, and his observation has merit.

Loosely paraphrased, those cartridges with velocities that range between 2,100 fps and 2,400 fps have been heralded as "the classics", as these will deliver a bullet within the bore diameter with a S.D. of .300 or greater at those velocities. When it comes to the cup-and-core bullet of yesteryear, there were little-or-no premature breakup or penetration problems when this muzzle velocity was adhered to; when things got faster than 2,400 fps, or the bullets got lighter, penetration became an issue.

This theory holds especially true when the game gets as large as Cape buffalo. The black beasts have overlapping ribs, thick muscle, and huge shoulder bones. The skin of the chest region is loose enough to make traditional softpoints 'upset' too early in the wound channel, compromising penetration. This is one of the reasons that the ultra-fast Weatherby cartridges gained a sketchy reputation early on: the velocity was too high for the strength of the projectiles. I've seen solids that have bent at right angles, and laid eyes upon the softpoints that have just about broken apart.

Now I don't want to sound like I'm picking on the Weatherbys and other cartridges that run at faster velocities, but the classics are classics for a reason. I firmly believe that the super-fast cases are best used for longer shots, where their speed gets a chance to drop off to that of smaller cases at a short velocity. Dangerous game, generally speaking, is taken at relatively short ranges, and today's premium dangerous game bullets make the classics just that much more effective.

That said, I know people who've taken buffalo with traditional softpoints in dangerous game calibers, and I'm certain it could still be done, but when on a hunt of that magnitude, I think you owe it to yourself, your family, and the animal to use the readily available premium bullets of suitable construction and weight.

To answer my own rhetorical question, I personally subscribe to the second scenario, where I carry a premium softpoint in the chamber, and solids in the magazine for backup shots when hunting buffalo. I want to know I can penetrate the length of a buffalo's body from any angle, and I like those North Fork Cup Solids as my buffalo solid. There are still those 'old school' professional hunters who insist on using nothing but solids, but they are becoming fewer and fewer, once they see the performance of the premium softpoints. I suggest you listen to the man to whom you're paying all that money, and use the bullet he asks you too.

There are a couple of points of interest about those blunt-point solids that we should discuss. First, some bolt-action magazine rifles don't like to feed them well from the magazine, and I think this has to do with the rifle's feed ramp. No matter what, you must be absolutely certain that you can feed cartridges into the chamber reliably, every single time, without looking at the rifle. In all sincerity, your life may depend on it. Second, not all solids will hit the same point of aim as their softpoint counterparts.

It will take some experimentation on your part (read that as time spent at the range with your rifle), but you can find a combination of soft and solid that will work for you. Remember, if you're using solids for backup, odds are that the

The gargantuan .500 Nitro Express, shooting 570-grain bullets.

shot will be on the close side, as most buffalo shots are taken inside of 125 yards.

I like to shoot three-shot groups from my buffalo rifles, using one soft and two solids. I understand there has to be some leeway in the group assessment, but I will say that one of the beauties of the .375 H&H is that it does a fantastic job of putting bullets of different weight, shape, and construction to very near the same point of impact. My .416 Remington does that as well, although it took a little bit of reloading work to get that to happen.

If you choose to get nostalgic and pursue Cape buffalo with a double rifle (which I would love to do!), bullet selection becomes much more critical. A double rifle can be a very finicky creature. It is not easy to get two parallel barrels to hit to the same point of aim. The barrels are soldered together, and are 'regulated' with a certain weight bullet, moving at a particular speed. If you vary too awful far from that, things can get weird. I've done some loading work for guys with doubles

that wouldn't regulate well, and with specific powder charges and experimentation with bullet shape, we corrected most of the issue.

It is with the double rifle that you probably need to take the most time and thought into a combination of soft and solid. This is where the folks at Hornady have stepped up to the plate yet again, with their DGX/DGS line of ammunition. The softpoints and the solids have the same nose profile, and they are available in many of the classic double rifles calibers, like .450/.400 3", .450 NE (Nitro Express), .470 NE and the massive 500 NE. Many manufacturers of double rifles are regulating their guns with the Hornady ammunition. Hunting buffalo with a double requires that you get a bit closer than you might need to with a scoped rifle, but the up close experience is worth it.

Should you be a fan of the fast Weatherby cartridges for dangerous game, consider the best premium bullets for use on that which will bite, claw, or stomp you. Traditionally, Weatherby stuff was loaded with good, heavy

The .460 Weatherby Magnum is not for the recoil sensitive.

The .500 Jeffery's, with 535-grain Swift A-Frame softpoints.

cup-and-core bullets, but they are better performers with a bullet that can withstand the higher velocities Weatherby cartridges produce. My pal Kraig Kiger has a Mark V Weatherby in the enormous .460 Weatherby, which will certainly generate the ballistics necessary to cleanly kill any buffalo.

He has a vintage box of Weatherby 500-grain softpoints, which should suffice, but load that giant case with a 500-grain Woodleigh, Barnes TSX or Swift A-Frame and you'll avoid any question of bullet failure. Considering that the .460 pushes a 500-grain bullet at 2,900 fps, it takes a muzzle brake and a pair of brass ones to shoot that cannon accurately, but if you can, you've got a stopping rifle for sure.

There are some good bolt-action rifles on the market, in calibers usually reserved for the professional hunters. If you have a desire to use one, please be sure and practice like crazy with it. The difference in size (although very significant) between the .375 H&H and the .500 Jeffrey's won't make up for poor shooting. A .375 in the right place will kill better than a .500 in the wrong place. And those .500s do kick!

LOXODONTA AFRICANA: THE AFRICAN ELEPHANT

Hunting the mighty African elephant is a source of controversy these days, but to help with the overpopulation of the species, and to better manage and keep a healthy herd, hunting is a very effective tool. Controversy aside, if you are lucky enough to be able to pursue a Jumbo with rifle in hand, you'll be shooting a solid for sure.

The most popular shot on an African elephant is the brain shot, which puts the animal down quickly and cleanly, but requires that you penetrate over two feet of honeycombed bone if you take the frontal shot.

George Gibbs' .505 cartridge, with Cor-Bon and Norma ammunition. (J.P. Fielding photo)

Now, our premium softpoints are fantastic, but for this kind of work we want the penetration that only a solid can deliver. Furthermore, I personally like the idea of the monometal solids, which have much less of a chance to bend, break or deform than the copper and steel coated lead models.

The flatpoint monometal solids have been giving incredible results when the autopsy is performed on a hunted elephant. They are giving straight-line penetration, and plenty of it at that. Be careful with these, because as good as they penetrate on the frontal shot, if you take a side-on brain shot the bullet can exit the skull and kill or wound animals behind your target.

It is pretty well accepted that the .375 H&H is the minimum accepted

The .458 Winchester Magnum, and its big brother, the .458 Lott.

cartridge for hunting elephant, and I'd tend to agree with that. Many lesser cartridges have killed elephant cleanly (the .318 Westley Richards and 9.3x62mm come to mind), but there have been many wounded elephant and many wounded hunters from trying to use too small a rifle.

In the .375 H&H and other cases with that bore diameter, I like the 300-grain

monometal solids, like the North Fork flatpoint solid, the Trophy Bonded Sledgehammer, Woodleigh Hydrostatically Stabilized, and the Barnes Banded Solid. They all have a fantastic reputation throughout Africa, and just about any PH on the continent will sing the praises of the penetration capabilities of those long 300-grain .375s.

The traditional solids will still work, such as the heavy full metal jackets produced by Woodleigh, but I have heard stories and seen photos of steel and copper-covered lead bullets that bent at right angles, or that were sent on a strange path once that bullet hit the honeycombed skull of the elephant. This has been known to result in an elephant that is knocked out by the shot, but eventually 'comes-to' and is none too happy about your efforts to kill him. One of the features of the .375 bores is that they are relatively easy to shoot, and accuracy is as important - if not more important - than bore diameter. A PH would much rather have a client who can shoot his or her .375 accurately, than a client who carries one of the big .458 cases and has a wicked flinch.

That said, there really is no such thing as "too much gun" when it comes to hunting elephant, and there are some classic choices as well as some new developments. The good old .404 Jefferys was a standard issue for decades to the game scouts of many African countries, and still makes a great elephant cartridge. The .404 shoots a .423" 400-grain bullet, at a sedate velocity of 2,100 fps. Not as impressive as its .416" cousins, but the lack of recoil makes the old gun a winner among elephant hunters, as the shot will definitely be under 50 yards.

Hornady's 400-grain DGS (Dangerous Game Solid), a flat-nosed bullet with lead core and copper-clad steel jacket, is available in their Dangerous

Game Series of ammo.

Those .416s (Rigby, Remington and Ruger, and even the wildcat Taylor) are certainly a solid choice (pun intended) when it comes to elephant, as they are much easier to shoot than the .458s, yet deliver a 400-grain slug at 2,400 fps, plenty enough to quickly dispatch the giant pachyderms. My own .416 Remington really likes the North Fork 400-grain flatpoint solid, putting three of them into a group of just about one inch.

The Cutting Edge Safari Solid should make for a most impressive choice on elephant, but for now they must be handloaded. Again, make sure that the flatpoint solids will feed reliably in your particular bolt-action, as some of them have been known to hang up in certain feed ramps.

The .458 Winchester Magnum, with Federal Trophy Bonded Sledgehammer solids.

There are plenty of solids to choose from in the factory

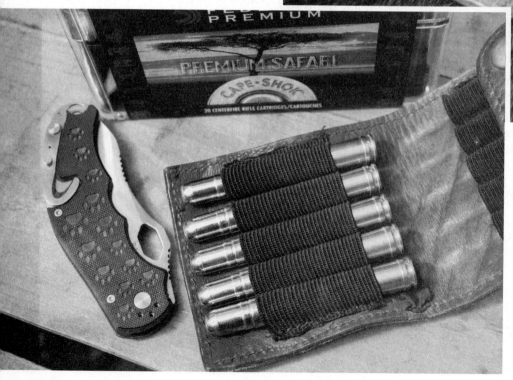

ammunition, including that wicked cool .416" 400-grain Woodleigh Hydrostatic Stabilized solid in the Federal Premium Safari line. The Ruger, Rigby and Remington are all represented in Hornady's Dangerous Game Series as well, giving an economical option for those who are pursuing Africana Loxodonta.

If you prefer a single-shot or double rifle in .40 caliber, the .450/.400 Nitro Express has seen a resurgence of late, especially in the Ruger No. 1 single shot. Shooting a .411" diameter 400-grain bullet at about 2,050 fps, there are some good choices for the el-

ephant hunter.

Kynoch still produces ammunition loaded with solids, but I like the Hornady DGS for this classic and the Barnes 400-grain Banded Solid will

A good choice for an all-around dangerous game rifle: the .458 Lott with 500-grain softpoints and solids. (J.P. Fielding photo)

certainly get the job done. The parallel-sided and flatpoint solids create a larger wound channel than do those of a more curved profile, and are well worth the investment should you need to stop a charge on an enraged elephant.

The .458 calibers are probably considered the classic elephant calibers, from the .458 Winchester Magnum and .458 Lott, through the .450 Rigby and .450 Watts, to the .450 Nitro Express and .450 No. 2, designed for the single-shots and double rifles. Using a good 500-grain solid, they run from around 2,100 fps to 2,400 fps, and they deliver over 5,000 ft.-lbs. of energy, and a nice big wound channel. They penetrate wonderfully on brain shots, and are good for side body shots as well. The older Kynoch-style solids have been with us forever, but there are better choices on the market today.

The Hornady DGX and the Trophy Bonded Sledgehammer are loaded in factory ammunition, and both are fully capable of taking an elephant cleanly. Woodleigh offers their classic full metal jacket bullet in 500 grains, and they will regulate very well in the many .45-caliber double rifle cartridges, and I firmly believe that they are, structurally speaking, a better choice than the Kynoch bullets while being of the same weight and shape. In .458" diameter, I like the way the parallel-sided and true roundnose solids shoot.

When we headed over to Tanzania on a buffalo safari, I loaded ol' GP some 500-grain A-Square Monolithic solids for his .458 Winchester, and they shot very well. It took a bit of handloading, and experimentation with several different powders, but I got that rifle to match the factory velocity of 2,150 fps. I understand the A-Square trio of Monolithic Solid, Dead Tough and Lion Load are available again this year, and I hope they are as good as they ever were.

Cartridges over .45 caliber, including the veteran .470 Nitro Express, .475 No.2 Jeffreys, .500 NE, .505 Gibbs and .500 Jeffreys, are usually in the hands of a professional hunter, not a client, but lately there seems to be exceptions to that rule. I had the opportunity to spend some time with my buddy Mike McNulty's Montana Rifle Works Model 99DGR in .505 Gibbs, and I wouldn't

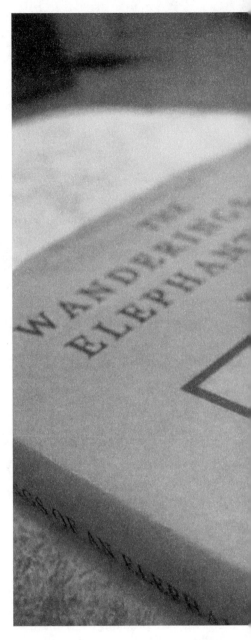

hesitate to use that rifle on an elephant.

Norma's African PH ammo, with a Woodleigh full metal jacket 600-grain solid at 2,100 fps was surprisingly manageable, and plenty accurate to hit the brain of an elephant. Many of the calibers in the class give the same, or at least very similar, levels of per-

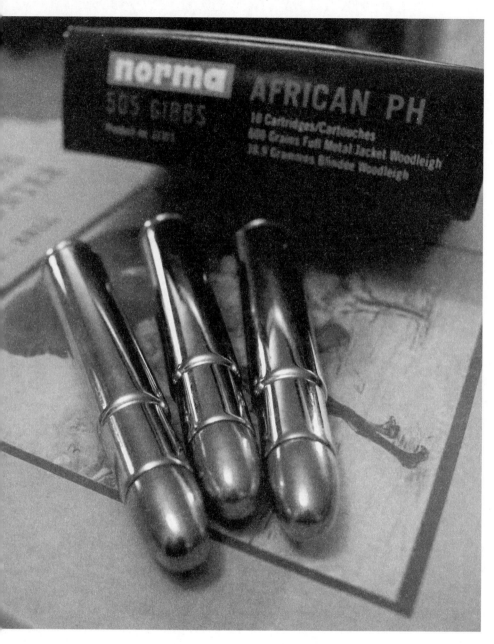

A true elephant stopper, the .505 Gibbs with 600-grain Woodleigh solids.

formance. The gist remains the same; when it comes to something as massive as an African elephant, get the best solid you can afford and put that ammo through rigorous testing to make sure it functions perfectly through your rifle. You can't be too prepared for a hunt like this.

RemingtonModel 700 SPS target rifle, in .338 Lapua Magnum.
(J.P. Fielding photo)

For those folks who love to punch paper more than anything else, accuracy is not just part of the game, it is the game. The post-impact construction of the bullet has no bearing on their decision, as it does in the hunting world, just so long as that bullet hits the tar-get at the same point every time. These bullets, whose job is to rip bullseyes at ranges out to and beyond 1,000 yards, require highly consistent dimensions and weights to attain that level of accuracy. Generally speaking, the bullets used by target shooters are called "match" bullets, and are some form of

TARGET RIFLES

hollowpoint, unless military FMJ bullets are required for service competitions.

As we will discuss, it was the target bullets that prompted many of the new designs of bullet ogive, using specific mathematical curve formulas to maximize efficiency, and minimize the effects of air drag and wind drift.

The target shooter doesn't give a hoot about kinetic energy, as paper rips easily, but velocity, especially consistent velocity, is paramount. Ammunition must be constructed carefully, and many target shooters are damned fine handloaders. Riflescopes are of the

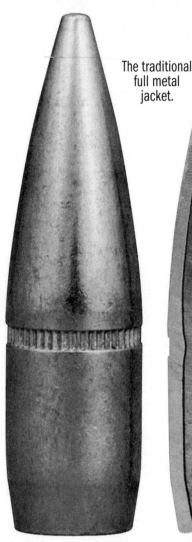

The traditional full metal jacket.

polymer tip that we talked about in the hunting bullet section, to resist meplat deformation and give consistent performance. With the exception of a handful of target bullets, there will be a boat-tail at the rear of the projectile (I use a couple of the flat-base match bullets regularly), and the ogive, or nose section of the bullet, will be

best quality affordable, triggers break if a squirrel farts, and rifles are tuned like a Ferrari motor. But again, it is the bullet that does the lion's share of the work.

Match-grade bullets are marketed by many companies, and just about any caliber can be used as and considered a target rifle. Accordingly, match bullets are made in almost every caliber up to .338", and usually in different weights as well. The most popular target bullets today have a hollowpoint design with a very small hole in the end, to produce a very small meplat and a high ballistic coefficient. Some will utilize the

Berger match-grade bullets.

long and pronounced.

I believe we should discuss some of the terms associated with target bullets, to better explain them and their relevance to choosing a proper target bullet. You'll read about 'tangent' and 'secant' ogives, about G1 and G7 models, and all of a sudden you're back in 9th grade algebra class. At least I was, until I delved a little bit deeper into what makes these bullets tick. Let me reiterate for a second: the curved section of the bullet, where it changes from its specified caliber and begins to taper to a point, is called the ogive. The curve itself is based on a mathematical formula (welcome back to algebra!), whether it's a portion of a circular curve, or based on the curve derived from plotting the algebraic functions of secant or tangent.

Now, I get mathematics, but shooting is much more fun, so let's put it this way- the math guys have done the

homework for you, and crunched the numbers, and what comes out of the other end of the slide rule is a precise ballistic coefficient figure. The higher the ballistic coefficient figure, the better the bullet will resist air drag and the effects of crosswind drift. This figure is very important, especially when the target is more than a half-mile from the muzzle.

Experimentation with various types of ogive curves (some of them are a blend of two algebraic functions) have resulted in bullets that perform very well at truly long distances. Ballistic coefficient itself is a non-static figure, as atmospheric pressure, elevation, and bullet velocity can all have an effect on the B.C., and change the game a bit. But for our purposes in choosing a bullet that will serve you best, let's use the B.C. figure published by the manufacturer. The boat-tail angle is often included in bullet descriptions, and deserves a quick explanation.

The boat-tail bullet tapers at its rear, and the angle of taper varies from model to model. A bullet with a 7° boat-tail has a longer taper than does a bullet with a 20° boat-tail. The longer tapered bullets get a boost in the B.C. figure, but that taper both cuts down on the bearing surface, and elongates the bullet. The long secant and tangent nose profiles have the same effect. Depending on the cartridge you're using, and whether or not you're single feeding the cartridges or using the rifle's magazine, the longer ogive bullets may pose a problem if you're trying to adhere to the SAAMI maximum C.O.L., and many paper punchers exceed that dimension in order to enhance the accuracy of the load.

The ballistic coefficient figures that we often see listed are a mathematical comparison to a model bullet. The G1 model I referred to earlier is a simple flat-base projectile, having a length of 3.28x caliber, and a curved nose with a radius of 2x caliber. The long, sleek

The SAAMI G1 bullet model.

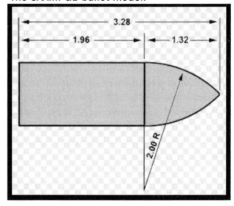

target bullets will have a very favorable B.C. in comparison to this model. However, the G7 model better mirrors the design of our modern-day target bullet, with a 7.5° boat-tail, a 10x caliber radius secant curve ogive, and a length of 4.23 calibers. This will help you understand why some bullets have two B.C. figures, and why the G1 figure is higher than the G7 figure. The SAAMI website and other internet sources will delve into the formulae required to derive at these figures. The mathematics involved in this derivation is a good cure for insomnia.

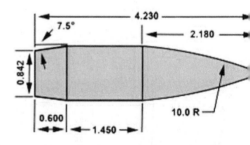

The SAAMI G7 bullet model.

Most match-grade factory ammunition will strictly adhere to the SAAMI C.O.L., but with a bit of research you'll find that many target shooters handload their ammunition to obtain a specific C.O.L. that their particular rifle likes best. Many factors are involved in this process, including the 'leade' of the rifle, or the distance within the chamber from the front of the cartridge case to the beginning of the lands and grooves.

The idea these shooters are using is to minimize the 'bullet jump' from the cartridge mouth to the rifling, keeping a distance of just about 0.015", and helping to better center the bullet in the bore. This is a process best left to experienced handloaders, as it can be dangerous should the bullet be touching the lands and grooves.

So, as a target shooter, I'm looking for a bullet that will perform well at the distances I intend to shoot, that will give a rather flat trajectory, and resist the effects of wind. I'd like a blend of high ballistic coefficient, good bearing surface, and wind-bucking ogive. There are several bullets that give exactly this.

THE STAPLES: CLASSIC MATCH BULLETS

When someone mentions match-grade bullets, there is inarguably one bullet that comes into my mind: the Sierra Match King. It was this bullet that introduced me to the world of match-grade accuracy. I had received a .300 Winchester Magnum as a gift for my 30th birthday, and I couldn't find a load that the rifle would shoot well.

Grumpy Pants emerged from the back room of our office with a box of 1970s-era 180-grain Sierra Match King bullets he'd been hoarding (there are still some in that box), suggesting in his less-than-subtle manner that I "try

GP's vintage box of 180-grain Sierra Match bullets. Note the $7.95 price! Those days are gone.

Sierra .22-caliber Match King bullets.

a real bullet" to see what was what. Well, I can't exactly say that it was the Match King that made the difference, as the next load I assembled shot less than ½" groups with that bullet and many others, but it certainly endeared me to the Sierra bullet.

When I purchased a Ruger Model 77 in .22-250 Remington, it certainly wasn't long before I looked to the Match Kings for a load that would give the ridiculous accuracy that this cartridge is famed for. I tried the 52-grain Match King, with the boat-tail, but the crown of my particular Ruger wasn't exactly perfect, and those and other boat-tails wouldn't group well. My pal Col. Le

Frogg suggested trying the 53-grain flat-base Match King (the only flat-base match bullet Sierra makes), and he had the right of it. The rifle will put three 53-grain Sierras into a 3/8" group or better, which is respectable from a sporter-weight barrel.

Mark "Pig-Newton" Nazi shoots a Remington Model 700 SPS in .308 Winchester that absolutely loves the world-famous 168-grain, .308-caliber Match King. I've shot this rifle, and to say that it is accurate is definitely an understatement.

It shoots some other bullets well, but not like those Match Kings. Mark also used the 250 and 300-grain Match

King in his .338 Lapua Magnum, printing three-shot groups that measure ¾", at a distance of 250 yards. I think that demonstrates the accuracy potential of Sierra Match Kings.

What goes into these bullets that make them so good? Well, first of all, the bullet jackets are extremely concentric, being drawn to tolerances down to 0.0003", with a weight consistency of 0.3 grains, although the bullets I've weighed usually maintain a tighter weight tolerance.

There are many models of Sierra Match King bullets, from .224" 52-grain to the .338" 300-grain. Sierra plays to many groups of shooters, from the backyard guys like me, to the Palma Match shooters who are restricted to using FMJ bullets of a particular weight. The 155-grain PALMA Match bullet is enjoyed by many military competition shooters, and this bullet shoots very well from the M1A1 rifles.

Federal's Gold Medal Match .308 load, featuring 168-grain Sierra Match King bullets.

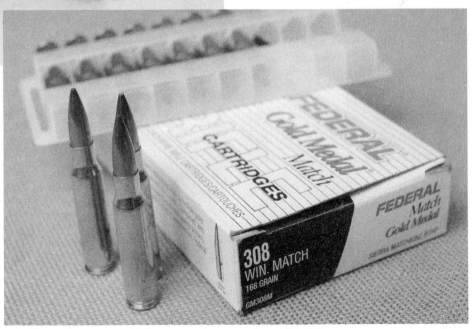

The .338 Lapua, with 300-grain Nosler AccuBonds and 250-grain Sierra Match Kings. (J.P. Fielding photo)

If you have a good target-grade 5.56mm/.223, Sierra makes some great heavyweight Match Kings in 69, 77, 80 and 90-grain weights. These bullets, if the rate of twist in your barrel can stabilize them, will give wonderful down-range performance. The 6.5mm bullets, with a legendary reputation for long-range accuracy and wind-bucking abilities, are represented in the 140-grain Match King, and the longer 142-grain Match King. I am awaiting the delivery of these bullets so I can load them in my 6.5-284 Norma and punch tiny little groups.

Federal Premium has seen the light, and loads the Sierra Match King bullets in their line of ammunition. The .30-06 Springfield ammunition, loaded with the 168-grain Match King, showed its accuracy potential at the underground range of the Federal facility. We were testing the penetration of several different hunting bullets into ballistic gelatin, and while the target bullet didn't penetrate worth a darn, the accuracy of this load when we sighted the rifle beat all of the other hunting bullets, hands down.

The other bullet widely seen at competitions (and championship photos) across the country, is the Berger line of target bullets. Berger has some fantastic designs, and all of them feature the famous J4 bullet jacket. This jacket is well-loved, and many of the boutique bullet companies, like Precision Ballistics, LLC, build their custom bullets around the Berger J4 jackets.

Berger has fully embraced the target community, and their founder Walt Berger is a highly-decorated target shooter himself. The famous VLD (Very Low Drag) design set the target world on its ear, and remains a bullet capable of ridiculous accuracy. Other models, like the Match VLD Target, Hybrid Target, Match Long Range BT Target and FULLBORE will ensure that target shooters of all disciplines have something to sink their teeth into.

One thing I like about Berger bullets is that they embrace the potential of flat-base target bullets (at least in .22 and .30-caliber) as being a contender in competition. The heavyweight Berger target bullets, like the .22-caliber 82-grain Match Long Range BT Target, and the .30-caliber 230-grain Match Hybrid Target have proven to be highly

Norma Match ammunition, with 168-grain Sierra Match Kings.

Berger's .30-caliber 185-grain OTM Tactical bullets.

accurate, should your firearm have the twist rate sufficient to stabilize them. My buddy Col. Le Frogg has a Ruger No. 1 in .300 Winchester Magnum that adores those long 230-grain Match Hybrid Target bullets, putting three into a ¾" group at 100 yards.

Berger bullets were a component item for as far as I can remember, but that has changed now. ABM (Applied Ballistic Munitions) now loads Berger Bullets products exclusively, in .308 Winchester, .300 Winchester Magnum and .338 Lapua Magnum, and all of the ABM stuff I've tried has performed very well.

(opposite top) ABM ammunition, .300 Winchester Magnum with 230-grain Berger bullets.

(opposite bottom) ABM ammunition in .300 Winchester Magnum and .308 Winchester.

Berger's J4 jackets have a similar tolerance to the Sierra Match King, in that they advertise a runout tolerance of 0.003", and a tight weight consistency, even from lot to lot. Depending on your caliber, and the type of target shooting, there is a Berger that will fill your needs. I have found that the Berg-

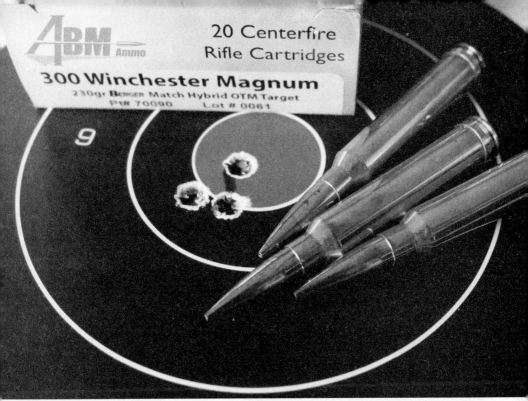

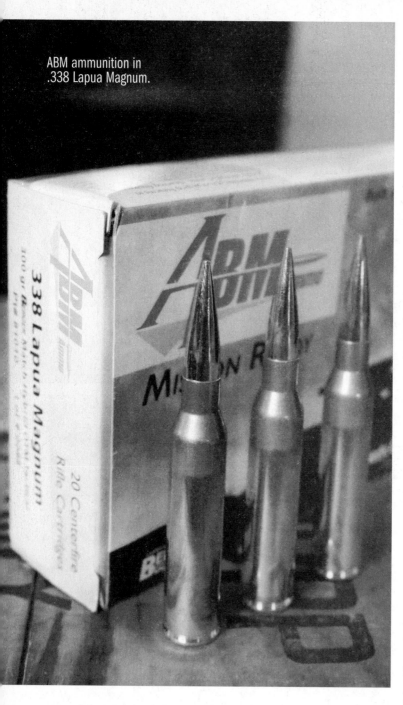

ABM ammunition in .338 Lapua Magnum.

very well.

Speer has been making bullets since 1943; they are among the oldest component bullet companies surviving today. Their line of match target bullets has diminished compared to past years, but there are noteworthy models that survive. The .22-caliber 52-grain boat-tail hollowpoint is a standby in that caliber. Well balanced, and capable of being stabilized even by the slow rate of twist of the .22-250 Remington and .220 Swift (I still don't understand why the twist rate of these rifles is so slow...), it will give fantastic accuracy, as Ol' Grumpy Pants can tell you.

His Remington Model 700 ADL will put three of these into less than a half-inch group at 100 yards. The 7mm 145-grain target bullet will

er models tend to be longer than other match bullets, due to the ogive designs, and that may pose a problem in maintaining a SAAMI specified C.O.L., but if your magazine can handle the additional length, Bergers will perform show you the accuracy potential of your 7mm Remington Magnum, or .280 Remington. Lastly, the .30-caliber 168-grain hollowpoint boat-tail will serve any of the accurate .30s very well. The 168-grain weight in .30-cali-

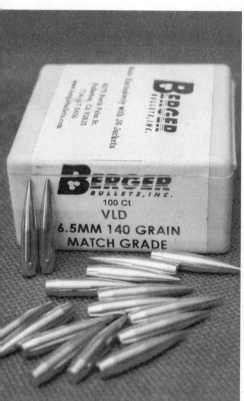

Berger 140-grain 6.5mm VLD bullets.

The .30-caliber 208-grain A-Max is making a very good reputation in cartridges from the diminutive .300 Blackout to the .300 Winchester Magnum as a fantastic long-range target bullet. It has a G1 B.C. of 0.648, derived from not only its shape, but also from its length, and at that weight it will retain velocity on the longer shots. For the .338 Lapua shooter, the 285-grain A-Max makes a good 'in-between' bullet, when the 250 is too short and the 300 is too slow. And, based on sheer cool factor, the 750-grain A-Max built for the behemoth .50 BMG is one bad hombre.

6.5 Grendel, with 123-grain Hornady A-Max.

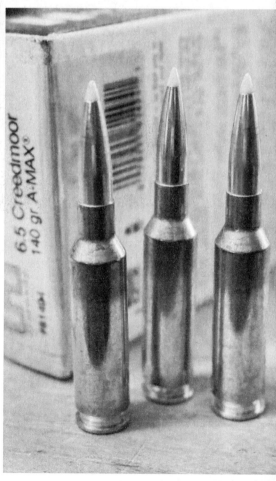

ber has been a standby for decades, and represents an optimum weight for an all-around target bullet.

NEWER MATCH BULLET DESIGNS

Hornady has been in the match bullet game for decades, but recently the line has been rejuvenated with the introduction of the A-Max bullet. These polymer-tipped gems use a secant ogive and the proprietary AMP bullet jacket, held to the same type of tolerances that Sierra and Berger hold. As much as I like the way the 53-grain flat-base boattail Hornady bullet shoots in my .22-250, I'm excited to shoot the 52-grain A-Max.

My 6.5-284 loves the 123-grain A-Max, and the 140-grain A-Max as well.

Hornady A-Max
.308 Winchester
match ammo.

Nosler has its Custom Competition line of target bullets, and they have been well received by the target community. They are a traditionally designed hollowpoint, with a lengthy boat-tail, and are available in standard weights, as well as the heavyweights that will require the faster rate of twist.

Produced in calibers from .224" to .338" they include the 8mm caliber, a rarity in today's market. Included in the Nosler line is the very popular 155-grain match bullet, designed for PALMA Match competition, requiring the 7.62mm NATO cartridge and a 155-grain bullet to ensure a level playing field. All the nice, long .22-caliber models are on the menu here, including the 69-grain, 77-grain and 80-grain bullets. That 80-grainer is over an inch long!

Barnes Bullets, famous for its revolutionary all-copper hollowpoints, has produced a line of match bullets, called Match Burners. Instead of modifying the all-copper design, Barnes decided to make a more affordable lead-core hollowpoint, complete with boat-tail. While most calibers are well represented, the bullet weights are limited. I haven't had the opportunity to shoot these bullets myself, but if they're anything like other Barnes products, they warrant a trip to the range.

One new company whose target bullets I find exciting is Cutting Edge Bullets. Their match bullets are lathe-turned, all-copper, and feature the Seal Tite band to help improve accuracy. These bullets are very uniform, and have proven to be very accurate in my

rifles. Mind you, I don't own a dedicated target rifle, but I know the accuracy potential of my guns, and the CEB stuff was among the best I've shot. Most of the MTAC (Match/Tactical) bullets are produced with their Seal Tite band placed in a location that will allow the reloader to maintain a SAAMI C.O.L. specification, but there are those bullets designated as 'Single Feed', and for those the band is located in a spot that will maximize case capacity, yet will be too long to feed through a magazine.

This single feed design will also minimize bullet jump, giving an accuracy advantage. Cutting Edge makes these bullet in the common target calibers such as .22, 6mm, 6.5mm, 7mm, .30 and .338, but also offers some nice heavyweights in .375, .416 and a very impressive 802-grain beast for the .50 BMG.

The Lapua Scenar has attracted a ton of attention among target shooters and its younger brother, the Scenar-L, will

(below) Sierra and Nosler Custom Competiton 168-grain .30-caliber match-grade bullets. (J.P. Fielding photo)

.308 Cal - 180

SINGLE FEED -

CUTTING EDG
BULLET

308 180

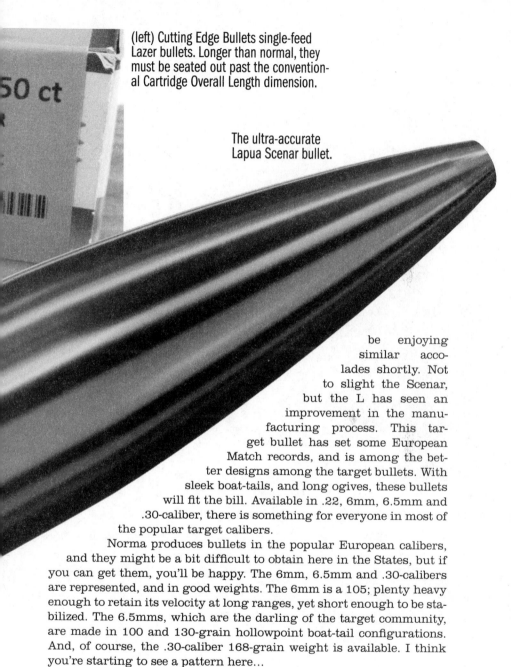

(left) Cutting Edge Bullets single-feed Lazer bullets. Longer than normal, they must be seated out past the conventional Cartridge Overall Length dimension.

The ultra-accurate Lapua Scenar bullet.

be enjoying similar accolades shortly. Not to slight the Scenar, but the L has seen an improvement in the manufacturing process. This target bullet has set some European Match records, and is among the better designs among the target bullets. With sleek boat-tails, and long ogives, these bullets will fit the bill. Available in .22, 6mm, 6.5mm and .30-caliber, there is something for everyone in most of the popular target calibers.

Norma produces bullets in the popular European calibers, and they might be a bit difficult to obtain here in the States, but if you can get them, you'll be happy. The 6mm, 6.5mm and .30-calibers are represented, and in good weights. The 6mm is a 105; plenty heavy enough to retain its velocity at long ranges, yet short enough to be stabilized. The 6.5mms, which are the darling of the target community, are made in 100 and 130-grain hollowpoint boat-tail configurations. And, of course, the .30-caliber 168-grain weight is available. I think you're starting to see a pattern here...

Realize that every barrel is a different animal, especially when target grade accuracy is concerned. Choose the bullet that best appeals to you, and the targets will tell you whether or not your rifle is happy with that particular load. Once you find that magic combination, hang onto it, and have fun printing tiny little groups at a variety of ranges.

CHAPTER 8

AR-STYLE RIFLES

Happiness is a pile of 5.56mm brass.
(J.P. Fielding photo)

The recent popularity of the AR-style rifles has spawned some interesting developments in the cartridges they fire. The traditional choice of 5.56/.223 Remington still dominates the playing field, but there are plenty of new kids on the block. They are generally de-signed to function in a standard AR15 magazine, so we're seeing some very short cases with long bullets (the .300 AAC Blackout is one example), and some fat cases with rebated rims (the .458 SOCOM comes quickly to mind), and all sorts of stuff in between.

The recent trend in subsonic ammu-

nition has only enhanced the performance of some of these cartridges, as it can be very difficult to get the smaller cases to push the heavier bullets very fast. There are some cartridges that have proven to be very accurate in shooting matches, and more and more AR-style rifles head to the hunting fields each year. Bullet companies have modified their designs to best serve the AR platform, and a crop of specialty bullets has popped up. "Tactical" is word I don't use often, but it seems to be a catchphrase that consumers enjoy. One thing is for certain, many shooters have embraced the AR rifle for many

Hornady's steel-cased ammo can be fun for days at the range. The 75-grain bullet needs a fast rate of twist.

different purposes, and its popularity continues to grow.

That little .223 Remington is the leader of the pack among the ARs, and depending on the rate of twist in your rifle, you can get some widely varying bullet weights in the factory loads. I think the 55-grain weight is still the top seller, and it represents a good balance of striking energy and velocity, with most loads rolling along at 3,500 fps or so. The lighter 40 and 45-grainers are available, as are the 60, 62, 69, 72 and even 80-grain heavyweights.

If you're hunting with your AR, the chapters on Varmint and Medium Game rifles will apply to you. If it's a target gun, find out what rate of twist your barrel was made with, and check with the bullet manufacturer to ensure your barrel can stabilize the longer bullet you may want for long-range shooting. The Berger VLDs, set to the proper SAAMI length so as to function properly through the AR magazine, have

The long-for-caliber 69-grain Sierra Match bullet, in .224 caliber.

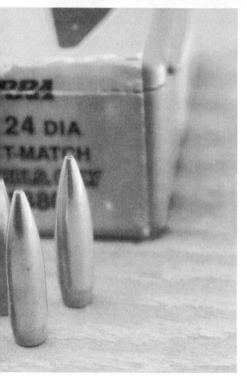

proven to be very accurate in the ARs that I've shot.

The inexpensive 55-grain FMJ boattail bullet, as produced in bulk by, say, Winchester or American Eagle, can provide hours of fun at the target range, or while plinking. This same bullet is often required for military-style shooting competitions.

The .25-45 Sharps is an interesting little cartridge, relatively new on the AR scene. Simply a .223 Remington case necked up to hold .257" diameter bullets, this case will push an 87-grain bullet to 3,000 fps, just like the old .250/3000 Savage cartridge, but this one will work perfectly in the AR platform. This newbie uses a bonded-core 87-grain bullet (I've heard rumors of an 87-grain Nosler AccuBond coming onto the market), and at that velocity it should improve on the Savage cartridge's performance, delivering plenty of hydraulic shock yet driving deep into the vitals. The bonding process

A pair of 6.5mm AR-based cartridges, the 6.5 Creedmoor and the 6.5 Grendel.

eliminates almost all chances of jacket/core separation.

I think the .25-45 Sharps will make a great deer/antelope cartridge for the ARs, giving a nice, flat trajectory when firing that 87-grain spitzer. Considering the performance of the .250/3000 Savage, I think the 87-grain Hornady InterLock or Sierra Varminter would make a good choice among the cup-and-core bullets. I've loaded both of them for clients in the Savage case, so the Sharps (at the same velocity) should shoot it just fine.

There's a pair of 6.5mm cartridges that have been designed to work well in the AR platform: the 6.5 Creedmoor, and the 6.5 Grendel. I am a fan of the 6.5mm projectiles, as they often have a high B.C., and are available in a decent variety of weights. The Creedmoor is based on the .308 Winchester, with a shortened case to allow proper seat-ing of the long and lean 6.5mm bullets. It is a well thought out design, and velocities are not far behind the larger 6.5 cases, giving plenty of speed for long-range trajectory. The 6.5 Grendel is based on the .220 Russian case, and was designed to better the downrange performance of the 5.56mm, yet still be able to fit double-stacked in the standard AR magazine.

Why the attraction to 6.5mm cartridges? I asked myself the same question, years ago. I mean, there are some great .25-caliber and .270-caliber bullets, so why not them? I think I've sort of figured it out, and it led me to purchase a 6.5/284 Norma bolt-action hunting rifle. The answer: downrange performance. America settled on the .30-caliber bullets for their ability to balance good velocity and wind-bucking trajectory.

However, the energy required to get

that performance requires a certain level of recoil, and a case size (read .308 Winchester) that holds enough powder to attain those levels. The beauty, and attractive quality, of the 6.5mm bullets, is that you get just about the same level of high B.C. (to buck the wind), at a better S.D. than most of the .30s, with a considerable reduction in recoil. This translates to a lighter package, and increased magazine capacity in the example of the Grendel. While certainly not a speed demon in comparison to the Creedmoor, the Grendel is still a fine performer in a very concise platform.

In both the Creedmoor and Grendel, I like bullets of 140 grains or less, as they will give a bit more room for powder within the case, yet the B.C. of 6.5mm 120 through 140-grain bullets is still fantastic. Hornady's 123-grain A-Max target bullet will make a good choice for AR target work, and their 139-grain SST will handle the hunting end of things if you drag your AR into the hunting fields. The Sierra 123-grain Match King is an awesome bullet for both of these cartridges if you're hunting paper, as the weight tolerances and jacket concentricity will allow you to eke the most out of your AR barrel. The Grendel will push these 123-grain bullets to around 2,500 fps, which is perfect for target work from 200 to 800 yards.

Hornady makes their A-Max bullet in a 123-grain configuration, which is a winner as well. The Creedmoor has a 300 fps velocity advantage, but suffers from a lack of magazine capacity. Hornady's Match ammunition has a 6.5 Creedmoor load that drives the 140-grain A-Max target bullet to 2,700 fps, and the longer bearing surface of this bullet, at a higher velocity, should prove to be a fantastic target bullet

The 6.5 Grendel can be double stacked in the AR magazine.

from your AR.

Hornady loads the Grendel with a 123-grain SST, and that should perform very well on deer-sized game at 2,620 fps. Ultimately, the choice in AR 6.5mm cartridges really depends on whether you're after firepower or speed, as both are highly accurate, as most 6.5mms are. The Barnes TTSX is another good choice for a hunting bullet, and I like the 100-grain variety in both the Creedmoor and Grendel. Should you take your AR hunting, this bullet can be driven to very respectable velocities, while the all-copper construction will guarantee bullet integrity and deep penetration.

Remington developed the 6.8 SPC (Special Purpose Cartridge) as a better anti-personnel round for the AR platform, and it is a solid design. Firing a .277" diameter bullet, in a case based on the century-plus-old .30 Remington, but shortened to be the same length as the .223/5.56mm, it was developed in conjunction with the U.S. Military as a potential replacement for the 5.56mm, giving better ballistics from a heavier payload. The SPC uses the same bullet diameter as the .270 Winchester, but primarily takes advantage of the lighter weights. Seems like folks enjoy the 5.56mm, but are always looking for a replacement, eh? The SPC is well respected among the military rifle fans, and with good reason: it offers performance much better than the .223/5.56mm and is easier recoiling and easier to carry than the .308 Winchester.

Oddly enough, while the U.S. Military was developing the replacement for the .30-40 Krag (as you know, the .30-'06 Springfield won that race), they looked at a modified 7mm Mauser case, holding .277" diameter bullets, so our military was very close to using the .270 Winchester as its standard issue cartridge. I look at the 6.8 SPC as a return to that idea.

For a self defense round, I like the Nosler Defense 6.8 SPC load using the 90-grain bonded solid-base bullet, as it will best use the case capacity of the SPC. You'll want to look for loads using bullets weighing between 90 and 120 grains, be they the DoubleTap 95-grain Barnes TTSX bullet, or the Hornady Custom 120-grain SST load. This cartridge is just about perfect for deer and deer-sized game, up to and including wild hogs.

There are several cool .30-caliber cartridges designed for use in the AR platform, and they handle the full gamut of the oh-so-popular .30-caliber bullets. The .30 Remington AR is the first, built around Remington's own AR offering, the Remington Model R15 rifle. Based on the .450 Bushmaster (cut down and necked down), the .30 Rem AR is ballistically equivalent to or better than the venerable .30/30 Winchester. There are some really cool loads for the .30

The 6.8SPC, shown next to the .223.

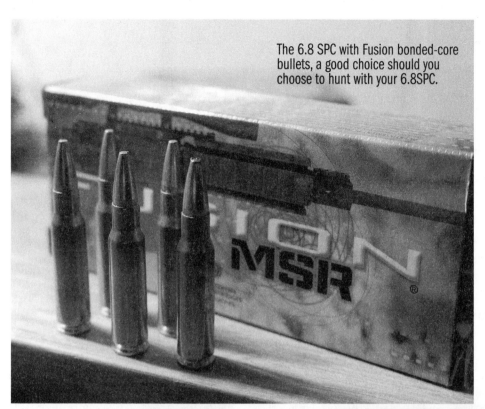

The 6.8 SPC with Fusion bonded-core bullets, a good choice should you choose to hunt with your 6.8SPC.

The .300 Whisper/Blackout.

Rem, including a 125-grain Barnes TSX, pushed to 2,800 fps, which will easily handle deer and hogs. Big Green also loads the 150-grain Core-Lokt soft point, and at just over 2,500 fps, will perform on par with the .300 Savage. Not too shabby.

The .300 AAC Blackout, and its step-brother the .300 Whisper come next, and both are the .223 case blown out to .30 caliber and severely shortened.

At a first glance, they seem almost, well, ineffective, being shortened so radically to utilize the AR magazine and yet push the longer .30-caliber bullets, but they offer the AR shooter some cool options. The goal of both of these cartridges was to better the subsonic ballistics of the 7.62X39 cartridge, for military operations requiring stealth. There is however, one inherent little problem with the Blackout/Whisper package, and it could prove detrimental, so I'll feel better pointing it out. It was brought to my attention by my friends at Western Powders. Being designed to function in any AR style magazine, there are some bullets (the shorter ones in particular), that allow the .300 to chamber in a 5.56mm rifle, using the bullet's shoulder in place of the 5.56's cartridge shoulder. Were the trigger to be pulled, hell itself would be unleashed, and the results will be tragic. Keep your .300 Blackout ammunition far away from your 5.56 ammo, and all will be well.

Hornady loads the Blackout with a 208-grain A-Max, and while designed to be subsonic (1,050 fps or so), it provides a lot of punch from the AR platform, especially as a target rifle. The 110 to 125-grain bullets, if properly constructed, will make a decent close-range hunting choice for game on the small side of things. Nosler Match Grade ammo uses their 125-grain Ballistic Tip at 2,250 fps. I've used this bullet (at 3,000 fps) in my .308 Winchester, and at the relatively low velocity this bullet should perform wonderfully.

Hornady gives the varmint hunter

an opportunity to use the .300 Blackout, building a load around the 100-grain V-Max at 2,350 fps, which should dump coyotes in their tracks. For the economy-minded shooter, Fiocchi offers the 150-grain FMJ at just under 2,000 fps, which should satisfy the hunger of any trigger-happy shooter, without breaking the bank. Handloading the uber-cool Berger bullets into the Blackout should be a ton of fun as well.

The 7.62x39mm cartridge, so popular in the AK47 and SKS rifles, has translated well into the AR platform. While this cartridge makes a good defense round, I haven't been impressed by the performance on game, or as a target cartridge. This may have been due to a couple of issues with the "39".

Some 7.62x39 rifles are manufactured with a bore diameter of .308", and other models use a .311" bore diameter, and if the bullets are mismatched, this can pose quite a problem in accuracy.

The 39 tends to perform best using 123-grain bullets, and many companies manufacture steel-cased, inexpensive ammunition using this bullet weight in a full metal jacket configuration. These steel cases can't be reloaded, but they perform well enough to teach good marksmanship. If you feel you want to hunt with the 39, pick out a decent hunting bullet to maximize your efforts. For example, DoubleTap loads the 123-grain Barnes TSX bullet, and Federal's Fusion line offers a bonded-core 123-grain bullet as well. Reming-

The highly popular 7.62x39mm.

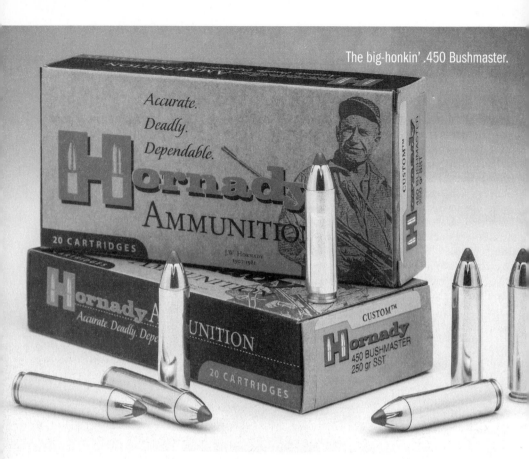

ton, Winchester and Federal all load a 123-grain pointed softpoint bullet that should have no problem handling the 39's moderate velocity, but again, due to that bore diameter issue, make sure your rifle gives the accuracy necessary for ethical hunting.

Bumping way up in caliber, we find a pair of powerhouses in .45 caliber. But be aware that they're not the same .45 caliber. Confused? Bear with me here for one second and I'll explain.

The .450 Bushmaster uses a case that features a rebated rim with the same diameter as the 5.56mm cartridge, but a much fatter body diameter, and uses the same .452" diameter bullets as the .45 ACP and .45 (Long) Colt pistol cartridges.

The .458 SOCOM is a bit longer than the Bushmaster, but has a similarly rebated rim, yet uses the .458" diameter bullets of the .45-70 Government and .458 Winchester Magnum. Both offer good bullet choices, and the choice will depend on whether you like the performance of pistol bullets or rifle bullets from your AR. I've done some handloading for the SOCOM, using 325-grain Barnes TTSX bullets specially designed for that cartridge, and they worked out very well.

Designed to expand properly at SOCOM velocities, they are probably my favorite hunting bullet for the SOCOM, as they are light-for-caliber (which will give good velocity) and yet are of monometal construction (which ensures deep penetration).

For the Bushmaster, I like the Hornady load featuring the 250-grain FTX bullet, because of the spitzer point. It will give better energy retention and flatter trajectories than contemporary flatpoint or hollowpoint pistol bullet designs. Remington's Hog Hammer line takes advantage of the 275-grain Barnes TSX, pushing it to 2,175 fps for a good short to mid-range hunting load. Remington also loads a more frangible 260 AccuTip bullet to 2,180 fps.

Rounding out the lot is the behemoth .50 Beowulf. A proprietary design from Alexander Arms, this beast has a severely rebated rim the same dimension as the 7.62x39 case, yet will function (in single stack mode) in an AR magazine. The moderate velocity (less than 2,000 fps) allows good performance with pistol bullets designed for the .50 Action Express. Hornady's XTP, Speer's Gold Dot and Rainier's FMJ are all loaded by Alexander. Based on the

performance of that Gold Dot in the big pistol cartridges, that 300-grain bullet at 2,330 fps should make a good hunting load for the Beowulf.

In a defense situation, Alexander loads the 240-grain Millennium Solid Copper split hollowpoint bullet, a design very similar to the Cutting Edge PHD bullet. A deep hollowpoint, and perforated walls down to the base of the cavity, combined with lighter weight and a bit higher velocity will guarantee near explosive expansion, and keep penetration to a controllable depth.

For larger game, the Alexander load that features a Hawk 400-grain bullet at 1,800 fps should pretty well mirror the performance of the .45/70 Government, and I don't think I need to explain how well that has worked for 140+ years.

Behold, the mighty .458 SOCOM!

The Lyman Great Plains rifle, deadly in GP's hands.

CHAPTER 9

The earliest firearms we American enjoyed were muzzleloading; they won the American Revolution with a bullet as simple as the lead round ball. The muzzleloading rifle is part of our American heritage, and each year many hunters head afield with a smokepole in their hands. But, that simple patched round ball, which I mentioned earlier has been improved (although I still use that original design), and has actually gotten quite technical in design, and is capable of delivering great accuracy and better energy figures.

A brief history, so you'll understand the development, is in order. The first rifles, which featured grooves in the

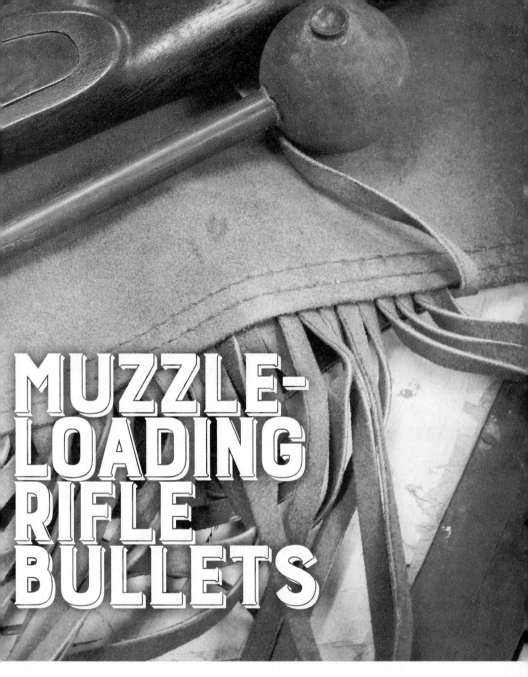

MUZZLE-LOADING RIFLE BULLETS

barrel instead of a smooth bore, needed a patch of cloth and a caliber-specific lead round ball to build pressures and seal in the burning gasses.

As time progressed, the early ballisticians realized that elongating the ball and giving it a longer axis about which to rotate would increase the accuracy. The Minie Ball, which had a hollow

base to allow the bullet to expand, to better contain the burning gases and take the rifling, offered a huge ballistic improvement to riflemen and soldiers in the mid 1800s. Better still were the longer, flat-base lead bullets that would stabilize well and retain energy better at longer distances. As the muzzleloading rifles gave way to breechloaders,

The clumsy round ball; it put tons of meat on the pioneer tables.

little attention was paid to the bullets that the old timers fired, until special seasons were put in place allowing hunters to use primitive weapons to spend more time afield.

At first, the plastic sabot, which is a simple cup that surrounds the bullet in the bore of a muzzleloader, was utilized so that muzzleloading riflemen could shoot .45-caliber jacketed pistol bullets from their Hawken-style rifles. This resulted in better terminal performance, but accuracy was, and is, sometimes questionable. The pistol bullets don't have the best S.D. figures, and while the B.C. of these bullets seems lacking in comparison to the sleek centerfire rifle bullets, they are better than that of a round ball.

It was the inline muzzleloaders that totally changed the game. The questionable ignition of the Hawken-style percussion rifles was near totally

solved, and the new-style barrels made from better steel could withstand higher pressures. One hundred fifty grains of black powder or Pyrodex (and other black powder substitutes) were not a problem to ignite, as the newfangled inline uses a standard shotgun 209 primer as its ignition source. These new velocities called for better bullets, with a higher B.C., and the market responded accordingly.

Accuracy was on par with the lever guns designed in the late 19th and early 20th centuries, and once the inline was scoped, they became a 200-yard and over rifle. Standard cup-and-core style muzzleloader bullets, in a plastic sabot, were the first offerings, and then the polymer tips, partitioned, bonded core and monometal designs began to show their faces as the market grew and hunters embraced the new technology.

Hunters like Jim Shockey pioneered

the use of the inline muzzleloader around the world, and many counties, states, and provinces that had previously only allowed the use of shotguns and slugs were allowing these very accurate inlines to be used, and deer hunters latched on to the opportunity.

The Knight rifles of the late 80s and early 90s and the Thompson/Center designs paved the way for what is now a huge hunting market with many rifle designs to choose from, but the muzzleloading bullet has experienced an even bigger overhaul. Let's look at some of the cool new designs, starting with the brand new stuff.

Powerbelt Bullets were a wonderful development, giving good hollowpoint expansion and a good gas seal from the plastic gas check on the rear of the bullet. These are still a popular choice among many muzzleloader hunters.

Federal has recently released the Muzzleloading Trophy Copper, using the same technology as their Trophy Copper rifle bullet designs, but with a special plastic sabot built to integrate with the rear portion of the bullet, for ease of loading. Federal calls this the B.O.R. LOCK MZ System, and it seems to be a solid design. The "obturating ramp" helps clean the fouling during loading, and the plastic cup slides over these ramps upon firing, to become the bullet's bearing surface within the barrel.

All this stuff equates to a very tight gas seal, to get the most out of the

250-grain .50-caliber PowerBelt bullets.

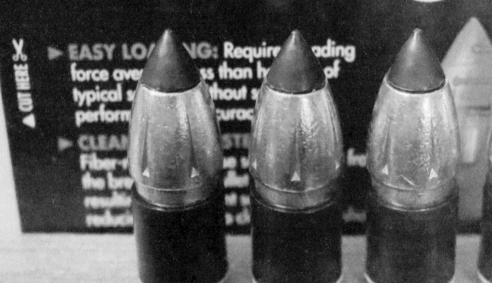

Federal's new B.O.R. LOCK muzzleloader system.

burning gases and increase velocity. A sharp polymer tip gives a good B.C. and at 270 grains, 200-yard accuracy is not out of the question in a good in-line muzzleloader. This bullet is showing its true colors in the hunting fields, with centerfire rifle type accuracy and all the penetration you'd ever want. Unless I'm very wrong, you'll be seeing quite a few people with the Federal Trophy Copper in their front loaders.

Cutting Edge bullets also has a new muzzleloading bullet, the MZL Raptor, and like their other bullets, they are all copper and lathe-turned. These beauties are offered in 160 grains and 250 grains, with a black polymer tip for an increased B.C.

The Cutting Edge design relies upon a deep hollowpoint and skiving that will give fantastic impact trauma, and maintain the caliber diameter of the rear portion of the bullet for deep penetration into the animal's vitals. Having tested the 250-grain bullets on paper out of Neighbor Dave's T/C .50-caliber Encore, we got under 2" groups at 100 yards, plenty enough accuracy for shots out to 250 yards or so.

I think these bullets are going to make quite the splash in the muzzleloading world, especially the 160-grain Raptor, which can be driven to higher velocities for long-range work. These 160s, although very light for caliber, will give the typical impact trauma wound typical of the Raptor line, and yet still send the remaining copper slug well into the vitals. I'd look to the 250-grain bullets for larger or tougher game, but I wouldn't hesitate to use the 160s on deer and deer-sized animals.

Barnes has long offered a muzzleloader bullet, but has expanded their line in recent years. The Expander MZ Muzzleloader bullet is essentially a larger version of the TSX bullet we all love in our centerfires. Instead of four petals causing impact trauma, the Expander MZ peels back into six petals, for plenty of blood loss. These bullets lack the grooves associated with the rifle versions, as the sidewalls of the muzzleloader bullets don't come into contact with the rifling, the plastic sabot does. That said, the Expander MZ is a field-tested winner, and is made for inline muzzleloaders of .45, .50. and .54 caliber, in very practical weights and ratios that will give the performance you're after.

Want that all-copper performance, but with a higher B.C. for long range work? We know that inline muzzleloaders are capable of handling shots out to 250+ yards, with the proper optics and ammunition, and for that job you'll want to look at bullets like the Spit-Fire MZ line. These bullets feature a nicely curved ogive to better resist air drag and wind drift, and three models are available, depending on your taste.

The three of them are only available for .50-caliber rifles, as this is the most popular muzzleloader caliber. The Spit-Fire MZ is configured like the traditional Barnes X bullet, but with a boat-tail and a curved ogive. The Spit-Fire TMZ has the same design, but with a blue polymer tip that serves to initiate expansion, as well as give a higher ballistic coefficient for the longer shots.

The only issue I have with either of these boat-tail offerings is that the true benefits of the boat-tail (a flatter trajectory and better retained energy) don't really take effect until 250 yards or so, so perhaps it is unnecessary. I do like the Spit-Fire T-EZ design, having the polymer tip and curved ogive, but with a flat base. The flat-base bullets have proved to be as accurate, if not more accurate, than the boat-tails and within 200 yards and perform just as well as any boat-tail ever designed.

Hornady has long made its Lock-N-Load muzzleloader system, with the 45-caliber 250-grain SST bullet and a special sabot that has a plastic rod for easy alignment of powder pellets, but they've also extended the FlexTip bullet into the muzzleloader line. Hornady

calls it the FPB bullet, and this is a completely new design, made to load easily, yet give a good gas seal without the use of a plastic sabot. There is a hollow cavity (much like the Minie ball concept) at the rear of the bullet, and upon ignition the burning gases will cause the base to expand to both seal the gases and better engage the rifling. For the traditional muzzleloaders, if it is legal to use anything other than a patched,

Hornady brings the polymer tip and sleek ogive of the SST bullets to the muzzleloader world.

round ball, this would be a great ballistic improvement. The FPB comes in 300 and 350 grains.

Nosler has also seen the wisdom of higher B.C. muzzleloader bullets, and they offer the Jim Shockey Signature Series Ballistic Tip muzzleloader bullet. Being .458" diameter, and almost an inch long, the 300-grain polymer-tipped bullet should prove to be a winner if Mr. Shockey has put his name to

it, as he is probably the greatest living authority on muzzleloader bullet performance.

There are many companies that produce a pistol-style hunting bullet for use in a .50-caliber sabot, and there is nothing wrong with using these, especially if your shots are under 100 yards. I like the premium pistol bullets especially, as they will handle some of the impact velocities better than the

The Hornady FPB, with its expanding base.

more frangible designs.

Load a Swift A-Frame .44-caliber 300-grain bullet in a .50-caliber sabot, and you've got a potent combination, even if the B.C. is lesser than some of the more streamlined designs. Any of the good pistol bullets that are discussed in the Handgun Hunting Bullet chapter, if they are heavy-for-caliber, will suffice for use in your muzzleloader.

Now, for the more traditional muzzleloader bullet designs, there are specialty choices out there for you as well. The patched bullet or ball is the original projectile, yet the specialty shops have changed the game as well. Thompson/Center, long in the muzzleloader game, makes the Maxi-Hunter bullet for traditional muzzleloaders. It has deep grease grooves, filled with Natural Lube 1000+ Bore Butter, to keep fouling soft and reduce the necessity for frequent cleaning. Depending on the size of the game being pursued, they are offered in 275, 320 and 350-grain weights in .50-caliber. The original T/C Maxi-Ball bullet has even deeper grease grooves, and still performs very well. A similar design to the Maxi-Hunter, the Maxi-Ball is a .50-caliber 370-grain tapered flatnose, and makes a great choice for those states that have special seasons that do not allow the use of a sabot.

I must admit that I don't spend an awful lot of time with a smokepole in my hand, as our muzzleloader season here in the Southern Zone of New York comes after our regular rifle season, and I've used up most of my available time, but when I do get out I use a Cabela's Hawken .54-caliber percussion lock. This particular rifle has shown a definite preference for .54-caliber patched balls and 90 grains of FFFg, and doesn't really like the 340-grain cast bullets that GP and I have made for it. His Lyman Great Plains rifle,

also a .54-caliber percussion cap rifle, absolutely loves those 340-grainers, and shoots the patched balls equally well. Rifles are finicky creatures after all, aren't they?

If you prefer the old school projectile, as I do, there are two choices: cast your own or purchase the projectiles. Hornady, Speer and Thompson/Center all make quality round balls, of very consistent diameter. The most important factor in obtaining accuracy in your front loader is finding the best powder charge for your rifle. There are many options, like traditional black powder, Triple 7, Pyrodex and Black-Horn 209. Take your time at the range, and you'll find the formula that works for you. Half the fun is making huge clouds of smoke!

The .54 caliber cast round ball.

CHAPTER 10

America's sweetheart, the .45 ACP.

Your choice of defensive handgun bullet is a very important one; your very life may depend on it. I've said it before, but I'll reiterate here: I hope to live out the rest of my days having never pointed a firearm at another human being with intent to kill, but I also firmly believe in the inalienable right to defend one's life, family, and property, and wouldn't hesitate to do so. Virtually any handgun, from .22 Long Rifle all the way up to the .500 S&W, can be used as a self-defense weapon. Some make more sense than others, but whatever the caliber, you'll be relying on the bullet to remove the threat to life and limb.

DEFENSIVE HANDGUN BULLETS

There are also other considerations to keep in mind. Shooting indoors can pose a threat of over-penetration, and unintentionally hitting someone in an adjoining room is never a good thing. So we are after a projectile that is tough enough to penetrate through clothing, skin and bone, but frangible enough to avoid over-penetration. When it comes to saving your bacon, I believe that pistols with a larger hole in the barrel will make a larger hole in the assailant, and that's a good thing.

There is also the balance of cartridge to portability. As much as I love to shoot my .45 Colt revolver, it doesn't make a good carry gun, and with a 7.5-inch barrel, it isn't really concealable

Hornady's Critical Defense .22 Winchester Magnum Rimfire.

at all. My Smith & Wesson Model 36, in .38 Special, with a 1 7/8" barrel is both lightweight and small enough to conceal, but lacks the ballistics of the bigger .45 Colt.

The numerous revolvers on the market give many options, and I like them for their simple design and reliability.

Personally, I carry wheelguns, but that doesn't mean that I don't enjoy and understand the benefits of the autoloaders, including the 1911 and its numerous clones, the family of Glocks, the Beretta line; there's literally something for everyone.

Regardless of how cool a bullet is, how strongly it is built or what the downrange ballistics look like on paper, one thing must be stressed: If you use an autoloading handgun, your chosen bullet must feed reliably. I have seen certain .380 Autos that simply would not feed certain bullets, and I know of 1911s that don't like the semi-wadcutters.

Now these issues may be specific to a certain firearm or model of firearm, but when it comes to self defense, a pistol that jams is

Hornady's Critical Defense Lite .38 Special load, with the 90-grain Flex Tip bullet.

(above) .44 Remington Magnum, with Federal Hydra-Shok ammunition.

(left) Speer Gold Dot loaded in the .45 G.A.P. cartridge.

The .380 Auto with Winchester 90-grain hollowpoints.

Cutting Edge Bullets Personal Handgun Defense ammo.

just about useless. It may take several boxes of ammunition at the range until you find a bullet profile that works for you, but that is some time well spent. When you need it, you need it, and no discounted price will look as sweet when the gun jams in an ugly situation.

Bullet structure, especially in the lighter handgun calibers, can make or break a shooting situation. I don't think I'd be overstating things when I say that the .45 ACP is one of the most relied-upon self defense calibers in existence. Though it lacks the look of fortitude, and its profile resembles Danny DeVito (no offense Danny!), it is one of the most useful defense cartridges ever invented.

This is not without

The Rainier total metal jacket bullets, with no exposed lead.

with no exposed lead to diminish the lead vapor possibility.

The traditional FMJ load commonly referred to as "Ball Ammo" (with the base having exposed lead), is a solid choice (pun totally intended), but the expanding bullets are definitely the way to go if you need to defend your life.

good reason; since 1911 the ACP has defended our nation across the globe. The traditional loading is a full metal jacket 230-grain bullet, at 850 fps, and there is absolutely nothing wrong with that. One of my favorite FMJ bullets is the 230-grain Rainier Ballistics bullet. It is not just a full metal jacket, in the sense that the nose has no exposed lead; this bullet is totally encapsulated in copper. While it makes a great defense bullet, it also complies with those indoor ranges that require a bullet

There are many good makes and models of expanding bullets for the .45 ACP, and we'll touch on many of them, but it would be impossible to cover them all without writing an entire book on that topic. I had an eye-opening experience at the Federal Premium plant this year, while testing three different models of Federal .45 ACP defense ammunition in ballistic gel.

We had a sweet Kimber pistol; plenty

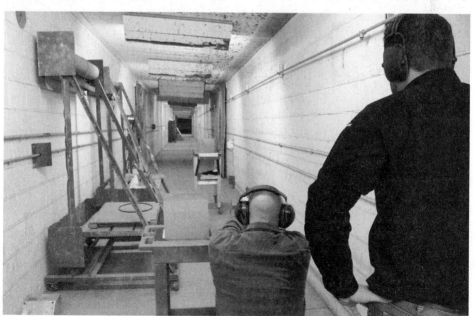

Testing the .45 ACP loads at the Federal Premium facility in Anoka, Minnesota.

The Federal Hydra-Shok ammunition.

Federal Guard Dog ammunition.

accurate and an absolute pleasure to shoot. There were boxes of 230-grain Hydra-Shok, 185-grain Guard Dog and 230-grain HST ammunition, and clean gel blocks to observe penetration and expansion.

The Hydra-Shok is Federal's classic hollowpoint, which is skived to promote expansion and features a small post in the center of the cavity. The Guard Dog is designed for indoor situations; it has a rubber insert filling the hollow cavity, and then the whole bullet is plated so as to appear like a flatpoint FMJ.

The HST bullet is also a skived hollowpoint, designed to expand into a flower-like pattern, and the high-antimony core holds well to the heavy copper jacket. These bullets were fired into three types of test media: gel alone, gel covered with an amalgam of clothing layers, and then through two pieces of drywall and into the gel.

All three of the bullets performed very well into bare ballistic gel.

Weight retention for the Hydra-Shok was 222 grains, Guard Dog retained a good amount of its weight, coming in 164 grains, and the HST did as well, weighing 228 grains after expansion.

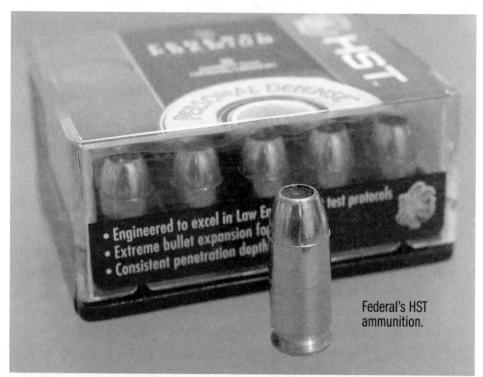

Federal's HST ammunition.

Hydra-Shok, Guard Dog and HST bullets, recovered from gelatin.

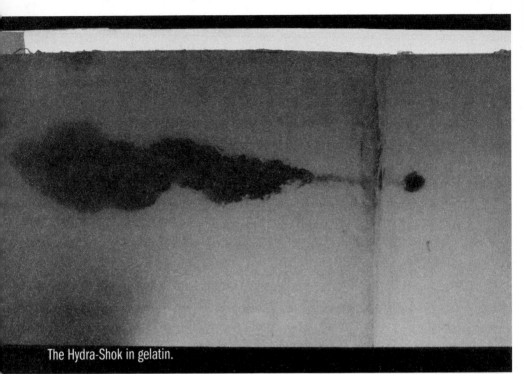

The Hydra-Shok in gelatin.

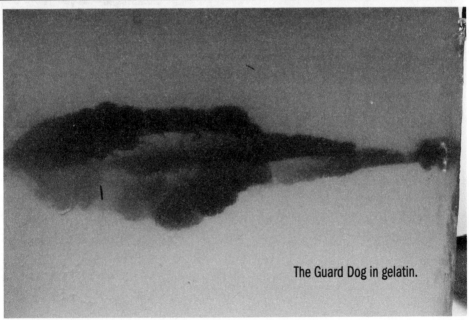

The Guard Dog in gelatin.

Expansion was consistent, with the Hydra-Shok measuring 0.65", the Guard Dog measuring 0.72", and the HST opening up to an even inch. Penetration was between 12" and 13" for the HST and Hydra-Shok, and 6 ¼" for the Guard Dog, so I really didn't have a favorite. Yet...

The clothing test revealed a bit of a different story.

The Guard Dog expanded reliably, to 0.70", and retained 163 out of 185 grains, but penetration was cut down to 8 ¼'". The Hydra-Shok retained 227 grains, but expansion was reduced to 0.65" and penetration was 13". However, the HST retained 227 grains, expanded to 0.82", and penetrated 14" of gel. I'm forming an opinion here.

The drywall, however, sealed the deal for me.

The HST in gelatin, showing a great wound channel and deep penetration.

Expanded .45 ACP bullets fired into clothing.

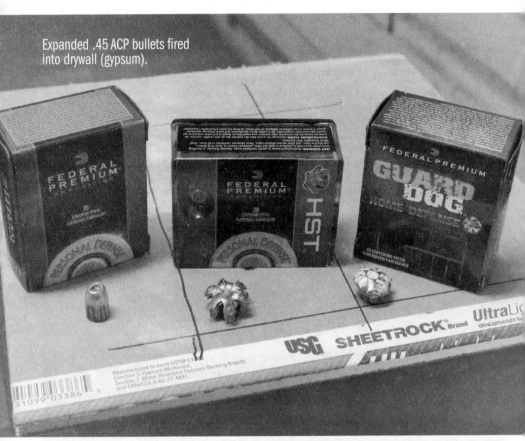

Expanded .45 ACP bullets fired into drywall (gypsum).

Removing the expanded bullets from the gelatin (can you smell the cinnamon oil?).

The Hydra-Shok didn't expand at all, and the bullet could more than likely be re-fired. The weight after recovery was 232 grains, as it was filled with gypsum. The bullet penetrated 24" of gel block, and was recovered downrange about 15 yards. The Guard Dog expanded to the same dimension of 0.70", and weighed 170 grains, but didn't penetrate more than 8 1/2", completely in line with the design of the bullet and loading.

The HST weighed in at 228 grains, despite the wallboard, and expanded to 0.81", with a full 8" of penetration. It was the jagged edges of the expanded HST, along with the nasty wound channel created in the gel, which made me favor this bullet.

If I was forced to shoot indoors, and over-penetration was an issue, I think the Guard Dog line of ammo might be your baby. But for an overall self-defense bullet, in the Federal line I prefer the HST, for the reason of the expanded shape. While the Guard Dog was very reliable, the HST, with those razor sharp petals, will undoubtedly decimate the enemy and "chastise with extreme prejudice", to borrow a military expression.

Now please keep in mind that this is a comparison of only three bullets, in one company's line of ammunition, but I feel it is very illustrative of the different characteristics of self defense bullets. There are a whole bunch of wonderful defense bullets on the market, and while we're going to highlight a bunch, you'll need to take a look at the construction of any bullet you're interested in, and see if (based on the information here) it will work for you.

The HST, expanded in ballistic gelatin.

An expanded Cutting Edge Bullets 9mm PHD bullet.

Among the newer bullet designs that I like for self defense is the Cutting Edge Bullets PHD, or Personal Handgun Defense, for a pair of reasons. One, the lathe-turned, all-copper hollowpoint is very consistent, and has proven to be plenty accurate. Two, the skived design of the walls of the bullet break off into four blades that create one hell of a lot of impact trauma, yet the resulting caliber-sized slug drives deep into the target. This line of bullets is generally light-for-caliber, with the .45 ACP load weighing 150 grains, yet

will penetrate as well as the 230-grain ball ammo. The additional velocity of the lighter bullets adds to the impact trauma. In a rifle bullet, velocity is the enemy of penetration, especially in a standard cup-and-core bullet, but when it comes to the monometals, that rule can sort of go out the window.

The Cutting Edge 150-grain PHD load has a muzzle velocity of 1,050 fps, which will guarantee decent penetration of the rear portion of the bullet (12"+), yet surely will get those blades spinning to create enough impact trau-

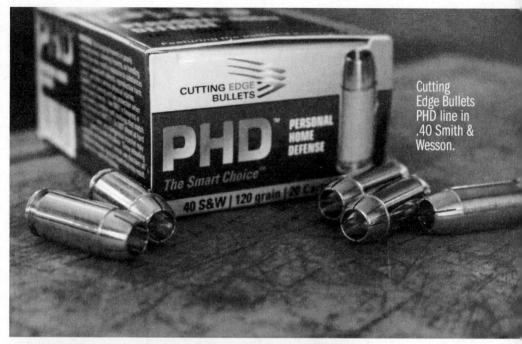

Cutting Edge Bullets PHD line in .40 Smith & Wesson.

The 10mm Auto, with 180-grain Hornady XTP bullets.

ma to stop any ne'er-do-well intruder in his or her tracks. Cutting Edge offers PHD ammo in .380 Auto, 9mm Luger, .40 S&W and .45 ACP. As good as it is in the bigger calibers like .40 & .45, it makes the .380 & 9mm a much more

reliable choice, adding a new dimension to the smaller concealed carry belly guns.

Hornady, a longtime leader in bullet technology, has the XTP (eXtreme Terminal Performance) bullet in its lineup, in many calibers. The .45 ACP is loaded with 185-grain and 200-grain XTP, and it's wonderful stuff. In my .45 Long Colt revolver, I absolutely love the 300-grain XTP at 1,250 fps as an all-around hunting/ defense load. It'll ring a 12" steel gong at 75 yards, even with iron sights and my aging eyes.

My little S&W Model 36 loves the .38 Special 158-grain XTP loads I've devel-

9mm defense ammunition.

oped, and there are other calibers that utilize this bullet well. The Hornady InterLock ring is present, and the heavy jacket that is turned well over the lead core, yet the bullet is hollow enough to initiate expansion. This bullet design has worked well for me in calibers of varying muzzle velocities, and remains among my favorites, whether for hunting or self defense.

Hornady loads their XTP in a wide variety of pistol calibers, from the .25 Auto, with a 35-grain XTP, to the behemoth .500 S&W with a 500-grain XTP. Part of the magic in this design is the controlled expansion, deriving great performance from a jacket of varying thickness. Thinner toward the front, and thicker at the base, I think you'll find the XTP to be a satisfactory choice, regardless of cartridge.

The Hornady Critical Defense line uses the FlexTip bullet, in a sharply-tapered flatpoint configuration. There is a red polymer insert at the nose, which prevents the hollowpoint from plugging up, and ensures reliable expansion. Bullets in this line of ammo generally run on the lighter side of things, to keep velocities higher, and the FlexTip bullet tends to operate well at higher velocities.

This line even includes a .22 Magnum load, for those who want to take full advantage of their rimfire pistol. The 45-grain FTX at 1,700 fps makes a viable load for the rimfire carry gun, and although the load doesn't carry a ton of energy, it will get you out of a jam, and a .22 Mag is better than no pistol at all.

There is also a Critical Defense Lite,

with very light bullets at a bit slower velocity, which makes a great tool for diminutive shooters or for training those new shooters who might not like

The Speer Gold Dot bullet, after expansion.

the recoil of full-house loads in a short-barreled revolver. My own belly gun, a S&W Model 36 in .38 Special, loves the 90-grain FTX load in the Critical Defense Line, shooting among the best groups of any ammo out of the 1 7/8" barrel.

The Speer Gold Dot Personal Protection is another of my favorite bullets for defense situations. Many of my friends in law enforcement choose to carry this bullet in their pistols, and that itself is a ringing endorsement. Built with a deep hollowpoint, bonded core, and a thick jacket that is crimped over the top of the meplat, it gives very reliable expansion and deep penetration irrespective of the shooting situation. Speer makes the Gold Dot in most popular pistol calibers from .25 Auto to .45 ACP, in some useful bullet weights. I love the 155-grain Gold Dot handloaded in the 10mm Auto, as the bullet is tough enough to withstand the high velocity of the Big Ten, yet has shown to be superbly accurate.

I also like the choice of the Gold Dot in the smaller calibers that are common in the concealed carry guns, like .32 Auto, .380 Auto and the like. It is the smaller calibers, like the popular 9mm Luger and .380 Auto, as well as the .32-calibers, that bullet construction is of utmost importance to ensure penetration. The Gold Dot will retain its weight very well, and perhaps save your bacon if, God forbid, you need it to do so. Speer is once again loading Gold Dot ammunition for those who don't reload their ammunition, and shooters should be rejoicing. Pick up a couple of boxes, and try some different bullet weights in your favorite pistol; I think you'll like their performance.

Speer also has taken into consideration that many concealed carry pistols are being made with shorter barrels these days, and while the performance of the Gold Dot has been great in these short barrels, Speer saw fit to revise the Gold Dot to best perform in the stub-

A wide selection of .40 S&W defense ammunition.

by. The bonded-core design has been tweaked to perform well at the slower velocities generated by the snub-nosed revolvers and compact carry guns. Gold Dot Personal Protection Short Barrel is a great concept, and worth a try in your belly gun.

Remington has also answered the call, loading the Compact Handgun Defense line, designed to operate at 100 fps or so lower than traditional loads. I'm glad the ammunition companies have recognized this situation, as pistols and barrels continue to become smaller and shorter. Big Green loads their brass jacket hollowpoint to per-

The Federal HST ammunition.

form at a slightly lower velocity, and the spiraled skives should guarantee good expansion at any velocity.

The Winchester Defender series also offers a notched-jacket hollowpoint in their defense ammunition, and as you can see, this type of bullet is the most-often used for defense ammunition. The rapid expansion of a good hollowpoint delivers plenty of hydraulic shock. There is a fine balance between too much penetration and too little penetration.

For an indoor situation, I prefer the more frangible bullets, with a thinner jacket, so as to minimize the possibility of injuring or killing someone innocent in an adjoining room. The previously highlighted Federal Guard Dog exemplifies this type of bullet, and if you spend a bit of time with it you'll see that there was a whole lot of engineering involved in the design of this particular bullet. And, as an added benefit, it is technically a flatpoint, and not a hollowpoint. This is important in states like New Jersey, which prohibit the use of hollowpoint ammunition.

For a carry gun, I prefer the stiffer hollowpoints like the Hornady XTP, Federal HST and Cutting Edge PHD in my chamber. My general rule is to find the bullet of this style that shoots best from my particular handgun; the concept being that a lesser bullet in the right place is worth much more than a stronger bullet that doesn't hit where it is aimed. That concept holds true for just about any type of shooting situation, so do some range homework and carry confidently!

Buffalo Bore .380 Ammo, in +P (higher pressure) configuration.

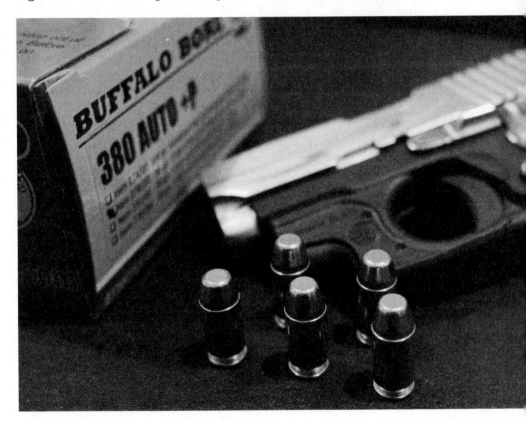

CHAPTER 11

Ruger Blackhawk in .45 Colt.
(J.P. Fielding photo)

T he sport of hunting with a handgun has gained a ton of ground in recent decades, and the development of pistol bullets has paralleled the popularity. From the days of Elmer Keith, when he developed the .357 Magnum and .44 Magnum, to guys like handgun hunter Gary Reeder, cartridge de-veloper J.D. Jones, and Jim Skildum, who had a huge part in Desert Eagle and Magnum Research, there is an undeniable appeal to the handgun hunter. Now, in most of the venerable handgun calibers, a standard cup-and-core bullet of sufficient weight will fit the bill. But, with the increases in handgun velocity came a development in better handgun

HANDGUN HUNTING BULLETS

bullets, of better construction, and designed to perform in the higher velocity handguns.

The recent developments, guns chambered for cartridges like .460 S&W, .480 Ruger, .500 S&W and the like, warrant a rethink of the bullets originally designed for the calibers of lesser velocity. Guys are hunting, with

great success, with the 10mm Auto, the .38 Special (in +P form), and .40 S&W. This is largely in part to the better bullet selection. Many of the hunting handguns are revolvers, but the autoloaders are making headway among the hunting handguns.

The makers of the premium rifle bullets have embraced the handgun

The .357 Magnum, with Hornady FTX ammo and American Eagle semi-wadcutters.

hunters, and have modified their designs to give satisfactory results in a hunting handgun. These new bullets will appeal to the shooters of the huge-cased revolvers, as well as those who still like using the classic cartridges. They also bring out the full potential of the heavy-framed, and often scoped, hunting revolvers. Choosing a proper bullet for your handgun, and by varying the power level, you can dramatically increase the versatility of the weapon.

The huge .460 S&W Magnum, with the .454 Casull ammo and .45 Colt ammo that it may also fire.

As an example, the .460 S&W is a monster cartridge, capable of taking just about anything in North America, but you certainly don't need that level of power all the time. A whitetail deer doesn't require the same amount of penetration or velocity as a brown bear, and the .460 S&W was designed to be a very flexible cartridge. The .460 is simply an elongated .454 Casull, and the Casull is nothing more than an elongated .45 Colt. This gives the owner of a .460 S&W hand cannon a wide range of choices.

My buddy Fred "Fritz" Shultz and I sat down the other day just before our New York deer season, and Fritz came to me with a problem. His .460 was making a bit of a mess of the deer he had taken when he was using full-house .460 loads. He asked me for some advice on how to lessen meat damage while still killing effectively. I handed him a box of Federal Fusion 260-grain ammunition, in .454 Casull. The slightly lesser velocity and bonded-core bullet solved the problem, and ol' Fritzy is a happier deer hunter.

HUNTING REVOLVERS

THE .357 MAGNUM

As a sensible minimum, I feel the .357 Magnum will comfortably handle deer and black bear-sized game, including wild hogs. Were I using it, I'd opt for a 158-grain or heavier bullet, of decent construction. I like the Hornady XTP

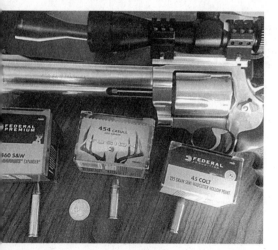

The Swift A-Frame pistol bullet, shown in section and expanded.

bullet, as well as the Speer Gold Dot. Both have a heavy jacket and are of hollowpoint construction, and will open just fine at .357 velocities. Swift makes

the .357 shine. Just like the lever-action rifle cartridges, Hornady produces the FTX spitzer bullet for the .357 (and the .38 Special as well), in a 140-grain configuration. This will perform better at the longer ranges, and will improve accuracy if you use a long-barreled, scoped handgun.

THE .41 REMINGTON MAGNUM

The .41 Remington Magnum fills the gap in revolver cartridges between the .357 Magnum and the beastly .44 Remington Magnum, and fills it well.

I really enjoy shooting the .41 Magnum, as it is has a bit less recoil than the .44 Magnum, but will still make a very effective hunting handgun. With a bullet range of 170 grains to 250 grains, there is something available for anything you'd

The .357 Magnum, with 140-grain FTX bullets.

their A-Frame bullet in .358" diameter, designed to open at velocities as low as 950 fps. It is offered in this diameter at 158 and 180-grain weights, so if you're looking for really good penetration from the .357, there is the option of the 180-grain bullet at a lower velocity.

Federal loads the 180 Swift A-Frame at 1,130 fps, and this load will make

The .41 Remington Magnum.

feasibly hunt with a handgun.

The traditional jacketed hollow-points, like Sierra's 170-grain JHC and 210-grain JHC, and the 210-grain Hornady XTP are available, and will work just fine at .41 Magnum velocities, especially for deer-sized game. If you're planning to use your .41 for anything with teeth and claws, I think the premium bullets make a wise choice. If you like velocity, there are some monometal hollowpoints worth looking at. Double Tap loads the Barnes 180-grain XPB for the .41 Magnum, at a muzzle velocity of 1,610 fps, and the proven all-copper design will give good results in a hunting revolver.

Cutting Edge Bullets makes a pair of good bullets in their Handgun Raptor series: 135-grain and a 180-grain. Due to the integrity of this bullet, the lighter model will handle medium game, and the heavier bullet will work just fine on the larger game animals.

The 210-grain Swift A-Frame is produced for the .41 Remington Magnum, and the Federal load leaves the muzzle at 1,270 fps and would make fantastic bear medicine. As with the rifle variety of these bullets, I feel the Swift A-Frame is one of the best bullet designs available today.

THE .44 REMINGTON MAGNUM

Like the .416 Rigby, which was relatively unknown until Robert Ruark made it famous in *Horn of the Hunter*, the .44 Remington Magnum was launched into infamy in the hands of 'Dirty' Harry Callahan. It was touted as the "most powerful handgun on earth", and the Smith & Wesson Model 29 became an instant success.

This cartridge is, in my opinion, Elmer Keith's shining moment as a cartridge developer. It will push the light-for-caliber 180-grain bullets to a muzzle velocity of around 1,600 fps, yet the heavyweight 300-grain slugs will still move at 1,100 fps from a revolver with a barrel of 6" long or longer.

I have found the .44 Magnum to be a very accurate cartridge. The Sierra 250-grain Full Profile Jacket Match bullet is capable of very tight groups, as this mid-weight bullet is made to exacting tolerances, and proves to be a great blend of bullet bearing surface (for better accuracy) and manageable recoil.

The Hornady FlexTip 225-grain bullet makes a great choice for the scoped Ruger Redhawks and Blackhawks, as it will give a bit of a flatter trajectory than the flatpoint bullets do out at

The all-copper Barnes XPB.

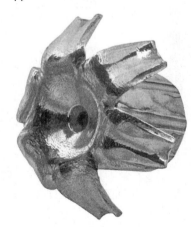

100 yards and over. I surely wouldn't hesitate to grab some of the Hornady 300-grain XTP ammunition in .44 Mag, especially if black bears were on the menu.

These bullets, along with the Speer Gold Dot, have a reputation for toughness and will make an irrefutable choice for a hunting bullet. The premium bullets, like the Swift A-Frame 300-grain pistol bullet, will totally ensure good hunting performance from your .44 Magnum. The bonded-core beast is .91" long, and the shallow hollowpoint will expand along the skives to give enough expansion on the front end to ruin any game animal's day.

A Barnes XPB in .44 Magnum, at 225 grains, will perform just as well. There is an obvious correlation between the lighter-weight monometal bullets and the heavier lead-core bullets. A monometal bullet, being constructed of a lighter metal, will be longer than a cup-and-core bullet of comparable weight, or to put it a different way, two bullets of the same length for any given caliber will have a heavier cup-and-core and a lighter monometal bullet. So, you can expect nearly identical performance from a lighter monometal as you would from a heavier cup-and-

core. The choice is yours, depending on how well either of the projectiles shoots from your rig.

The .44 Mag is one of those cartridges that lends itself well to the cast lead projectiles, especially in the heavier weights. Hard-cast lead bullets, with higher antimony content, in weights of 320 to 340 grains, with a broad, flat point, can make for a very dependable hunting load, especially on larger game. These bullets, at a lower velocity than their lighter counterparts, can give all sorts of penetration.

It was this principle, the heavy and slow theory, which led Elmer Keith to develop the .44 Magnum in the first place. Grizzly, Cor-Bon and Buffalo Bore all produce great factory loads, but it is always possible to pick up a set of Lyman bullet dies and cast your own bullets. Lyman's No. 429421 bullet mould will yield the famous 245-grain "Keith" bullet, which Elmer found so accurate in both the .44 Special and .44 Magnum. A semi-wadcutter design, the Keith bullet, if cast of sufficiently hard materials, will give great hunting performance.

The .44 Remington Magnum, with 240-grain hollowpoints.

THE 45's AND BEYOND

The .45-caliber handguns make fantastic hunting guns, and there's plenty to choose from here. The .45 (Long) Colt has been with us since 1873, and has proved to be a fantastic handgun cartridge, especially in the stronger-framed handguns like my beloved Ruger Blackhawk. Colt's design is capable of firing ammunition made for the antiquated .45 Schofield. But folks like to tinker, and decided that a faster version was needed.

The thicker-walled .454 Casull adds 200-300fps to the velocity of the .45 Colt, and gives the shooter great confidence if a defensive handgun is needed while fishing the trout streams that big-honkin' bears love so much. But we aren't finished yet. Smith & Wesson saw fit to improve upon the Casull design, offering a further elongated case that they call the .460 S&W, which can safely fire .45 Schofield, .45 Colt, .454 Casull and .460 S&W. That's versatility!

The .454 Casull can shoot its own ammo, .45 Colt and .45 Schofield, but not .460 S&W. The Colt can shoot Schofield and Colt, but not Casull or .460. Got that? Good.

Depending on the velocity of your chosen cartridge, and upon the size and tenacity of your quarry, you have a whole lot of bullets to choose from in .452" diameter. My Blackhawk, in .45 Colt, loves both the 300-grain Hornady XTP and the 300-grain Sierra JHP, and I'd take either one along on any given hunt that I'd use a handgun for.

Federal makes the Fusion bullet I told you about earlier for the .454 Casull, and all reports from the field are positive. The bonded-core bullet will combat the higher velocity of the Casull, cleanly taking game without making a bloody mess of things. The Fusion ammo I've fired has been wonderfully accurate, in both rifle and pistol cartridges.

The Casull case head, which uses a small pistol primer.

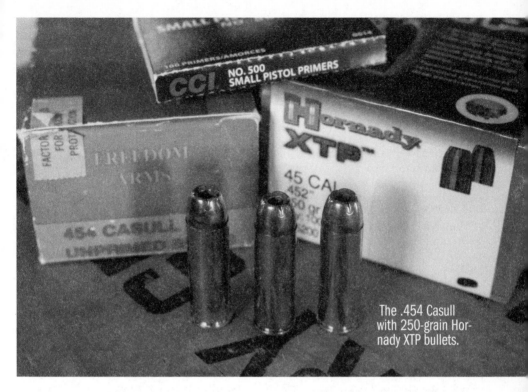

The .454 Casull with 250-grain Hornady XTP bullets.

The huge .460 S&W clearly demands the best bullet technology money can buy. This huge case can push the 300-grain bullets over 2,000 fps, while my Colt will push them to 1,300 fps. With that dramatic increase in velocity comes a huge increase in recoil, as well as additional stresses on the bullet. Federal Premium loads the 300-grain Swift A-Frame pistol bullet in the .460 S&W, and at 1,750 fps, this bullet will easily stand up to the test. This combination will take almost all game on earth, including grizzly bears and the like. Federal also loads the 275-grain Barnes XPB in the VitalShok line.

Starting to see a pattern here? The choices, among the premiums, amount to a heavy bonded core, or a bit lighter monometal. The .460 S&W also shoots the heavy hard-cast lead bullets very well. Grizzly and Buffalo Bore both offer a 360-grain flatnose bullet in .460 S&W, at a velocity right around 1,900 fps. This very nearly equals the performance of the .45/70 Government, but from a handgun. What a load for bison, elk or moose!

Speaking of the .45/70, I had the privilege of meeting Mr. Jim Skildum, of Magnum Research, on a recent hunt in Minnesota. Jim was hunting in an adjoining camp and happened to stop into the camp I was hunting with for a cocktail, and it wasn't long until we started talking hunting guns. I asked him what his favorite hunting revolver is, and he quickly responded "The BFR, in .45/70." The BFR (Big um, unprintable Revolver) is a large-frame, superduty revolver, capable of handling fantastic pressures.

This gigantic wheel gun is specifically designed to handle the longer cases normally reserved for rifles, like the .450 Marlin and .45/70, and in the longer-barreled gun it generates respectable velocities. You can refer to the rifle section of this book to select a good bullet, as the revolver will handle the same types and weights of bullet that the rifles will. Serious cool factor here.

The .480 Ruger jumps up to an impressive bore diameter, and that will equate to a larger wound channel. The .480 Ruger uses .475" diameter bullets, and the cartridge is based on the wildcat .475 Linebaugh, which in turn was based on the .45/70 Government. Designed in conjunction with Hornady, the .480 Ruger can give performance almost comparable to the .454 Casull, but with a larger frontal diameter, but it seems to be fading away.

Hornady loads the 325-grain XTP, a great choice for this cartridge at 1,350 fps or so, and there are some heavier cast lead choices. Personally, I see the .480 Ruger as a good choice as a cartridge for a sidearm in the hunting woods where bears are present, but the .460 and .500 make better choices for a large hunting caliber. With the rather moderate velocities of the Ruger case, pick a decent bullet between 300 and 425 grains, and performance should be rather consistent.

Now, that .500 S&W I mentioned is a horse of an entirely different color. Developed jointly between Cor-Bon and Smith & Wesson, it launches a ½" diameter projectile of between 300 grains and 700 (yes, seven hundred) grains, all at respectable and useful velocities. I can't find fault with you if you find yourself asking "Do I need a .500-caliber handgun?" but if that revs your motor, so be it.

For hunting lighter game, or if you like the fast and light way of thinking, give the Hornady FTX 300-grain bullet a look. Driven to over 2,000 fps, and delivering over 2,800 ft.-lbs. of energy at the muzzle, this should be a perfect deer/black bear load. The Hornady XTP, perhaps my personal favorite handgun hunting bullet, is available in a 500-grain flatpoint configuration, with a muzzle velocity of over 1,400 fps. This is a serious big-game load, fully capable of taking all of North America's game, including Kodiak brown bears.

Federal loads a pair of premiums for the .500 Smith: the 275-grain Barnes XPB, a cool monometal, and the partitioned, bonded-core 325-grain Swift A-Frame. Either will make a good choice, and although the bullet weight is lighter than the true heavyweights for this caliber, the construction of this pair will guarantee both good expansion and deep penetration. Grizzly ammunition loads the 400-grain flatpoint Hawk bullet, a bonded-core, flatpoint affair driven to 1,400 fps that should engender all sorts of confidence while fishing the Alaskan streams or while actively pursuing those with claws and fangs.

If you (like me) enjoy shooting the heavier bullets for any given caliber, Grizzly has a load for you: a 500-grain, hard-cast lead flatpoint, driven to 1,550 fps! Mind you, this will generate some serious recoil in addition to the 2,300 ft.-lbs. of muzzle energy, so be sure and start with some lighter loads to become familiar with your handgun before subjecting yourself to this level of ferocity.

Matt's Bullets, out of Arkansas, loads a 700-grain gas check bullet for the .500 S&W, marketed as the T. Rex cartridges. Having a flat point, with a very wide meplat, this bullet should hit like a sledgehammer. As the website states, a cylinder full of these is ½ lb. of lead. Woof…

HUNTING AUTOLOADERS

THE 10MM AUTO

In an autoloader, I totally dig the 10mm Auto. Originally designed as an FBI-issued defensive round, the recoil proved to be a bit too much for the more diminutive agents, and was shortened into the .40 S&W that is so popular in carry guns today. That aside, the 10 Auto is a damned fine hunting round if you like an automatic. Plenty of velocity to deliver high striking energy, and a bullet selection heavy enough to penetrate into the vitals of deer and hogs, the Big Ten delivers the goods as a hunting round.

The brand-spankin'-new Federal Premium 10mm Auto load features the 180-grain Trophy Bonded jacketed softpoint bullet, and I had the privilege to play with this load out at the Federal plant in Anoka, Minnesota. Recoil was very manageable, and accuracy was exactly what you'd want from a handgun, but the bullet performance is what impressed me the most.

As you can probably tell if you've been following along thus far, I'm a huge fan of the bonded-core bullets, especially in the hard-hitting cartridges. If you like your velocities on the higher end of the spectrum, there's really no reason to use a bullet that may not respond well to those velocities. Bond the core to the jacket, and you've got a recipe for success under a myriad of hunting situations.

Ideally, with any hunting bullet, you want enough expansion to create a large wound channel, yet a structural integrity that will give enough penetration to reach the vital organs.

Arguments have gone on for decades, and can get rather heated, as to whether or not you want a bullet to exit a game animal, or whether you want all of the bullet's energy expend-

The Federal 180-grain Trophy Bonded bullet, in 10mm Auto.

ed within the animal. I am completely fine with either scenario, as the first scenario will leave a large blood trail and end the animal's life quickly from blood loss, and the second scenario delivers a whole bunch of shock, which kills equally well.

Or, with regard to the most common game animals at sane distances, we could look at it this way: a bullet like the Trophy Bonded will more than likely exit on a thin-skinned animal like a deer, yet give you the penetration you'll need to get through the gristle plate of that fantastic bacon factory, the wild hog. But, I digress....

The 180-grain bullet is a good middle-of-the-road choice for the 10 Auto, as there are lighter bullets that travel at a higher velocity, and heavier bullets moving slower, but I feel the 180 represents the best balance of both qualities. The Federal load moves along at 1,275 fps, and DoubleTap offers a similar load moving at 1,305 fps. The DoubleTap bullet is a controlled-expansion jacketed hollowpoint, which should give performance that is more than acceptable at this velocity. Odds are you'll get a bit more expansion and a touch less penetration in comparison to the bonded-core Federal load, but it won't perform poorly at all.

If you like velocity in favor of bullet weight, I suggest looking at the monometal bullet choices. In 10mm Auto, DoubleTap loads the fantastic 155-grain Barnes XPB bullet, at the increased velocity of 1,400 fps. With a conventional bullet at that speed, you might be testing the strength of the marriage of jacket and core, but not so with an all-copper bullet. Some all-copper bullet designs won't expand properly at lower velocities, but 1,400 fps is more than enough to obtain proper expansion. This is a very potent hunting load, and should give sufficient accuracy to any distance you'd be comfortable shooting an iron-sighted autoloader.

Grizzly Ammunition loads a nice

180-grain controlled expansion jacketed hollowpoint, which I wouldn't hesitate to use as a 10mm hunting round. At 1,350 fps, it should make a good choice as a deer and hog load for close ranges.

THE .50 ACTION EXPRESS

The famous Desert Eagle handgun comes chambered in .50 Action Express, and as far as autoloaders go, this a fine choice as a hunting round. The .50AE shoots .500" diameter bullets, usually of 300 to 350 grains, at a

velocity of 1,400 fps or so. Look for a good jacketed hollowpoint bullet, with a decent tapered meplat, so the bullet will feed well from the magazine. The flat-point, hard-cast projectiles will more than likely give you feeding problems. That 300-grain Hornady XTP I mentioned in the .500 Smith section is designed to perform well at .50AE velocities, and should feed perfectly.

Magnum Research, developers of the Desert Eagle, load a 350-grain jacketed flatpoint in their line of ammunition. The bullet has a sound reputation as a hunting bullet, dispatching hogs neatly and quickly. Speer loads the 300-grain Deep Curl bonded-core hollowpoint at 1,550 fps, and that should make a fine choice for the big Desert Eagle. With a skived jacket that extends down and throughout the shallow hollowpoint, completely covering any exposed lead, the Deep Curl should give more than enough expansion on the front end, yet the bonded core will prevent any jacket separation to guarantee good penetration.

The .50 Action Express and the .500 S&W.

Colt Target .22.

Ah, plinking! Countless afternoons have been spent assassinating tin cans, water jugs, and paper targets with handguns happily in hand. Plinking and/or target cartridges can range from the little rimfire rounds we all love up to and including the large magnum calibers.

The main focus of plinking is to spend time familiarizing yourself with your handgun, while target shooting is a more precise measure of the accuracy of you and your gun. Generally speaking, plinking rounds are those that lean toward inexpensive, while the target ammunition is designed for precision.

HANDGUN PLINKING AND TARGET BULLETS

In the rimfire handguns, for plinking purposes, just about any configuration will suffice, providing you can find any .22 Long Rifle at all. I like the inexpensive wax-coated lead bullets, like the Remington Thunderbolts. If it's a target bullet you're after, look at the Lapua Match ammo to feed those Ruger Mark I and Browning BuckMark pistols.

For plinking and target rounds for the revolver crowd, the wadcutter bullets are a fun and inexpensive choice. They are often set flush with the mouth of the case, and feature a hollow cavity at the rear of the bullet, to act as a gas seal. The wadcutter bullet, with a totally flat meplat, usually punches a

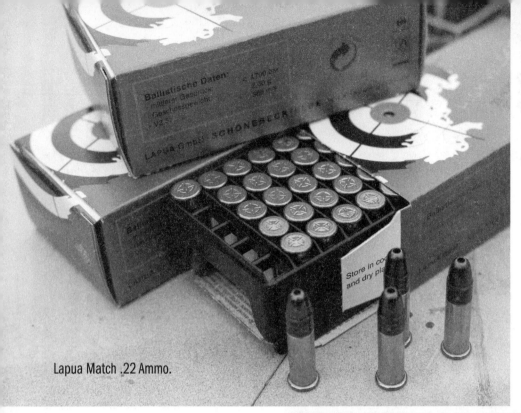

Lapua Match .22 Ammo.

very neat, caliber-sized hole in the target. This makes scoring a group size much easier, and allows the shooter to easily assess the accuracy of his or her shooting.

While a rather unsightly cartridge, the wadcutter projectile is an inexpensive proposition, and can be seriously accurate in revolvers. My S&W Model 36 absolutely loves the 148-grain pure lead wadcutter, and delivers surprising accuracy from a 1 7/8" barrel. Unfortunately, the semi-automatic handguns do not like to feed this type of cartridge worth a hoot.

However, the semi-wadcutter, having a slightly truncated cone for a nose section, will feed very well in the larger autoloaders. These bullets can prove to be very accurate as well; in fact some of them can rival the target bullets. Falcon Bullet Company makes a fantastic 185-grain semi-wadcutter in .45 caliber, that I have seen print groups that are nothing short of jaw-dropping. These hard-cast bullets are very affordable in addition to being very

.357" caliber wadcutters.

consistent. They also offer a Fal-Coated option that will reduce the problem of barrel leading, and keep your cleaning chores to a minimum.

I've gotten to know David Moore, owner of Falcon Bullets, rather well over the years, and he takes his hard-cast lead bullets very seriously. They produce a bullet that is both afford-able and accurate, something that is rare in the shooting world. I love the 230-grain roundnose bullets they make for the .45 ACP, as they maintain the same profile as the military FMJ style bullet that the .45 ACP was designed for, at a fraction of the price of the jack-eted stuff. This makes target practice and plinking much easier on the family budget. They have good bullet choices in the most popular pistol calibers of 9mm/.380 up to .45.

I like the little 95-grain roundnose

for the .380 Auto, the 158-grain semi-wadcutter in .38/.357, the 180-grain truncated flatpoint in .40S&W/10mm Auto, and the 200-grain roundnose flat point for my .45 Long Colt. The only issue that comes along with Falcon is that they must be handloaded; they aren't loaded in any factory ammuni-tion. Take a look at the Falcon website, and give their bullets a try at the target range, even if you have to get someone to load them for you. You'll be happy you did.

Another inexpensive option for high-volume pistol shooters is the full metal jacket bullet. A simple bullet, mass-produced for military purposes, there are many companies producing relatively inexpensive loads that use the FMJ bullets.

All the major ammunition compa-nies will offer an FMJ round for your pistol, and for plinking purposes they will work just fine. But, if you'd like to use your pistol at the many indoor pistol rang-es the traditional FMJ bullet may not suffice.

You see, the indoor ranges are trying to cut down on the lead vapors, and while the military ball ammunition has no exposed lead on the sides or nose, the base of the tra-ditional FMJ has no copper jacket, and is exposed to the burning gas-es of the powder charge, creating lead vapors. There are bullets, howev-er, that are totally

.38 Super 140-grain ball ammo, in +P configuration.

AE38S1

AMERICAN EAGLE

encapsulated in copper jacketing material. These bullets are often referred to as TMJ, or total metal jacket bullets.

Rainier Bullets is a company that comes quickly to mind, and their bullets make a wonderful choice for indoor shooting. Rainier makes a bullet in TMJ configuration to match just about all of your favorite exposed lead choices, and once you shoot them, you may not want to shoot anything else.

My Dad, Ol' Grumpy Pants, is not one to buy into my love of new bullets very easily, but when I showed him the Rainier .45 ACP 230-grain roundnose bullet, he didn't hem or haw over having me load him some. GP has a wicked cool WWII-era government-issued M1911, and the old girl puts those 230-grain Rainiers into nice, tight little groups.

Speer offers a TMJ as well, and the time-tested company delivers a winner here. The 124 and 147-grain 9mms, the 158-grain .357s, the 155 and 180-grain .40s and the 200 and 230-grain .45s; all have been proven at the range to be very consistent and highly accurate. They even offer a 300-grain bullet for the huge .50 Action Express, giving the Desert Eagle fans a high-quality yet affordable option.

Here's another option for the high-volume handgunner: casting your own lead bullets. It can be a rewarding hobby, even if it is time consuming. There are a couple of caveats; firstly that lead fumes are extremely toxic, so be sure and melt your lead in a well ventilated area (read: never indoors), and secondly; it isn't hard to make some ugly looking bullets until you get the hang of it.

The good thing about casting your own bullets is that you can easily melt down your mistakes and reform them. There are good bullet moulds available, from companies like Lyman and Lee. They come in many different configurations, from single cavity to four cavity moulds, and in virtually all bullet profiles. This will allow you experiment

9mm 115-grain ball ammo.

with the various possibilities for your handgun, without breaking the bank. And in a pinch, when ammunition and components are rare (as they have been for the last two years) you always have the option of casting your own.

I like the 158-grain semi-wadcut-

ter bullet for my .38 Special that I cast from my Lee mold, as well as the Lyman 255-grain Keith semi-wadcutter for my .45 Colt. You can cast the lightest 9mm bullets, or feed the behemoth .500 Smith & Wesson. Like the Falcon cast lead bullets, your own cast lead bullets will require handloading, but it sure is fun to shoot accurate groups with bullets you've cast and loaded yourself.

Then there are those training rounds where the bullets are comprised of a sort of compressed metal dust, which drastically reduce the risk of ricochet because the bullets will disintegrate upon impact. While certainly not any sort of a long-range affair, these cartridges are plenty accurate enough for the close-quarter ranges at which pistols are fired.

(above) 38 Special, 158 grain semi-wadcutters.

(below) Training ammo, in .357 Sig, made of a compressed metal 'dust'.